Transplanting Hope

A Journey Through Pain, Addiction, and
the Miracle of a Rare Surgical Procedure

Becky Young Miller

In memory of Hazel Buhrman, Cherie Riggs, and Jim Wescott. During their final months on earth, these three individuals showed me how to live.

CONTENTS

Preface

Part I: The Jagged Journey with Undiagnosed Pain

Part II: Diagnosed Pain – and a Terrifying Plan

PREFACE

The following memoir is based on my recollection of events and thoughts. It is not meant to diagnose or treat any medical conditions. If you are having a medical issue, please seek the advice of a medical professional.

I had both positive and negative experiences on my journey. I mean no malice toward any individual or institution. This book is not a critique of hospitals and the care they provide.

The following names (listed alphabetically) are pseudonyms: Allan, Dr. Abet, Dr. Albert, Dr. Cole, Dr. Ogrite, Dr. Slope, Dr. Sport, Kayla, Lauren, Mary, Megan, Ruth, and Zach.

PART I:
THE JAGGED JOURNEY WITH UNDIAGNOSED PAIN

CHAPTER 1

ADMIT

"Admit," muttered someone in a white coat with the letters "M.D." after his name. The word rolled off his tongue automatically, as if he were saying his name. With drugged and heavy lids, my eyes blinked long and slow. *What?!* I thought, struggling to comprehend. *Admit is for people who are confessing something. Admit is for VIPs invited into an exclusive club. Admit is what doctors say to patients who are really sick.*

I looked down in confusion at my one-size-fits-no-one hospital gown. I had donned these gowns before for checkups and occasional emergency room trips, but this time was different. I did not understand what was going on. Why was I hooked up to so many monitors? I was having abdominal pain, not a heart attack. I felt a wave of anxiety wash over me. The tubes all over my body made my fuzzy mind think of a lab rat, then a tangled pile of spaghetti.

I had an extreme fear of spending the night in a hospital. I am not sure where this fear stemmed from, but I have always been afraid of the needles, nauseating smells, and blank walls. In my mind, hospitals, nursing homes, and prisons were lumped into the same category. They were okay to visit, but I never wanted to be a resident.

My first trip to the emergency room for abdominal pain had been over seven years ago, while I was attending college. Back then, I was fiercely independent and thought I was smarter than my parents (and had told them so). Little did I know that God was already taking me on a journey that would humble and mold me – and push me to my physical limits. In college, I had called my mom out of the blue to tell her I was scared. I was having pain every time I ate and had gone to the hospital for testing. After an ultrasound, CT scan, and HIDA scan, the doctors determined that my gallbladder was barely functioning. They scheduled an endoscopy and colonoscopy to rule out stomach cancer. The two "C" words (colonoscopy and cancer) scared me to the core and vaporized my tough 21-year-old façade. My mom drove seven hours and stayed with me in a hotel room for nineteen days as I underwent tests and then recovered from having my gallbladder and appendix removed. That surgery left me with gastric issues that periodically sent me to the ER, although I tried to avoid it at all costs. My doctors regularly chastised me for waiting too long before seeking medical care, but I always hoped that the pain would pass on its own.

Then, as now, my mom had selflessly dropped everything to be with me. Seeing my mom beside my hospital bed now reminded me of her unconditional love and unwavering support. Yet even in her loving presence, my extreme anxiety did not evaporate. My fighting spirit, which usually helped me wrestle my fear into something manageable, was absent. My mind was swirling. Why this? Why now? Was it the exhaustion of working a full-time job and three part-time jobs simultaneously? Or the constant drain from being in over my head in debt? My mind – which typically analyzed and then overanalyzed everything – could not process these simple questions. In my fog, I struggled to piece together the events that had brought me here. All I knew was that I was in the grip of tremendous fear.

My week had begun the same way it had for the past five years. I put on a suit, packed my lunch, and headed out the door. The ten-minute commute was a blur as my mind was preoccupied with the dozen things I needed to get done after work. I was always trying to think of ways to earn more money and spend less. Money. It overshadowed everything – my friendships, my marriage, even my faith.

Ironically, I had graduated college six years earlier not focused on money, but instead with a dream of helping those who did not have the same educational opportunities or financial resources that were available to me. With degrees in mathematics and dance, and not a single education class, I had joined a program called Teach for America and was assigned to teach math on a Navajo reservation in New Mexico. As the "token" white teacher, I felt true isolation for the first time in my life. For reasons entirely unknown to me, the majority of the students, faculty, and parents hated me and told me so on a daily basis. As a peacemaker and a people pleaser, I found it hard not to be liked. I had no community or support system. I lived 45 minutes away from the closest fast food chain or grocery store. I had a determined spirit, and some of my students advanced four grade levels in one semester with me. I thought that over time I could earn respect and affection. The students did eventually warm up to me, but the faculty and administration did not. After a semester of living on two hours of sleep a night, eating all of my meals alone, and having my safety threatened, I made the dream-shattering decision to return to my hometown.

Emotionally wrung out, I took a position as a credit analyst in the commercial loan department of a community bank. It would just be temporary, I was sure; after what I had experienced on the reservation, I needed a job that would not ask anything of me emotionally and would allow me to leave work at work. Within a year of working at the bank, my emotional scars had slowly begun to heal, and I went on a blind date with a sweet man named Jack. In August 2008 I married Jack, and he began seminary that same month.

For the first three years of our marriage, we lived a very modest life while he completed seminary courses. Hard as it was financially, I found the schedule even harder on our marriage. Friday nights were the only evening that Jack and I had dinner together. All the other nights of the week, he had classes or commitments at the church where he worked part-time. I felt like I was married to a hologram. I convinced myself that life after seminary was going to be much better, with more time together, more income, and a family. I fantasized more about his graduation than I had about my wedding day. Yet when that day finally arrived, I was depressed rather than elated.

A few weeks before graduation, Jack had met with the financial aid person at his seminary to discuss his student loans. I knew he had financed his education, but because many churches help to satisfy that debt, I was not worried. However, when Jack told me the grand total of his graduate and undergraduate student loan debt, I was shocked. His student loan payments were larger than our mortgage payments.

I became distraught, and then quickly went into fix-it mode. Jack and I got creative about how to fill the deficit in our monthly budget. My sister moved in with us to help pay our mortgage. In addition to working at the bank, I started taking on side jobs, tutoring in high school math and SAT prep on evenings and weekends. I did house cleaning for extra money. Jack signed up and trained to be a substitute teacher.

For the first time in my life, I felt the strain of debt. It was a boulder crushing me. As a pastor's wife, I appreciated on an entirely new level the grace and gift Jesus gave by taking on all of my iniquities, so I could be debt-free from sin. Unfortunately, my faith growth was overshadowed by fear and confusion. I could not stop asking God, "What did I do wrong? Where did I go wrong?" Despite my best efforts, every month our savings shrank.

Only a year earlier, Jack and I had begun the paperwork to adopt siblings from Ethiopia. We both had a passion for orphans, and the hope of adoption gave me added purpose. My drive to "fix" our financial situation was fueled by my desire to provide for our future "forever children." Unfortunately, I was running on fumes. It seemed I was on a treadmill that kept going faster and faster. As a rule follower, I wanted to keep the Sabbath, but I did not trust God to provide. The only rest and break I allowed myself was a few hours of sleep at night. Daily I prayed for a miracle – a lump sum of money to pay off the debt.

On the morning of September 26, 2011, I arrived at the

bank, a three-story building in the suburbs. Even though the burden of financial debt weighed heavily on me, I flew up the steps two at a time to make it to my desk by 8:00 a.m. I did not punch a clock, but I hated to be late – and yet was also notorious for pulling into the parking lot without a minute to spare, because I had tried to squeeze in one more chore before I left the house.

I forced a smile, said my hellos to co-workers, and then quickly began tackling the stack of business financials that had remained at my desk from Friday. All day long, I ran numbers to calculate how much money the bank's customers and prospective customers could afford to borrow for commercial loans. Ironically given my work, my personal cash flow was negative. I did not want to be here, and I hoped no one could see through my cheerful façade. My employer had recently acquired another bank, so my familiar co-workers, whom I had grown fond of, were now located at many different offices. The environment had also grown more stressful, as several positions had been cut. Everyone was on edge. I was certainly not working my dream job, but with the economy in a recession, I was thankful for employment and benefits.

I generally sat at my cubicle, in my zone, oblivious to what was happening around me. I stayed at my desk and only got out of my chair to go to the copier or the restroom. I had a few mementos on my desk: a framed picture of my husband and me on our wedding day, an Audrey Hepburn calendar, and a few inspirational quotes. Otherwise, my work area was pretty bland.

As I settled in that morning, my mind worked through the numbers in other people's financial profiles. I resented them. How could other people have such high salaries and so little debt, while I was working multiple jobs to barely make ends meet? I knew I needed to find a higher paying job and had recently started studying (during my precious little spare time at home) for the first of ten exams necessary to become an actuary. I had made this decision purely for financial reasons, not because I felt called to actuarial work. Looking back, I realized that I had never prayed about this decision. Exhausted, I hated to admit my joy was gone. Of course, with the exception of my parents, my sister, and my husband, no one knew I was looking into a career change. I could not afford to lose my current employment.

The day was predictable and ordinary. Then suddenly, a stabbing pain took away my breath. The pain ripped through my ribcage and shot down my back, but it disappeared as quickly as it had come. "Oh well, must be stress and indigestion," I thought. I dismissed it and went back to my calculations. But the next morning at work, the same shooting pain coursed through my body. This time the pain lasted a few minutes and caused me to hunch over my desk. *Okay*, I thought, *I don't have the money to spend on a doctor right now, but this isn't good!* I called my doctor's office and got an appointment that afternoon with a physician's assistant. It was her first day, and I certainly gave her a challenge. After a thorough exam, she concluded that my gastroparesis (delayed stomach emptying), a consequence of my earlier surgery, had flared up. She prescribed a mild pain medicine and I was on my way. The next morning, on Wednesday, I took that pain pill as a preventive measure and experienced no pain. *Ah, problem solved!* I was sure.

Once again on Thursday, I took the pain pill as a preventive measure before leaving for work. But while crunching numbers at my desk, the pain ripped through my body. I leaned over my desk, took deep breaths, and silently pleaded to God for the pain to stop. After several minutes of constant pain, I knew it was not going away. I debated going to the ER, but I knew I would have to wait for a long time before being seen. I decided to call my doctor's office for advice. They said they would see me immediately.

Afraid of passing out from the pain, I called my mom to pick me up from work. There was no way I could drive in this crippled position – hunched over and unable to stand up. I thought, *I'm only twenty-eight! What is happening to my body?!* No one would ever guess that I was a lithe dancer.

I quickly zinged an email to my new boss saying, "I am in horrible pain and going back to the doctor." I was afraid of what my new boss might think of me. Two doctor appointments in one week seemed absurd even to me.

My mom picked me up and drove me to the doctor's office, where I was seen by the same physician assistant. She took one look at me and instructed me to go to the ER. Thankfully, she called ahead to the hospital and they were ready for me.

When we arrived at the ER, staff transferred me from a wheelchair to a bed, and shortly after some initial blood work, they inserted an IV into my arm – along with a dose of strong narcotics. Instantly the pain subsided, as the meds took me away to a nice place, far, far away. Once I was resting, my mom called Jack at work and filled him in on the details.

Later as my eyes fluttered open and began to focus, I realized Jack was sitting next to me, holding my hand. His profile reminded me of Tom Hanks, which made me smile. But we hardly had a moment together before the hospital staff wheeled my bed from one room to another. They took X-rays and scans and called my gastroenterologist. Several ER doctors came to see me. I quickly lost track of all the doctors and tests.

Thankfully, my mother and husband were my advocates. In my drugged state, I was in no position to ask questions, let alone to understand the answers. But the truth was that everyone had more questions than answers. No tests were coming back positive. No one knew what was wrong with me.

I had faith in the doctors and faith in God that I would be okay. But as a mathematician, I enjoyed *solving* problems – and the faster, the better. I had not signed up for this. Spending time at the hospital was not on my agenda. I had meals planned for the week, students to tutor, someone else's house to clean, actuarial practice exams to take, and a dog to walk.

I slowly began to acknowledge my lack of control. Maybe it was the narcotics or maybe it was the fact I had not had a vacation in thirteen months, but my surroundings reminded me of a hotel room. The spacious hospital room had a couch and a bathroom. There were even prints of artwork on the walls and a spectacular view of the city – my beloved city, where I had lived for the majority of my 28 years.

Lancaster, Pennsylvania, the oldest inland city in the United States, is known to most tourists for its Amish community. But for me, the more urban Lancaster was full of memories. In this city, I grew up going to dance classes and dreaming of being a businesswoman. From my hospital bed, I had a view of the steeple of the very church where I was married. Some of the brick buildings below housed art galleries that I enjoyed lingering in, and cafes where I loved to catch up with friends.

Of course, the shrill beeping and the bitter, metallic taste in my mouth reminded me that I was not at a local café. The smell of hand sanitizer alerted me to yet another staff member entering. How many people had to touch me and move me? All I wanted to do was sleep.

Even when I was not being tested or poked, it was hard to rest. A blood pressure cuff periodically squeezed my arm, and machines beeped to alert the nurses when my breathing or pulse dipped, or if a bubble formed in my IV bag. Of course, the worst alarm bell of all was the intense abdominal pain jerking my body awake. The IV pain medicine typically kept me comfortable for three and a half hours. Unfortunately, I could only receive pain medicine every four hours. This thirty-minute window six times a day became brutal. I would scream, cry, and beg to receive the pain medicine early.

I was extremely grateful to have a hand to squeeze and not to be alone. Jack and my mom took turns sitting next to my hospital bed, doing their best to distract me by finding something on TV, reminding me to take deep breaths, or reading to me. They sacrificed their own sleep so that I could get pockets of rest. I do not remember what I watched, or much of what they read to me. However, one devotional that Jack read stood out to me, and I would repeat to myself as I drifted off to sleep: "Rest is a form of worship." I had never heard this before. This nugget of truth provided peace and combatted my guilt about being unproductive. I would smile as the pain medicine entered my veins, and I knew soon I would be "getting my worship on."

After five days in the hospital, I concluded that every square inch of my body, inside and out, had been examined. In this area I was thankful for the fog the pain medicine provided. It prevented me from putting up a fight, feeling overly violated and flushed with embarrassment, or remembering many details.

With the pain still constant and as yet unidentified, doctors were unwilling to discharge me from the hospital. Clearly this was not going to resolve on its own, and I desperately needed to know what was wrong. Then, as if in answer to prayer, a gastroenterologist entered my hospital room with a reassuring confidence. He began by reminding me and my family members present that they had "completed a thorough investigation" over the past five days. I felt like a crime scene. He also needlessly reminded us that they had discovered nothing specifically wrong.

However, when I heard the words "game plan," my ears perked up and I sat up in bed. The doctor thought that my pancreas duct was not fully open and that my Sphincter of Oddi duct needed to be cut. I did not even know that I had a Sphincter of Oddi. He proceeded in an informative tone, "The Sphincter of Oddi is the duct connected to the pancreas. If the duct gets blocked, the enzymes that the pancreas produces to break down food cannot escape to the stomach and the enzymes end up inflaming the pancreas. I believe your extreme pain is the result of an inflamed pancreas. However, the only way to confirm this hypothesis is to go inside your pancreas. There is a specialized endoscopy called an Endoscopic Retrograde Cholangiopancreatography – or ERCP for short – that can not only go into the pancreas, but if needed can place a stent in the Sphincter of Oddi to open the duct."

I was bobbing my head, excited that the culprit to my pain could be solved with an endoscopy. I said, "Great, when can we schedule this procedure?"

He paused. I never liked hesitation. He explained, "An ERCP requires the skill of someone who does many ERCPs on a regular basis, because precision is vital. Unfortunately, this hospital does not perform ERCPs."

I interrupted the doctor and urgently asked, "Where can I get an ERCP?" while simultaneously thinking, *What good is a solution if we can't implement it?!*

"Temple Hospital in Philadelphia performs ERCPs. I will have the nurse provide you with the contact information."

Oh, thank goodness, I thought. Temple Hospital is only a few hours away. I could have this procedure done and be home the same day. I did not want to use up all of my paid time off at hospitals or to spend money on airplane tickets.

"Until this procedure can be completed," the doctor continued on, "you will need to stay on pain medicine. It is available in oral tablets. I will write you a script, so you can get unhooked from the IVs and return home this afternoon."

I was elated! Eagerly, I asked, "Can I return to work?"

"You cannot drive while taking this medicine. In addition, the medication may make it difficult to function. However, as long as you feel up to it, you can return to work."

I thought to myself, *This doctor has no idea how stubborn and motivated I am.* Even through the fatigue of intravenous pain medicine in the hospital, I had tried to work through actuarial flashcards to refresh my brain on the calculus, statistics, and probability concepts that I had learned in college more than five years ago. My hope was to take and pass the first actuarial exam the following month.

As soon as my IV was detached, I felt like a prisoner whose shackles had been removed. As far as I was concerned, I was no longer a patient. I was free! Of course, there were formalities. Jack received the contact information to schedule the ERCP, and I was given my discharge instructions. I zoned out as the nurse went through what I would consider common sense, but not always practical, steps. "Drink plenty of fluids, rest, call your doctor if your symptoms get worse," and so on. Rest was for the elite or lazy. I did not have time to rest. I planned to return to work the next day.

The very next morning, Jack drove me to work. As Jack

dropped me off, he reminded, "Now, don't overdo it." We both expected that I would be flooded with backlogged work. I was instantly greeted with well wishes and genuine concern by my co-workers. I quickly reassured them, "I am truly fine. The only reason I was in the hospital for so long was because the doctors had trouble determining the issue. Now I just need a minor outpatient procedure and I will be as good as new." Not only did I say this, I believed it.

I almost fell over when I opened my file drawers and saw that the projects I had left partially completed were gone. First, horror swept through my body. Was I fired? Had I been replaced? I had great job security before the bank merger, because I was the only credit analyst. Now there were three of us – Allan, Zach, and myself. Allan and Zach were significantly older and had more than double my years of experience as an analyst. Allan was a peacemaker, like me, and Zach loved confrontation. I certainly was not feeling up to a battle, so I did my best not to reveal fear as I asked Allan, "Do you know what happened to my files?"

In a soft, gentle voice Allan graciously informed me, "Zach and I completed them. The commercial lenders were anxious. You know how they are." We chuckled in agreement at the impatience of loan officers. They were always in a hurry to see if their prospective client met the bank's loan approval guidelines. I felt a flush of gratitude. I was familiar with being part of a team. However, never before had anyone actually completed my work.

I tried to get back into my old routine as quickly as possible, but the doctor had not exaggerated when he warned about the side effects of my new pain medication. I entertained the idea of quitting the pain medication cold turkey, but although it did not eliminate the pain, it lessened it considerably. My mind felt sluggish, and all my body wanted to do was sleep. I typically could remedy fatigue with caffeine, but I was having no such luck. Because I was not allowed to drive while on this medication, my mom would pick me up at lunch and I would eat quickly, so I could squeeze in a nap at my parents' home.

My sister would then pick me up from my job at the end of the day on her way home from work.

I temporarily stopped tutoring and cleaning. It took all of my energy to get through the workday at the bank. Jack, my sister, and I would have dinner together, and then I would go straight to bed. I was typically asleep by 6:30 p.m. and would wake up to my alarm clock the following morning. I imagined this was what mono felt like. Even after twelve hours of sleep, I still woke up exhausted.

Jack quickly called to schedule my ERCP at Temple Hospital, only to find out the first available appointment with the referred doctor was not until December. Two months seemed like an extralong time to wait in my lethargic state.

Still, I saw all these problems as short-term. My long-term goals were still intact. I may have grumbled about detours off the path I had prepared for, but I was not discouraged during my first week back to work. Like many people, I always wished I could know the future – for the primary purpose of being better prepared. Surprises made me feel queasy and anxious. The unknown opposed my desire to be in control.

But looking back, I am glad I did not know what was ahead. There was no way I could have planned or prepared for the literal and figurative gut-wrenching journey ahead.

THE FIRST STEP

Nine days after being discharged from the hospital, I sat at my cubicle crying silently. I grabbed a tissue from my desk and hurriedly wiped my eyes. I had only cried in public a handful of times. I was usually good at suppressing my emotions, so much so that sometimes I wondered if my tear ducts worked. There had been times when I sensed it would be appropriate to cry, and I wanted to cry, but I could not produce a single tear. But now, no matter how much I tried to control it, the awkward tears just would not stop.

I did not know what to blame my waterworks on, but I had several choices. I was exhausted despite tons of sleep. I was discouraged and overwhelmed that I could not be seen at Temple Hospital until December. I did not know if I had the stamina for two more months of pain and grogginess. Plus, there was no way I could take the actuarial test with this pain medicine in my body, as the medicine affected my cognitive skills. This meant I could not take steps to change careers, pay down our debt, and prepare for my future children. I felt hopeless and stuck. I had asked a few friends and family to pray for me.

That same afternoon at work I received a call from Temple Hospital. There had been a cancellation, and the scheduler asked if I would like the now available timeslot on Monday, October 24th. Despite a large lump in my throat, I managed to say, "Yes, please." I felt God had heard my petition and pleas that I just did not have the endurance to wait until December. I looked at the beautiful, calm image of Audrey Hepburn on my cubicle calendar. She had always been a source of inspiration and role model for me, especially her dedicated work with UNICEF. I counted: six more days of work until I go to Temple! I thought to myself, *I can make it.* Relief, joy, and hope swept over me.

I took a few deep breaths to help calm my emotions, and I returned to spreading financials until my sister arrived to pick me up from work. The lump returned to my throat as I shared the good news with her and Jack over dinner. Without the strength to make calls to close friends and family about the good news, that evening I sat down on the couch, picked up my laptop, and started to email them.

As I was typing it occurred to me, *What if I send a mass email out to friends and extended family?* I typically only sent out mass communication once a year, and that was through a snail mail Christmas letter. It was out of character for me to reach out in such a generalized way; I always wanted friends to feel special and much preferred to give them my individual attention. During college, I had gotten up at 5:00 a.m. to decorate some friends' dorm room door with crepe paper, balloons, and signs for their birthdays. I enjoyed putting notes through the campus mail to encourage my friends. I liked to think of myself as a cheerleader, but without the pom-poms.

Helping others had always been easy. I had learned from both of my parents. We took flowers to those in the hospital and baked cookies and delivered them to homebound members of our church. I helped my mom bake apple pies for new neighbors when they moved in. My parents' love and self-sacrifice for my sake instilled in me a strong desire to pay it forward. On the other hand, asking for help did not come naturally to me. It felt like defeat and humiliation tied together. If there was any way I could overcome an adversity on my own, I would.

Further, over the past few years, especially the last five months, I had really lost touch with many friends. I was embarrassed to admit it to myself, but I had allowed money and work to consume all of my time and energy. I felt a twinge of guilt about emailing them now in my hour of need. Still, I had received email newsletters from friends in ministry with updates and prayer requests, and I thought, *I am definitely in need of prayers.* I believed prayer was a powerful tool. So perhaps this was not asking too much. Plus, it occurred to me, *If I ask for prayer, then I can send a follow up email describing how the prayers were answered and glorifying God. Maybe my purpose for this health hiccup is to provide a gateway to strengthen friendships and bring glory to God.* I thought, too, about my future "forever children." What wouldn't I do for them? As hard as it was to ask for help, I swallowed my pride, and with newfound energy I humbly sent out a mass email to many friends, providing a little update and asking for prayers, especially for my appointment at Temple Hospital on October 24th. I was hopeful that at this appointment I could schedule an ERCP, the specialized endoscopy. I fully expected this to be a short-term prayer request.

I also added an odd request for CD mixes. As a young girl, I had enjoyed cassette tapes with a variety of artists. The Shell gas station sold them, and we would listen to them during long car rides. Once CDs came out, I started making my own mixes and sharing them with friends. Music energized and comforted me. It could take on so many different emotions that I sometimes struggled to express. Often when I was feeling lonely and isolated in a situation, I would listen to a song that articulated how I was feeling, and it would really lift my spirits. Now it had become even more of a lifeline. With extra fatigue, it was one of the few things I could enjoy while my eyes were shut.

After hitting that small send button on my email, I immediately began to feel like a VIP. I received tons of emails, cards, packages, and lots of encouragement and affirmation. One friend took bright orange, red, and yellow artificial fall leaves and wrote personal words of affirmation about me on each leaf, so that when I felt discouraged, I could pull one out and combat fear and doubt. I also received lots of CD mixes, and even homemade cookies for Jack!

With my dormant friendships reignited and so many prayers

at work, I was confident that I would have good news to share by the end of October.

CHAPTER 3

BUSINESS OR PLEASURE?

On a crisp, sunny Sunday afternoon, Jack put our overnight bag in the car and we headed east towards Philadelphia. He popped one of my latest CD mixes into the stereo. Despite feeling anxious, nervous, and excited, I was asleep just ten minutes into our drive. The warmth of the sun and the gentle movement of the car were the perfect aids for an afternoon nap.

Jack had learned early in our dating relationship not to take offense at my napping. I fell asleep during the first movie we watched together, and I even fell asleep once listening to his sermon over the phone!

My parents joked that I had only two speeds: on and off. Any time I sat down and was not engaged in an activity, I would fall asleep. Insomnia was a foreign concept to me; when my head hit the pillow, I was out. Conversely, my first grade teacher had put on my report card, "Becky doesn't sit at her desk. She hovers." I was never very good at sitting still. Maybe that is why I tired so quickly.

However, since my latest ER visit, taking the daily pain medicine had put my mind and body into extra slow gear. I only had a few thoughts going through my head. First: have the ERCP done, so I could get off of pain medicine and resume my part-time jobs. Second: continue to find ways to pay down our debt. Third: prepare for our future children. The first two steps were prerequisites for the third.

Even with the grogginess of the medication, my goals had not changed. I wanted so much to be a mother and had desired to adopt for as long as I could remember. My heart hurt every time I saw pictures or heard stories about orphans. God had put orphans on my heart in so many surprising ways. My parents sponsored a child in Africa when I was young, and we sent letters back and forth. My dance teacher had started out as an orphan in Russia. Classmates of mine went on mission trips to serve in orphanages. Jack also shared my passion for adoption; he had volunteered at orphanages in Zimbabwe on two separate occasions.

We had started the process to adopt two years after our wedding, confident that although we were far from perfect, we could provide a warm and loving home. We had connected with a national Christian adoption agency, figuring the process would take a few years. We understood that when Jack received a call from a church to be their pastor, it might require us to move. By partnering with a national agency, we hoped to prevent any delays or disruptions in the process.

Our decision to adopt from Ethiopia was a process of elimination. We had heard horror stories and knew couples who had adopted domestically – but then the birth parents had changed their minds. The social worker at the adoption agency confirmed that, if we pursued domestic adoption, there was no guarantee this would not happen. I knew that I would be devastated if this situation occurred. Plus, I really yearned to help a child in need. There were long waiting lists for a healthy newborn in the United States, but options and opportunities for orphans in developing countries were limited.

In Russia, the process for adoptive parents included meeting the child, returning to the United States for four to five months, and then flying back to Russia to bring the child home. I could not imagine holding my child and then leaving him or her for several months in an environment devoid of stimulation and touch.

To adopt from Columbia, one parent had to stay in the country for eight to ten weeks. I did not want to be apart from Jack for that long, and I was not sure we could financially both take off that much time from work.

Jack and I did not qualify to adopt from China, because we

had not been married for more than five years.

Consequently, adopting from Ethiopia seemed best. The adoption process there was moving quickly, with an average wait time of only eight months after completing the lengthy paperwork. I also appreciated that the orphanages in Ethiopia were often staffed with loving and kind caregivers. In Ethiopia, the adoptive parents meet their child in a group setting. Within two weeks, the adoptive parents may bring their child home. After seeing the long checklists and the cost to adopt, we had decided to adopt siblings, so that we only had to go through this process once. Jack and I planned to visit his friends in Zimbabwe during the two-week waiting period.

If the entire adoption process took two years, we would be parents a year or so after Jack was an ordained pastor. This was the plan, and it motivated me. I had grown up with two parents who were definite planners, so I had understood the value of planning from an early age. My dad researched and planned our family vacations so that we got the most mileage out of our trips. My mom kept track of menus and schedules, so that we were always well-fed and never late. Now whenever I felt tired, I pressed on because I wanted to be prepared for my future children. I had even created a baby registry.

Now all of our adoption paperwork was completed and in Ethiopia; we were just waiting for a referral. Even though we did not know the gender of our future children, Jack and I enjoyed discussing possible names. We decided if we were blessed with one girl and one boy, we would name them Grayson and Adelaide. Since I did not know if Grayson or Addie had been born yet, I prayed daily for their family and caregivers.

The idea that any day we could receive a referral provided energy, motivation, and strength – along with a little fear. I thought once the student loan debt was paid off, we should have sufficient income to provide for more than just the bare minimum needs. But I was afraid that now we might receive a referral but not have enough income to provide for their needs. I feared that if we couldn't pay off the debt quickly, I would have to work 60 hours a week and never have time with Grayson and Addie. My heart's desire was to provide for my children and to have time with them. Ironically, I was not afraid of my health hindering my childcare abilities.

Jack leaned over, kissed me softly, and whispered gently, "We are here." Thank goodness that the first thing I saw when I woke up from my nap was Jack, because nothing around me looked familiar. We were in a huge parking lot that was surrounded by barbed wire. It looked like an airport parking lot. I was thankful that Jack was with me and that I did not have to face a new doctor alone. Of course, I still didn't know what to expect, and that made me nervous and anxious. How could I prepare for the unknown?

We walked through the parking lot and entered a ritzy Hilton hotel. Even though I felt out of place in my sweatpants, I was thankful for the stretchy waistband. A year or so earlier, I had switched to maternity pants for work, because my waistline could expand literally four dress sizes within a day. No doctor had been able to give a concrete answer for this phenomenon. It was dismissed as bloating from my delayed stomach emptying, but it seemed a little extreme to me. I could start off the day in size four pants, but to be comfortable in the afternoon, I needed a size twelve! When I was not at work, I now lived in sweatpants. This was really out of character for me. In college, I had never worn drawstring pants outside of my dorm room. I dressed in knit sweaters and jeans, because I believed that a student's attire impacted her performance. "Dress for success" had been my motto.

Thankfully there was no sign on the hotel door refusing service to those dressed in sweatpants. Jack handed our hotel confirmation paperwork to the lady standing behind the desk. My dad had won a million Hilton points, so we were staying for free thanks to his generosity and good fortune.

A jolly middle-aged woman wearing a nametag that read "Ruth" asked the simple question, "Are you here for business or pleasure?" The fog from my nap had not fully worn off, but I certainly would not have said we were here for pleasure. Jack replied, "My wife has an early appointment tomorrow at Temple Hospital."

I could usually pull off a happy and peppy personality regardless of how I felt, but more recently I had discovered that acting happy required a lot of energy. I had none to spare. I smiled sheepishly at Ruth.

Ruth cheerfully responded, "In that case, I am going to change your room. We have an open suite on the top floor." What a gift! Only God knew how special top floor, corner spaces were to me. I loved God's attention to detail!

In my vulnerable state, I suddenly felt that Ruth was more like an aunt than a new acquaintance. Jack asked for dinner recommendations. There were some chain restaurants nearby, but Jack always liked to go for authentic local eateries. I admired this about him. The old stereotype that "opposites attract" applied to us in this realm. I always got the same thing when I went out to eat, and Jack always tried something new.

Ruth recommended a few small eateries in an eclectic neighborhood nearby called Manayunk. Later it dawned on me that the first four letters of this town's name are Mana – sounding just like the name of the food God provided the Israelites in the desert. How appropriate!

We took the elevator up to the top floor to drop off our things. Our suite had a little kitchen, a couch in a sitting room, and a huge bedroom that looked out over water. I could have spent the rest of the day curled up there, but Jack was ever the explorer.

As we walked around charming stores in Manayunk, it started to feel like we were here for pleasure. One store had journals made out of old records. We loved seeing things repurposed.

Jack spotted a used bookstore. As he pointed from across the street, he exclaimed with excitement, "Hey, we should check out that store!"

I sarcastically asked, "Jack, do you have an internal compass for these? You seem to have a magnetic pull towards them!" Since we were on a date of sorts, I gave in to his request. But I secretly hoped they were closed.

Jack and my sister both love books. I, however, have never understood reading for pleasure. I only read with a specific purpose in mind. I had recently read three books for our adoption class. I found books interesting, but rarely had the time – or rather, *made* the time – to sit and read. Plus, unless there was a deadline or test, I would fall asleep reading.

As he went happily off to explore, I gravitated toward the children's book section, searching out some gifts for our future children. A little balloon of hope rose up in me as I imagined wrapping Christmas presents for Grayson and Addie and pictured their excitement and joy.

Dinner in Manayunk was good, but dessert was amazing. We stopped at a small self-serve frozen yogurt place called "Whirled Peace," which offered all sorts of low-fat yogurts and toppings. I do not just have a sweet tooth; I have a mouth full of sweet teeth. I felt like Goldilocks sampling until I got the flavor that was "just right." For me it was definitely their New York cheesecake. Yum, it felt so refreshing. I did not know all of the triggers to my pain, but I did know that fat was one of them. This low-fat yogurt that tasted high-fat was a true treat.

After walking and exploring the quaint town, we headed back to our suite. I had temporarily forgotten our purpose for being in Philadelphia, and there was a spring in my step. I could not remember the last time Jack and I had been on a date. When we arrived back, we thanked Ruth for all of her great suggestions and shared with her all the places we had gone. We had never heard of Manayunk before, and thanks to her recommendations, we felt like we had been let in on one of the best-kept secrets.

The following morning we woke up bright and early. I was on edge as we made our way toward the hospital. Our GPS nearly directed us into a cemetery, but thankfully Jack has a great gift for navigating and we did not get lost. I laughed nervously at the GPS error, but my stomach was in knots. We were pleasantly surprised as we entered the huge hospital and found clear signage and people to help with directions.

We were led to a hospital waiting room filled with uncomfortable chairs that had weird stains and odors. The morning news was on the TV, but I was not interested. Instead I was intrigued by the several different languages being spoken around me. I quickly realized that individuals from around the world were here to receive care. This encouraged me. I thought to myself, *Hopefully this hospital puts more of their money into research than into the aesthetics. Certainly no interior decorator would want to claim ownership for this drab setting.*

A nurse took us back to a cold exam room. There were no windows or wall decorations. The room had two chairs, a desk with a computer, and an exam table, but I felt claustrophobic. I like natural light. I feel like a boy scout without a compass in a room without windows.

I grew up being taught that "hate" was a strong word and that I shouldn't use it. However, I truly hated meeting new doctors. I was an introvert, so meeting new people was always taxing. And with doctors, history had taught me what to expect, and it was not pleasant.

After a knock on the door, Dr. Albert entered. He looked like a mad scientist, with wiry hair sticking out in various directions. He introduced himself and shook our hands. I thought this was fairly standard procedure, but I would later meet a doctor who did not even have time for this nicety.

Dr. Albert's personal skills were lacking. He asked questions and then repeated my answers into a microphone and did not even look at me. This was a first for me. Usually I had heard doctors recording dictation after an appointment, not while I was sitting right there.

I appreciated all of the technological advances that allowed us to transfer medical records. But for some reason, all the doctors that I met for the first time wanted to start from scratch and redo my tests. I wondered why they even requested medical records to be faxed to their office, because it appeared that the doctors never even looked at them. Thus, I was not surprised to have to answer a million questions and then be touched. I dreaded the words, "Hop up on the exam table and let me take a look."

Most doctors either did not believe me or did not listen when I warned that I had a tender abdomen. I would warn doctors every time I went to the ER, and they would always ignore me. They would push and poke, and I either jumped off the table or went pale with nausea.

Once again, I explained that I had a tender stomach. And as usual my warning went unheard. I leapt off the table as Dr. Albert pressed firmly on my very sore abdomen.

Dr. Albert replied with shock, "Oh, you weren't kidding. Your abdomen is really tender." As I gagged and tried to hold back breakfast, he asked, "Do you need a basin?"

I attempted a half-smile as I replied, "No, I will be okay." What I really wanted to shout was, "Next time, listen to your patients!" I hoped his diagnostic skills were better than his listening skills.

After reviewing his notes on the computer screen, he said, "I want to rule out a few possible rare, but serious issues. The nurse will get you scheduled for some tests, and then I will see you back in a few weeks."

Dr. Albert was ready to leave when Jack quickly asked, "Assuming it is not these rare ailments, what would we be looking at?"

"Either a pacemaker for her stomach or an ERCP," he responded in a monotone voice. "Of course, we need to see what the tests show first."

"Of course," Jack said, as we both nodded in agreement. Jack wrote down notes. He would later learn to come to every doctor's appointment equipped with written questions. However, at this point we just thought we were here to be seen and then to schedule an ERCP. I was discouraged that this process was being dragged out, but I was not worried. I doubted that anything rare or serious was wrong with my body; I assumed that the doctor was just trying to be thorough.

The nurse that had shown us to the exam room looked at our paperwork. We stood in the hallway as she made several phone calls. She was able to schedule three tests for that day and three more for the following Monday and Tuesday. I was surprised at how quickly these tests could be scheduled, and I was thankful to be moving this process along.

I was not thrilled to have more tests, but I certainly wanted whatever was causing this mess to be resolved once and for all. I needed to be able to say, "Good riddance!" to this stabbing pain, and fast – because my future children needed a strong and healthy mother.

The first two tests were a blur. Jack was with me and held my hand. But the instructions for the third test shocked and horrified me: "Please remove all of your clothes, change into this gown, and then go down the hall to the waiting room on your left marked 'women only.'" Whoever decided to call hospital gowns "gowns" had a real sense of humor, I thought. I was certain that everyone around me knew that I had nothing on under the paper-thin gown. I felt extremely vulnerable without any ID except for the wristband on my arm. I also dreaded being separated from Jack.

For once, I was relieved that there were no windows. However, the room was very cramped. Two rows of chairs faced one another. There was only one chair open, and it was smack in the middle of a group of gabby ladies in the same gorgeous gowns. If I had been able, I would have crawled under the chair.

I assumed these ladies were friends, because they were joyfully involved in conversation. But I quickly discovered that none of these ladies had known each other prior to that day. Their topic of conversation also surprised me. What were they talking about? How good the Lord is.

On the TV, the news was talking about Representative Giffords from Arizona, who had been shot in the head but had recovered and was back at work. One woman said, "What man intended for evil, God made good."

Another agreed, "God's angels were protecting her."

Another lady said, "It can only be the Lord, because I typically have ten cups of coffee a day, and for my test I haven't eaten or had any coffee in two days, and I haven't hurt anyone."

We all laughed and encouraged one another. One lady was shivering, so another lady ventured into the hallway to find a nurse to request a blanket. I felt like I was in the Book of Acts, where acquaintances were all looking out for the wellbeing of their neighbors and sharing whatever they had.

I was a minority in this group; I was the only Caucasian person and the only one under the age of sixty. But these ladies easily welcomed me into their conversation. Instead of feeling like I was in a cold, depressing waiting room, I felt more like I was at the spa with girlfriends. Instead of being cranky or grumpy, these ladies were rejoicing in all the ways God was working. It felt like a little slice of heaven.

After returning from the X-ray, I had a smile on my face and could not wait to share with Jack the most recent blessing. I felt encouraged and inspired, and thanks to these ladies' positive outlook, I was reminded of answers to prayers every step of the way.

CHAPTER 4

TRICK-OR-TREAT

My second round of tests at Temple Hospital was scheduled for Monday, October 31. I was disappointed we would miss handing out candy to children that night, but thankfully, Jack and I were able to keep another October tradition alive: carving pumpkins. For the past six years I had carved pumpkins with two delightful and sweet children, Julia and Gordon, from our church. Their mother, Chris Snyder, had intentionally gotten to know my sister and me and was even able to keep our names straight. I don't believe that my sister and I look alike, but we are often asked if we are twins. In fact, we are 22 months apart and I am younger – although I always liked to be mistaken for the older one. Chris's effort to tell us apart really drew us to get to know her and her family better.

The first time Jack had met Julia and Gordon was three years ago, when they were ten and six. Jack and I had gone to pick up Julia and Gordon to go select pumpkins for carving – and Jack referred to the children as George and Lois. Julia quickly realized that Jack was being silly, but poor Gordon kept politely trying to correct Jack by softly saying, "Um, excuse me. My name is Gordon." Jack would just reply with a hearty laugh and say, "Oh, George, your dad said you were a jokester!"

As the years passed, Jack continued to call them George and Lois, and they loved it. Each year as we carved pumpkins, we also always ate a lot of junk food. Similar to Gordon and Julia's parents, my parents had avoided having highly processed foods (full of sugar and empty carbs) in the house. Therefore, it was a real treat to order pizza, eat chips, and make sugar cookies. I felt like a cool aunt. This year as we stayed toasty with the oven going and a fire in the fireplace, it snowed outside.

Another tradition with Julia and Gordon had begun on the day I had settled on my first house, before I had met Jack. Julia and Gordon's parents drove them across town in their Halloween costumes to ring my doorbell and say, "Trick or Treat!" They did not do this on some arbitrary day; I had settled on my house on October 31, 2006. Many years I would run out of candy, because I would drop one piece of candy in over 400 children's pillowcases and bags. However, I always held in reserve a solid dozen pieces of candy for both Julia and Gordon. When I dreamed about Grayson and Addie, I dreamed they would be like Julia and Gordon – exceptionally polite, and appreciative of the littlest things.

This year it was going to be hard to not be home for Halloween and to miss seeing all of the children dressed up. But most of all, it was going to be hard to not see Julia and Gordon.

On Sunday, October 30, exactly a week after our first departure for Philadelphia, Jack and I once again placed an overnight bag in the car and headed east. In many ways it felt like *déjà vu*. I fell asleep in the car and woke up in the barbed-wired parking lot. However, this time I felt more peace than anxiety because I had been here before, and it felt familiar. In addition, I could not wait to return to Manayunk.

At the same time, I was beginning to worry about returning to work on Wednesday. I was not one to let my body affect my life. Similar to the mantra, "mind over matter," I would often tell myself, "mind over body."

In the last seven years since my appendectomy and the removal of my gallbladder, I would sometimes experience excruciating abdominal pain – feeling like knives were being thrust and twisted all over my torso. Fortunately, this intense pain typically only occurred once or twice a year, usually in the evening. Each time, I would reluctantly surrender to the pain and go to the ER. As much as I dreaded going to the emergency room, the trips were fairly predictable. Each time, doctors would do tests and scans, but they never found anything life-threatening. They would give me some intravenous pain medication, I would feel better, and I would go home. Normally I would leave the ER around 2:00 a.m., sleep for a few hours at home, and head into work. In follow-up appointments, doctors never had any solutions; they only ever offered tweaks to things like my diet.

I rarely allowed my body to dictate my work schedule. I had never imagined needing to take time off for health issues. Vomiting was the only symptom that would keep me from going to work. But I seemed to be growing wearier with every passing day. If I took more time off from work now, that would mean a reduction in our income. And I could lose my job. I tried to push these thoughts out of my head as we walked from the car to the hotel lobby.

Jack and I were delighted to again see Ruth behind the desk at the Hilton hotel. She had truly gone above and beyond with our last stay, so we had picked up a little memento to give to her. My typical "love language" is to do things for others – but in this case, a gift seemed most appropriate. We brought quilted potholders, each with a star in the center, made by Amish individuals. I told Ruth, "It may sound corny, but you were a bright star in our journey last week. I was scared to go to Temple Hospital, and you made us feel welcome." I wished we had greater resources, because I really would have loved to give her a quilt. However, Ruth's stunned response was as great as if we had given her a quilt or some lavish gift. I was just glad we could express our appreciation and she could know what a difference she had made in our lives.

I am not sure if Ruth had scheduled us to return to the same suite prior to our arrival, but we were certainly ecstatic to get the room number and open the door to the exact same spacious suite. It was starting to feel a little bit like a home away from home. We spent the afternoon browsing and admiring the eclectic shops in Manayunk and grabbed a simple dinner.

This time, I felt ready and confident to return to Temple Hospital, like a school child returning to the same school after a year. I was not intimidated or overwhelmed as we entered the hospital; once again, familiarity brought peace. I anticipated facing the same typical hospital tests with IVs and big machines. Not pleasant, but not horrible. Experience had also taught me that I would not receive results until my follow-up appointment with Dr. Albert in two weeks, so I did not expect immediate answers to my health mystery. However, I had no idea the "treats" awaiting me on this Halloween morning.

The first test was a total breeze. I just had to blow into a new bag every fifteen minutes for three hours to determine if bad bacteria were growing in my intestines. A little timer would go off every fifteen minutes, and a nurse would appear from behind a curtain with a fresh bag and straw. In the interim, I got to watch TV. The worst part was lying in a hospital bed with an almost sheer curtain separating me from a patient in the bed on either side.

The second test, however, can best be described as torture. A tube had to be inserted in my nose, down my throat, and into my stomach. This would not have been a big deal if I could have been asleep. But not only did I have to be awake and swallow liquid, I was not allowed to take any pain medicine for twelve hours prior. I almost passed out from the pain, and I drenched my clothes in sweat and tears. I pulled muscles in my back from dry heaving so much. The technician's encouragement was a huge blessing. She kept saying, "You are doing great... Just a few more swallows... You are very brave." I had never felt so much pain in my life and believed it was only by the grace of God that I completed the test. Thoughts of my future children also played a part; they were my inspiration. Jack held my hand and kept encouraging me to persevere for Addie and Grayson.

Returning to the hotel was a blur. I did not feel like having dinner, but Jack encouraged me to check out the complimentary dinner that was being served. It turned out to be one of my favorites, Chicken Marsala. After dinner, Jack said he wanted to return to Manayunk. I thought, *Haven't we had a long enough day? I just want to go to bed.*

But Jack pulled out his most adorable smile and said,

"Please?"

I agreed, thinking I was doing Jack a favor – but in actuality, he had a treat planned for me. We returned to Whirled Peace, the frozen yogurt shop. Oh, how soothing the frozen yogurt felt on my throat, which was sore from the tubing.

After we had returned to the hotel and were lying in bed, I processed the day out loud. I lamented that this had not been my favorite Halloween, and I wished we were back in Lancaster. Jack encouraged me that maybe next year we would be out trick-or-treating with Addie and Grayson. I liked the sound of that.

Then, for the first time, I expressed to Jack my concerns about my ability to return to work on Wednesday. I felt like the day's tests had more than emptied all of my energy reserves – leaving a deficit. I could usually bounce back from hospital tests, but there was no elasticity left in me.

"I think you're overreacting," Jack said. He encouraged me to get some rest and see how I felt in the morning.

I wondered out loud, "Why did I have to endure that torturous test today? Why is God allowing this health issue to continue? What is the purpose of all of this?"

Jack replied thoughtfully, "Maybe our future children will have health issues, and you will be better able to relate to and care for them, because of this health issue."

I sharply declared, "That is a horrible thought!" Like all mothers, I wanted healthy children. I could not bear the thought that after I survived this hellish health issue, I was then going to have to watch my children suffer. No, thank you. I would rather die. I knew Jack's suggestion was not meant to be malicious, but it felt like a cruel idea – and now Jack was burdening me with something else to worry about. I was already praying that Addie and Grayson would be safe and well cared-for; now I felt the urge to start praying that they would have no major health issues. I turned away from Jack and shut my eyes. It took me a little while to fall asleep, as I was still processing the day and Jack's responses. I felt scared and alone.

The following morning I awoke still feeling really weak and

ready to go home. If it had been up to me, I would have stayed in the hotel bed all day and just pulled the covers over my head.

Thus, I did not enter Temple Hospital with as much zest as the day before. But I gave myself a little pep talk: "Becky, you just get this done and then you get to go home. You can do this."

I changed into the familiar unflattering and inadequate hospital gown and this time had an IV inserted in my arm. This test included an injection of radioactive stuff via the IV, and then X-rays over a period of several hours. Once again, no pain medicine was allowed. Jack could not stay with me because of the exposure to the radioactive material.

Fortunately, I was blessed with an amusing technician. He asked, "What brought you to Temple from Lancaster?"

I replied honestly, "My doctors were out of ideas and highly recommended Temple."

The technician replied with a mock serious tone, "People tell lies all the time." We both laughed. His sense of humor helped me get through another round of pain.

As I lay still with radioactive dye going through my IV – "glowing," as Jack liked to put it – I had a lot of time to think. I really could not imagine having the strength to return to work. The truth was, I was not feeling better; I was feeling worse. I prayed that God would give me the strength to return to work and to keep plugging along until my health mystery could be solved.

Meanwhile out in the waiting room, Jack fixed the room's TV and was rewarded with a free parking pass for the hospital. This was an eight-dollar value!

More blessings came that afternoon, in the form of a stop at Trader Joe's on our way back from Temple. Trader Joe's is my favorite grocery store, because their products do not have artificial junk in them. In the past few years, I had discovered that artificial colors and preservatives exasperated my digestive issues. Unlike many health food stores, however, Trader Joe's prices were very reasonable. We did not have a Trader Joe's nearby our home, so getting to stop at one was always a special treat – and I really needed a treat after Temple Hospital.

When we walked in, I think I looked about as good as I felt: terrible. I was hoping to purchase and then indulge in my very favorite product, salted dark chocolate caramels. These were a seasonal item, so I was not sure where to look. I decided to ask a friendly employee. (By the way, I have found all of the employees at Trader Joe's to be incredibly friendly and helpful.)

"Excuse me, could you direct me to the salted dark chocolate caramels?" I inquired.

The employee politely replied, "Unfortunately, they are not out yet. However, they should be out in a day or so."

I flatly let out an, "Oh, okay." My shoulders automatically slumped, and the little bit of pep in my face drained. "We actually do not live nearby," I explained.

I am not sure if the employee caught sight of my hospital bands on my wrist, or if I just looked that pathetic, but he whispered to me, "They arrived last night. How many do you need?"

In my little world, it felt like a holiday had just been declared. Excitement rushed back into my weary body. I replied, "Two boxes would be wonderful!"

The employee then stated with a bit of humor, but also an edge of seriousness, "One stipulation. You must hide them in your cart and not let anyone else see them."

"Deal!" I agreed. "Thank you so much!" I added.

The employee disappeared for a few minutes and then reappeared with two boxes containing the most delicious food I believed could enter a mouth. I quickly slipped them underneath the other items in my shopping cart, and I had the biggest grin.

After checking out, we returned to our car. Once the doors were shut, I turned to Jack and spilled my guts. "Jack, I am really scared. As happy as I am to have my chocolates, I am utterly exhausted," I started crying as the words came out of my mouth. "There is no energy left in this body. I don't have the strength to do anything, let alone return to work. I am not sure what to do."

Admitting this felt like total defeat. Jack calmly and lovingly responded, "Take a deep breath. Everything is going to be okay. Why don't you give Dr. Granger's office a call and see if he will complete paperwork to document a medical leave? Then once this health issue is resolved and you feel stronger, you can return to work."

I hesitantly picked up my cellphone and dialed the number to Dr. Granger's office while Jack drove us back to Lancaster. I spoke to a nurse and explained the situation. She said she would relay the message to Dr. Granger and be back in touch.

As sick and as weak as I was, I still worried what others thought of me. What would Dr. Granger's response be? Would he think I was lazy and just wanted an excuse not to work? I had just met Dr. Granger for the first time five days earlier. The family doctor that I had known and adored for years, and who had helped us complete our adoption paperwork, had moved out of the area a few months earlier to be closer to his aging parents.

But Dr. Granger had surprised me and impressed me. Prior to his first meeting with me, he had looked back through my chart and had a list of questions for me. This was a first. Usually, I was the one with the list of questions. He had discovered some inconsistencies that no other doctor had either picked up on or mentioned. As a result, Dr. Granger ordered some additional lab work. Over the past five plus years, I had not encountered any doctors who moved so quickly and persistently to solve this health mystery. However, my pain had never been so intense for such an extended period of time either. I was grateful for Dr. Granger's thoroughness. Little did I know that he would become my advocate and medical translator for many months to come.

Before Jack and I returned to Lancaster, I received a phone call back from Dr. Granger's office saying that a letter had been written and signed, explaining that I was not well enough to work at this point. I called Human Resources and asked what they needed for me to begin short-term disability. By the time we got off the highway in Lancaster, the appropriate paperwork was ready to be picked up at the doctor's office.

I felt relieved about getting the time off, but I still wondered whether I was making the right decision.

CHAPTER 5

DIVINE TIMING

I pulled out comfortable shirts and sweatpants from my dresser drawers. I neatly folded them and placed them in my suitcase. I gathered pill bottles and double-checked that there were enough doses to last me a week. I looked over my packing list to make sure I was not forgetting anything important, like underwear or pajamas.

I packed as quickly as my body would allow. I never knew when the next round of pain would strike. For the first time, I was losing my pep and positive attitude. My nights were now interrupted with bad headaches and stomach pain, as well as pain up my back, down my legs, and in my feet. Pain medicine helped to make the pain bearable. However, both the attacks and the medication left me weary.

Before departing on our road trip, I sat down at my laptop and sent out an update to friends and family. I announced that I would be doctor- and needle-free for at least ten days, and my follow-up appointment at Temple was set for Friday, November 18. I concluded my update with the epiphany, "I have heard that God only gives you what you can handle. I believe God only gives you what your support group can handle." I thanked my friends and family for all of the ways they were supporting and encouraging me.

A friend of my mom's, Judy, gave me a decorative box to take with me on my trip. She had purchased a variety of pampering items and wrapped each one in a different brightly colored piece of tissue paper. Her note with this creative gift invited me to either open one or two gifts a day, or all of them at once. I chose to open a gift or so a day. The small gifts included nail polish, nail files, face masks, lotion, and bath salts. The gifts helped me to remember to celebrate each day and helped me feel special and beautiful.

The gift also reminded me of fond memories from college. As a college student, I would invite friends over to my dorm room to put on face masks, and I would paint everyone's fingernails and toenails as we enjoyed "chick flicks." At a bridal shower, my maid of honor recreated this college spa experience. Judy, the lady who gave me the care package, had no way of knowing my special connections to pampering. Once again, God was interweaving themes and paying great attention to detail "behind the scenes."

Prior to being on disability myself, I probably would have been confused by hearing someone on short-term disability say she needed a vacation. However, this was exactly what I needed.

I had officially been on disability for a week. However, I struggled to relax at our home, because there were always piles of papers to tackle, or a project to work on, or just regular chores like cleaning and laundry. A vacation would remove the temptation to be productive.

Even though I had not planned to be on a disability leave, I had anticipated this vacation for many months. And what a time it was! The vacation began with my cousin's wedding in North Carolina. It was wonderful to spend time with family that I had grown up visiting every Thanksgiving, but as an adult hadn't seen all together in almost ten years. Celebrating with family was more than a distraction from my pain, it was a gift.

After the wedding festivities, Jack and I drove further south to Hilton Head Island in South Carolina. This was my third trip to Hilton Head; it was one of my favorite places to stay. Hilton Head does not feel commercialized in comparison to oceanfront places in the Northeast that I have visited. Bright lights and large signs are not allowed. This, along with many trees, gives a feeling that it is not overdeveloped. My parents have several timeshares, and they generously gave us a week to use wherever we wanted. Hilton Head was an easy choice.

Not only was the location ideal, but the weather was, too. This time of year, it was sunny and in the 70s. To a Pennsylvania girl, this was extraordinary November weather. We were able to relax by the pool and at the beach. In trips past, we had rented bikes and enjoyed traveling the winding bike paths all over the island. But not this trip; I tried to conserve as much energy as possible.

The frosting on the cake of our visit to South Carolina was getting to spend time with very dear friends, Beth and Colin Kernaghan. Jack had met them first in college, but they felt very much like my friends, too. As we were completing our adoption paperwork, we needed to make many hard decisions – but selecting the guardians for our children if we died was not one of them. Jack and I both immediately thought of Beth and Colin. We love them and admire Beth and Colin as individuals, as a couple, and as parents. They are the type of friends that feel like family.

As we visited at Hilton Head, Beth was seven months pregnant with their second son. We all enjoyed a slower pace and taking naps. Watching Duncan, their firstborn who was almost four years old, enjoy the pool and play in the sand was mesmerizing and magical. It reminded me of how much joy children can find in simple things. I looked forward to bringing Addie and Grayson to this resort location.

Even in an environment with zero stress and the company of sweet friends, my body experienced drastic changes in pain and confirmed my decision to go on short-term disability. One moment I would be feeling peppy and fine, and the next moment I would be doubled over in excruciating pain and exhausted. Even though this happened daily, I was always surprised. It was like a switch was flipped. There were no warning signs.

I truly gave myself permission to relax. I realized I could not take the actuarial exams while on disability. First, it might put my disability pay in jeopardy. Second, with all of the pain medicine my brain felt like mush. I was thankful for this buffer of rest and relaxation before we needed to return to Temple.

Less than a week after returning from Hilton Head, Jack and I set out for Temple Hospital. This trip was different from the start. We did not go down the night before. I did not sleep the night before, either. I was restless with anxiety and nervousness. I did not know what to expect. My mind was flooded with questions. *What if I had some serious problem? How long would it take to schedule one of the surgeries? What would the recovery from surgery look like? How long until this pain would be gone and my energy would return? When would I be able to get off of pain medicine? When could I return to work?*

We were unsure how heavy traffic would be on a Friday morning, so we allowed plenty of time for the drive. We arrived at Temple early and sat in the hospital waiting room. This was becoming one of my least favorite places to be. I felt like I was at an airport terminal waiting to get on a plane, but did not know when the plane was going to leave or where it was headed. I saw the sweet technician from the torture test, and I had flashbacks. I could not bear any more tests like that, I thought.

As our appointment time came and went, I became even more nervous. I tried to tell myself that sometimes emergencies come up, or maybe a patient needed some extra time with Dr. Albert. I attempted to have grace even though the delay was fueling my anxiety.

Finally a nurse opened the door into the waiting area and said, "Rebecca Miller." I was getting closer to the answer.

Jack and I were shown back to an exam room. We waited for another long gap of time. Eventually we heard a tap on the door, and someone besides Dr. Albert entered. It was a young woman who had more personality than Dr. Albert. She explained that Dr. Albert had gotten backed up with patients, so she was helping him out. I cannot remember if this individual was a nurse practitioner or a resident. Bottom line, she was not a full-fledged medical doctor.

Once again, my face and body language said it all. I think Jack also verbalized our exhaustion. We had sat for several hours and wanted to see Dr. Albert. What were the test results?

What was the action plan? This other individual could only take notes on my current symptoms. I felt like I was starting from scratch yet again and was being passed around.

I tried to calmly explain that the pain was getting more intense and more frequent. I did not have the strength and energy I had had just a few weeks earlier. The woman appeared very compassionate and took thorough notes. She was an active listener, asking questions and making sure she fully understood the situation. She said that she would prep Dr. Albert and he would be in shortly.

Again we waited. I felt like I was part of a lab experiment. How long can a patient wait before she starts climbing the walls or just leaves? We did have a window, which we could look out. Otherwise there were no distractions in this tiny exam room, except for a few posters showing human anatomy.

Finally after we had waited a total of three hours, Dr. Albert entered. He did not waste any time. He opened my chart, skimmed it, and stated, "All of your tests came back normal, with the exception of the bacteria overgrowth test. It appears you have bacteria overgrowth. You will need to take two different antibiotics for two weeks." He continued on in a monotone voice, "I will see you back here in three to four months."

Dr. Albert stood up to leave. I was paralyzed with shock. We waited three hours to hear this!? I had dealt with bacteria overgrowth before, and I knew what those symptoms were like. This was not the same.

Jack quickly asked, "Will the antibiotics help with the pain?"

Dr. Albert replied flatly, "No," as he reached for the door.

Jack asserted himself once again, "Can she start taking pancreatic enzymes? My sister has Cystic Fibrosis, and the enzymes help her tremendously. If Becky does have a problem with her pancreas could this help?"

Dr. Albert said apathetically, "Sure, she can start enzymes after she finishes the antibiotics. I don't think it is her pancreas, but taking enzymes certainly won't hurt her."

I felt like a significant withdrawal had just been drafted from my "hope" account. I was getting a loud message that my current health status was not important. The hospital scheduler informed us that Dr. Albert's next available appointment was not until May. I could not keep living like this for six months without any steps being taken to find a solution. Beyond the intense pain, this was also a financial hardship. I was angry. Was my health issue not life-threatening or rare enough, that it was okay for me to wait in pain for half a year? What about quality of life? Was I being punished for an error or wrong choice I had made in the past? Was this some sort of sick, twisted nightmare?

As we headed home, I was a mess of emotions. I was furious that we had waited patiently so long and then had received such poor care. I felt like an inconvenience or a hypochondriac. Did Dr. Albert not believe me? Would he want to wait six months in this kind of pain? How could this be acceptable? Was this what others experienced? This fit under the umbrella of Things No One Teaches You in School. I was never offered a course in high school or college on how to be a medical patient. It seemed my quality of life did not matter. I was twenty-eight years old, not one hundred and eight. I felt a huge blow to my self-worth. Somehow Jack managed to hold it together and drive. My vision was blurry from the tears I was attempting to hold back.

Thankfully we had a stop at Trader Joe's to look forward to. We pulled into the congested parking lot by Trader Joe's and started circling to try and find a parking spot. Then, to our great surprise, Jack spotted dear friends of ours from Lancaster. Trader Joe's is over an hour away from Lancaster, so we certainly were not expecting to run into our friends, Don and Rila Hackett.

Don was the minister who officiated our wedding. Don had also been Jack's mentor during seminary. Now Jack and Don were co-workers at the same church.

Years before, Rila had shared in church about a dark season in her life that occurred right after college. Her vulnerability had opened the door for me to muster enough courage to ask her if we could go to breakfast together. At a bustling family-style restaurant one Saturday morning in July 2006, we had breakfast in a booth. I shared my deepest fears. My fears encompassed a variety of areas, but they boiled down to one thing: fear of never being whole or complete. My time as a teacher on the Navajo reservation had left me raw and shattered. The healing process seemed to be moving at a snail's pace, if at all. I was too fragile to dream, because my greatest dream and passion of helping others, specifically disadvantaged children, had left me devoid of hope and self-worth. And so I was stuck, emotionally and spiritually. As I shared, I was amazed that Rila was not disgusted or repulsed by my explosion of tears.

During that first breakfast together, I had no idea that two years later, I would be a pastor's wife like Rila. But over the years, breakfast together became our tradition. I would call up Rila and ask her to join me, and I would share my struggles. She was a true mentor. We seemed to be wired similarly in some ways, and Rila was a great listener and asked thought-provoking questions. She also was willing to share some of her experiences and insights. Although she didn't look it, she was almost double my age – and had a lot of wisdom to share.

I do not think Jack and I could have chosen a better couple to cross paths with right after our frustrating appointment at Temple Hospital. After a rude number of honks, finally Jack got their attention; Don told us that he hadn't known why that car kept honking at them! They pulled into a spot next to us and got out of their minivan. I think the floodgate of my tears clued them in to the fact that we had not had a good appointment. Jack shared; I was unable to form words about what had transpired. Don and Rila hugged us and prayed with us.

Up to this point, I had been unaware of the toll all of this took on Jack, as my brain was on overload with so many questions and thoughts. Jack had stayed strong and positive around me, but in the presence of the Hacketts, he let down his guard. He not only verbally expressed his weariness, but his slumped shoulders and tired eyes reinforced that he was also experiencing a harsh beating from all of this.

The timing of seeing Don and Rila reassured me that God had not forgotten us and that we were going to be okay. Later as I typed my mass email about the appointment to friends and family, I realized that if the appointment had happened on time, we would have missed seeing the Hacketts. As frustrating as it had been to wait, I was grateful for the well-timed meeting at Trader Joe's. I was starting to see how truly the timing I wanted might not always be best, and that delays might be conduits for divine appointments.

CHAPTER 6

THANKSGIVING

Thanksgiving is one of my favorite holidays, because growing up it was the one time of the year that I saw many of my extended family members. My parents, my sister, and I would travel four hours south, other family members would drive north, and we would all meet up in Virginia at my great-aunt and great-uncle's house to enjoy a huge meal together.

My family members would be spread out over three or four tables, with folding chairs and card tables spilling out of the kitchen and dining room and into the living room. Orange and yellow tablecloths helped to unite the multiple tables. Many times the centerpieces on each table were handmade. Everyone helped in some way.

My great-aunt and great-uncle lived in a cozy ranch-style home, and the aroma from the many dishes – including sweet potatoes, rolls, green beans, and ham – would permeate the small house. Some years we did not have a turkey, because certain family members preferred ham and chicken. But the absence of a turkey on Thanksgiving did not bother me. It may sound like a greeting card, but even as a child I really felt and believed that being with family was what mattered most.

As Thanksgiving approached this year, I had lots to be thankful for. I was blessed that with every battle and challenge, God's presence was revealed in a new and creative way. I was constantly humbled and encouraged by sweet cards, notes, emails, and many prayers from friends. Then, the Sunday before Thanksgiving, the grand finale of blessing occurred.

Each year on the Sunday evening before Thanksgiving, our church held an apple pie auction in conjunction with a talent show. This annual tradition helped to support youth mission trips. The youth baked a ton of pies, and a church member, who was a professional auctioneer, auctioned off the pies in between performances of music, dance, and other forms of talent. The bids were known to get pretty high. It was not uncommon for a pie to go for three hundred dollars – and then be given back to be auctioned off again. The evening also included a bake sale and other items for purchase. Lastly, raffle tickets offered opportunities to win baskets full of goodies. It was an extremely fun evening that I looked forward to each year.

This year's event was just two days after my frustrating appointment at Temple. Jack and I donated a basket full of our favorite Trader Joe's products. I thought this was enough of a contribution, but Jack wanted to purchase some raffle tickets as well.

Sunday morning, I looked around at the different baskets, and one caught my eye. It was a basket labeled "serenity" with an incredibly soft and fluffy blanket, wind chimes, tea, a few books, a journal, a soothing CD, and other items. I knew our chances of winning anything were slim, because we were not purchasing many tickets. However, I secretly hoped for this basket.

That evening, I was too sick to go to the event. But the next day, Jack told me that we had won a piece of original art and the serenity basket. I couldn't believe it! I am a math person. Odds were low that we would win anything – let alone two items. When I took off the cellophane from around the serenity basket, a note inside explained that the contents had been donated by the Thursday morning women's Bible study group. Some serious prayer warriors from my church who had been praying for me were participants in this group. I felt like a small child with my favorite blankie. I wrapped myself up in this serenity blanket and took it with me to my parents' house each day, where I rested while Jack was at work. I liked to envision that I was wrapped up in prayers.

The blanket was extra comforting as I had returned from

Temple with a head cold. At first, I was not sure if my congestion was a result of crying. However, the sore throat and runny nose persisted. Then, the day before Thanksgiving, on Wednesday, November 23, 2011, I woke up with a urinary tract infection. It may seem silly or strange, but I was thankful for the infection, because it forced me to make an appointment with my primary care physician, Dr. Granger. I called Dr. Granger's office and was able to be seen that same day.

As sick as I was, I continued to be concerned with what other people thought, including individuals that I did not even know well. The friendly receptionists at Dr. Granger's office knew my name before I even signed in. Equally crazy, I was starting to remember their names. Did they think I was a hypochondriac? Did they wonder why I was there so often? I was even more concerned about what Dr. Granger would think. Would he agree with Dr. Albert and not want to see me for several months?

My appointment with Dr. Granger contrasted drastically with my recent appointment with Dr. Albert. I did not wait long in the exam room before Dr. Granger walked in and sat down, faced me, and showed genuine concern. Dr. Granger not only prescribed antibiotics to combat the infection, but he also prescribed some new medicine for nausea. The very best medicine he provided, however, was hope and empathy. Unlike my appointment the week before, I no longer felt abandoned for months on end. Dr. Granger desired to help me get to the root of the issue, so I could receive permanent relief and resume my quality of life.

Dr. Granger believed I had pancreatitis and that the enzymes would help. He prescribed CREON, which are pancreatic enzymes from pigs. I did not previously know much about the pancreas and was receiving quite an education. I learned that the human pancreas should secrete enzymes into the stomach every time a person eats, to help break down the food. If the enzymes aren't able to leave the pancreas, they not only cause inflammation and pain in the pancreas, but they also prevent food from being digested properly, which can cause malnourishment. Dr. Granger hoped that the prescribed enzymes would aid in my digestion and absorption of nutrients. I was losing weight, and my slender frame could not afford any more weight loss.

Unfortunately, I could not start taking the enzymes until I completed the two-week round of antibiotics for the bacteria overgrowth. But I could not start *those* antibiotics until I completed the antibiotics for my urinary tract infection. I felt like dominos had to be set up, and I could not just knock down one in the middle. The waiting was hard. I really wanted to skip the antibiotics and immediately start taking the enzymes, but I trusted and followed my doctor's instructions.

Dr. Granger also suggested I see a specialist somewhere else, so I made an appointment at Johns Hopkins Hospital to see a pancreas specialist. The first available opening at Hopkins was not until December 27. Even though this required another month of waiting, I felt like I had an action plan and an advocate in Dr. Granger, and this helped to restore my hope.

Dr. Granger was a real gift, because on top of the physical pain and the emotional rollercoaster I was on, I had another battle: my disability provider through my employer kept denying my approval for short-term disability and continued to require additional paperwork. I wanted to shout at the disability company that *I* wanted to be back at work even more than they wanted me to be. My disability pay was a third less than my regular salary, and our money was awfully tight. We really could not afford this decrease in income. In addition, the disability company was not helping my health improve by stressing me out. I did not understand why my doctor's word, my medical records, and my frequent hospitalizations were not proof enough.

As a peacemaker and person who avoids conflict, I found it very taxing and exhausting to have to argue and fight with the disability company. It also fueled the judgment I projected on others, sure that people must think I am lazy and that I just did not want to work. After all, I did not know a single peer of mine who was on disability. For brief periods I would even think that maybe if I just tried harder, I could go back to work. These thoughts would last for a few minutes – until I got up to do something and realized I had no energy, or I experienced another serious wave of sharp pain.

When I would get frustrated, which happened often, I would try to redirect my focus to my blessings. Dr. Granger was definitely at the top of the list.

Since I couldn't travel this year, on Thanksgiving Day Jack and I woke up early and headed to church. Typically we had been out of town on Thanksgiving Day, so this was the first time either of us had attended a Thanksgiving worship service. It was a small gathering of forty or so individuals in the former gym of our church. The only sign of the space's former life was the high ceiling. The church had removed the basketball hoops quite a few years back, and the floor was covered with carpet. A permanent stage had been added and was illuminated by professional lights. An enclosed sound system was partitioned off on the opposite wall of the stage. This space was now used for weekly contemporary services, while the main sanctuary continued to hold traditional worship services.

This Thanksgiving service was similar to Sunday morning's contemporary service, with musicians along with vocalists leading worship on the stage. The stage was typically filled with guitars, music stands, a drum set, piano, and six or seven people.

We sang some songs and had an opportunity to give thanks. It was a simple and brief service. Jack got to sit next to me. It was a rare treat to worship at church next to Jack, because he usually was leading worship up front. During the service, however, I started to feel intense pain. After the service ended, I told Jack I was not feeling well. The pain was surging through my rib cage. Fortunately, the church was only a few blocks from the Emergency Room. Jack drove me straight from church to the ER.

The pain was horrific and quickly escalated to unbearable. I cried from pain and also because I was upset to be in the ER on Thanksgiving Day. I profusely thanked the nurses, doctors, and staff for working on Thanksgiving Day.

After I received a round or two of narcotics via IV, the pain receded and my brain was in a fuzzy state. Jack called my mom to let her know that we were in the ER and would not be able to make it to Thanksgiving dinner. My mom decided to postpone our Thanksgiving festivities by one day. I was discharged from the ER around 6 p.m., just when my sister, her boyfriend Michael, Jack, and I had planned to meet at my parents' house for Thanksgiving dinner. I was afraid I had ruined Thanksgiving. Jack did not complain, but I felt bad that he had to eat a microwavable dinner. I had no appetite.

The next day, my mom reheated the previous day's dishes and we celebrated Thanksgiving. My parents, sister, Michael, Jack, and I sat around one table in my parents' dining room. A beautiful golden tablecloth was the backdrop to the china, sterling silverware, cloth napkins, and crystal.

I was still feeling rather guilty for postponing Thanksgiving. My sister encouraged me by saying, "Becky, I am rather glad that we are having Thanksgiving today. I don't know how I could have eaten two Thanksgiving meals in one day." She and Michael had eaten a Thanksgiving meal in the middle of the day with Michael's family. She continued on, "Thanks for helping to spread out Thanksgiving eating and celebrating." This helped to lift my spirits.

Typically I would fill my plate and then go back for seconds – but this year I only ate a few bites before feeling full and nauseous. I did not even want dessert. I excused myself early from the table and reclined on my parents' couch. I was feeling weary from the attack of pain the day before. Sitting up for extended periods of time was exhausting and added to my rib and abdominal pain.

With this Thanksgiving holiday experience, I hoped and prayed that my illness would not also ruin my family's Christmas celebration and festivities. I also knew that the Christmas season was Jack's favorite time of the year, and his love language was gifts. I worried about how I would make Christmas special this year with very limited energy and resources. I never would have guessed the ways God would provide and shower us with blessings during the Advent Season.

CHAPTER 7

TWELVE DAYS OF CHRISTMAS

A week after the apple pie auction and talent show, the contemporary worship space at our church looked more like a community theater. A downtown city canvas backdrop of row homes and storefronts replaced music stands, a drum set, and a piano on the stage. It was three days after Thanksgiving and the start of Advent, the season of anticipation of Christ's birth. We, along with about seventy others, had come to watch a special drama. There was excitement and energy in the air.

A handful of youth and a few adults performed the drama. Jack had written the script entirely in rhyme. It depicted what a variety of individuals from different socioeconomic backgrounds were doing the night before Christmas. One character slowed down enough to see – and help – someone in need. This compassionate character then reflected on the real meaning of Christmas.

It was always easy for me to get wrapped up in the decorating, baking, and holiday shopping, so the skit was a perfect way to kick off the Advent season with the right focus. I loved seeing my husband's creativity utilized, and it was fun to see familiar friends from church take on character roles that for some were drastically different than their true personalities.

Further, as much as I enjoyed the drama, the activities that followed were the true highlight of the evening for me. For the hour after the drama, Jack offered attendees three choices; we were welcome to do any combination of the activities and spend as little or as much time on each as we wanted. For one activity, the youth minister, who was also an artist, had outlined a nativity scene on the floor-to-ceiling windows located at the front of the church. These windows looked out over a main city street. Folks could help "paint" the windows to create a stained glass window effect.

The second option was to write cards to homebound members of our church community. Card stock, stamps, and stickers were available to create festive cards, to let those unable to come to church know that they were remembered.

The third option was to create two-toned fleece blankets by knotting the fringe of two pieces of fleece together. I spent the entire time working on these fleece blankets. My parents, Beth (my sister), Michael (Beth's boyfriend), Michael's parents, and Michael's three aunts also chose to work on the blankets. The blankets were larger than a card table, and so we sat around long tables knotting the fringes. It reminded me of pictures I had seen of ladies quilting. Obviously this took less skill and concentration than quilting, for which I was extra grateful with my mushy brain.

This was my first time meeting Michael's family. They are Greek Orthodox, and I admired them for coming to a different church denomination and participating. Michael's mother and her three sisters all liked to talk simultaneously and loved competition. Their favorite argument was which of them was the tallest. All four ladies hovered around the five-foot mark.

I had always believed that each individual person could make a difference. However, I was even more energized and inspired when a group of people came together and got a lot accomplished in a short amount of time. By the end of the evening, the group had completed 28 sizable blankets, along with the faux stained-glass windows and dozens of handmade cards.

Each completed blanket had a personal note pinned to it. I loved reading the creativity and thoughtfulness expressed on small sheets of paper: "May you know you are blanketed in love," or "Know you are wrapped in love." The blankets with their hand-written notes were donated to a local homeless shelter.

I appreciated that the three activities were accessible to

people of all ages. I loved seeing a five-year-old work alongside a sixty-year-old. I looked forward to doing activities like this with our own children.

I was extra proud of my beloved husband for organizing and pulling off this event in the midst of me being terribly sick and needy. I was also incredibly grateful to be present and to participate, because the following day I experienced horrible pain and spent the entire day in bed.

This year the countdown for Christmas was overshadowed by my countdown to seeing the pancreas specialist at Johns Hopkins. The majority of December was a blur, primarily because I slept a lot. Some days I would only get out of bed to go to the bathroom and to eat. My energy continued to decline, and my pain continued to increase. To combat the pain, I had to take pain medicine that made me drowsy.

Jack and my mom made a lot of Christmas cookies. I had always enjoyed baking and taste testing, but this year every time I ate, I feared that I would have pain. My mom did the shopping and wrapping of Christmas gifts for me. I helped my mom and Jack on good days, but other days I truly felt like an invalid. Of course, both my mom and Jack showered me with grace and encouragement. They never implied that I was an inconvenience or a burden.

One Saturday morning in December, to my great delight, I woke up without feeling horrible pain. Jack asked if I wanted to go to Central Market, our local farmers' market, to pick up some fresh produce and see the market decorated for Christmas. It was only a few blocks from our home, and typically we would walk. However, with my energy being limited, Jack drove us. As we opened the doors to walk in, a flash mob began singing the "Hallelujah Chorus." I felt like I was in a movie. The timing was perfect. I had seen videos of flash mobs on YouTube but had never experienced one live.

Then the most magical series of events began twelve days before Christmas. Every evening once it was dark, our doorbell would ring, and we would find a gift on our stoop. Each gift had a typewritten note, but no explanation of who was giving the gift. We were even instructed not to spy – or else the gifts would stop.

The gifts were lavish. One night we had a huge basket on our stoop filled with fresh fruit. Another night we received a $50 gift card to a favorite restaurant. It was clear the gift giver knew us well and knew what we liked. This generosity was extra special because money was so tight. Plus, the thrill of the surprise was exhilarating each evening. Jack and I tried to guess who might be up to this.

On Christmas Eve at church after the service, as Jack and I were hanging up the costumes from the children's pageant, Julia and Gordon (our pumpkin carving buddies) along with their parents handed us our final "Twelve Days of Christmas" gift. They had partnered with another member from our church to shower us with gifts. We were so humbled and shocked. We could not wait until the following Christmas to "pay it forward" and surprise another family.

CHAPTER 8

DECEMBER 27

Most people do not give their pancreas much thought, but when mine became a prime suspect for my mysterious pain, I found out as much as I could about it. I also discovered that someone I had known for years also suffered from pancreas problems. My hairdresser, Tami, had experienced similar problems with intense abdominal pain that took a while to diagnose and had sent her to the ER on numerous occasions. Tami is a petite lady with lots of freckles. I always picture her with red hair, although her hair's length and color actually change as often as the seasons. She is outgoing, but she's also an amazing listener.

Tami had been my hairdresser since I was a preteen. She helped me get through the awkward adolescent years. She even showed me how to put on makeup for special events. Tami could always lift my spirits – and not just by giving me a new hairdo.

When I returned from teaching on the Navajo reservation and felt defeated, Tami connected me with a veteran teacher who also had taught on a Navajo reservation. This other client of Tami's had taught locally for many years before accepting a job on a Navajo reservation. But even with years of experience, she was still only able to teach for less than a month on the reservation, because the conditions were so horrible. This helped release me from terrible guilt and shame.

Tami felt like a cool aunt or big sister to me. She had a few more years of experience, which gave her perspective I valued. I had always imagined Tami would do my hair and makeup on my wedding day. Unfortunately, Tami had health issues and had been unable to work for several years because of pancreatitis. But she had seen Dr. Cole at Johns Hopkins, and under his care she was finally able to get relief from pain and eventually return to work. I was optimistic that I would receive relief, too; I was going to see the exact same pancreas specialist at Hopkins.

After cutting my hair for over fifteen years, Tami knew me well. She knew I did not like surprises. She had seen her share of doctors, so she could empathize with the anxiety of meeting yet another new one. Tami shared that the first time she met Dr. Cole at Johns Hopkins, she only had a doctor's appointment scheduled. However, he had tests done the same day, and then she ended up having surgery the following day to remove a cyst on her pancreas. Thus, she encouraged Jack and me to pack clothes for several days. I was optimistic that Dr. Cole would provide me with relief quickly via an ERCP. This year throughout all of December, my eye had been set on December 27th and going to Johns Hopkins Hospital. As much as I loved the festivities and gift giving, I really was ready for a permanent solution to my pain.

So, two days after Christmas, Jack drove me down to Baltimore to meet Tami's pancreas specialist, Dr. Cole. We plugged the address into our GPS. According to our GPS, his office was a little over an hour away, but we allowed extra time in case we hit traffic or had trouble finding a parking space. I was confused when our GPS said we had arrived. We were in a parking lot surrounded by shops. There were several upscale brick buildings with boutiques, hair salons, clothing stores, and restaurants occupying the first floor.

Since we had neither hit traffic nor had trouble finding a parking space, we decided to check out a few stores. Our favorite was a stationery shop that had funny cocktail napkins, gag gifts, unique children's toys, and of course, gorgeous stationery. Jack was naturally drawn to the Christmas clearance section. I had to remind him we did not have any room for additional Christmas decorations.

Jack was doing his best to keep me distracted. However, I kept glancing at my watch. When it was fifteen minutes before my scheduled appointment time, we stopped window shopping and rode the elevator up to the third floor. The cherry wood paneled elevator reminded me of a fancy hotel. The elevator opened to a hall with office suites. The place did not feel like a doctor's office – until I opened the door to Dr. Cole's suite. The waiting room had individuals who looked to be in terrible health. Many were frail and clearly were not concerned with their appearance.

The ladies behind the glass counter took my insurance information and then had me take a seat. I had only been sitting for a few minutes when my name was called. A nurse took my temperature, blood pressure, and weight, but then she sent me back to the waiting room. False alarm; I was not about to see Dr. Cole.

Waiting rooms seemed to taunt me. Just as their name says, I did a lot of waiting and wondering in these rooms. Even in this classy, upscale building, the waiting room furniture looked shabby and was uncomfortable. There were brochures about different kinds of medication treatment options for horrible-sounding diseases and conditions. Not exactly coffee table reading material.

Thankfully, I had brought a book to read. However, between the narcotics in my system and being nervous, I had difficulty concentrating. I am sure I read the same page a dozen times and still had no comprehension of what was occurring in the story. Every time the door opened, I would look up and hope the nurse was going to call me back. Finally, a nurse called my name, and Jack and I went back to the exam room.

Dr. Cole listened, made eye contact, jotted down some notes, and flipped through my chart. He also examined my abdomen, but he was gentler than previous doctors. *Hooray, he was listening!* I thought. I was experiencing sharp pain during the appointment, which was helpful. I could point to specifically where I felt like knives were stabbing me. I felt a little psychotic explaining, "The pain is sometimes on the right side and sometimes on the left side, but always in my rib cage. Sometimes it feels like it is going from the front of my ribcage to my back and down my spine." Many times the pain would be so intense that I just felt pain. My entire body felt in pain. I was not sure how to articulate this to Dr. Cole.

I was not completely surprised, but I was definitely frustrated that Dr. Cole wanted to repeat some tests and also do some additional tests. One of the tests was an endoscopy. This would be my sixth endoscopy, and my most recent had been just three months earlier. My thoughts were, *Really? What do you think you are going to see that wasn't seen before?* However, I nodded my head in agreement.

What Dr. Cole said next crushed my spirit, like someone crumpling up an empty soda can. He stated, "I am a pancreas specialist, and I don't think there is anything wrong with your pancreas. To be safe and thorough, I am ordering these three tests. However, my guess is these tests will confirm that your pancreas is fine. If your pancreas is fine, then I will not be able to help you. Do you understand?"

"Yes, thank you," I softly responded. I understood that a pancreas specialist would only help patients with pancreas issues. What I did not understand was how Dr. Granger could think my pancreas was the culprit and Dr. Cole could be so sure it was not. I was not so concerned with which organ or system was malfunctioning; I simply desired to pinpoint the issue and have a resolution.

I sat at the checkout desk and waited while the receptionist called and scheduled the three tests. I had hoped we would be scheduling my ERCP today to put the stent in my pancreas duct – and I could begin the New Year with a new focus and outlook. However, one test was scheduled for 4:00 PM on January 9th, and the two other tests were scheduled for the afternoon of the 17th. We scheduled an appointment to review the tests with Dr. Cole on January 24th.

Before I had experienced horrific, chronic pain, waiting four weeks to follow up with a doctor seemed an acceptable amount of time. However, now every single day seemed to drag on indefinitely. I was experiencing extreme attacks of pain multiple times each and every day, and this was with strong narcotic pain medicine. I was horrified to think how wretched my body would feel without pain medicine. Even after each sharp attack would subside, I was left feeling like I had bruises all over my body.

I did not even have the energy to cry. I wanted to wave the white flag and surrender. I could not take any more. Where had I gone wrong? I had many friends and family praying for this appointment. I had all of my records forwarded to Dr. Cole's office. I was polite and courteous. I had good health insurance and paid my bills on time.

I wanted a fast pass. I had been experiencing pain without a break for over three months. This was beyond cruel and usual punishment. I knew the doctors were not inflicting the pain, but by their non-urgent response, I felt like they were saying, "It is okay for you to suffer."

I slept most of the next day, due to the exhaustion from traveling and receiving disappointing news. My sister called me from Florida, where she had spent Christmas with Michael and his family. She exclaimed that Michael had proposed, and she asked me to be her matron of honor. God gave me strength and energy to enthusiastically produce some squeals of joy over the phone. I was ecstatic for my sister. I did not mention the outcome of my appointment at Hopkins. I wanted all energy and focus to be on her.

Discouragement sank in, but I continued to send updates to family and friends and ask for prayers for strength. I was clinging to the words of the psalmist who wrote, "But I will sing of your strength, in the morning I will sing of your love; for you are my fortress, my refuge in times of trouble" (Psalm 59:16, NIV).

I also continued to be comforted by music, and I loved listening to Mandisa's song, "Stronger." I prayed and hoped I would come out stronger from these experiences. I trusted and believed that there was purpose in my suffering, but it was hard not being able to see how all of these puzzle pieces fit together. One dear friend at church reminded me, "It is darkest before the dawn."

CHAPTER 9

GRATITUDE SCAVENGER HUNT

"A new year and a new you." I have always loved the idea of New Year's resolutions. I enjoy fresh starts and blank slates. It's like a new journal with blank pages, or an Etch A Sketch after shaking it.

I love the opportunity or challenge to make self-improvements. My past resolutions had included giving up soda and fried food, initiating the habit of flossing my teeth daily, and reading the Bible in a year. Like most individuals, I had not been successful with all of my resolutions, but that never stopped me from making new ones each year.

In December my dear college friend, Annie, mailed me a copy of *One Thousand Gifts* by Ann Voskamp. In this book the author talked about various examples of miracles and healings performed after Jesus or someone gave thanks. For example, a Leper returned to thank Jesus after his healing and then received full healing; Jesus gave thanks before Lazarus was raised from the dead; Jesus gave thanks for the loaves of bread and fish before they miraculously multiplied; Jesus praised God even at the Last Supper when he knew he was going to die, so that we could receive salvation. This author also talked about the Greek roots of the word Eucharist – grace, thankfulness, and joy. She believes that gratitude is the key to joy. I thought, *I cannot eliminate pain with joy, but having eyes of gratitude will certainly help make the days more enjoyable.* My spirit had been slipping, and this book helped me get back on track.

One Thousand Gifts prompted me to start the New Year with a gratitude journal. Diet and exercise were not realistic areas for me to focus on during this season, but keeping a

60

gratitude journal was something I could do.

I became energized by the thought of continuing to read *One Thousand Gifts* and put into practice what I learned. It was like taking a new course. I took out a journal where I had jotted down items I was grateful for on a sporadic basis. Now I turned to a new page and entered the date: January 1, 2012.

I had no idea what events and observations would fill these pages. I longed for the day when I would record "pain-free day," or "health issue named and resolved," or "referral for forever children from Ethiopia," or "debt-free." As much as I desired these events, I was determined to record blessings each day. It was like a scavenger hunt challenge. I may have to look twice to find a hidden treasure that was disguised by its surroundings.

I liked to start each day, before getting out of bed, by declaring, "This is the day the Lord has made; I will rejoice and be glad in it!" from Psalm 118:24. I was never very good at memorizing Scripture, but this verse had stuck with me since childhood. As I reflected with my gratitude journal, I realized that most days I had not embraced the truth that this day, *today*, was a day to rejoice. I had habitually looked at the day ahead as an opportunity to be productive and cross items off of the ever-growing to-do list. Now, I was challenging myself to look at each day as an opportunity to rejoice – purely based on the fact that God was with me. I had little to no control over whether the day would be productive or whether I would have pain. Therefore, having the constant of God's presence brought me great peace and comfort that I had previously overlooked.

This gratitude journal also kept me accountable each day. I had assigned myself to find and record at least one blessing each day, and I found that the more I looked for blessings, the more I saw and recorded. The blessings ranged from a short line at the pharmacy, an item on sale at the grocery store, or a close parking space, to life-pivoting experiences.

One of these pivoting experiences happened on Friday, January 6. I had an appointment to have blood drawn. As someone who is scared of needles, I always dreaded blood work. The mere thought of needles made me lightheaded and queasy. On this particular Friday, I was looking forward to later accompanying my sister as she tried on wedding gowns; I was positive that trip would be my day's highlight. I didn't expect to list anything in my gratitude journal from this blood work appointment.

Fortunately, I did not have to go to the hospital to have lab work done. An office in the suburbs near my mom's house was tied to the hospital, but it did not have the weird smells or sounds that I associated with a hospital. All they did at this office was blood work, so I also mentally felt more comfortable going there, knowing that whoever was going to stick me had a lot of experience drawing blood.

Each time I had blood drawn, I could never watch as the nurse would stick me and fill up vial after vial of blood. I looked away from the needle and would always ask the nurses questions about their family and interests, based on pictures in their cubicles. This served two purposes. First, it helped to distract me. Second, since I spent a lot of time at home, this interaction helped to assuage some of my cabin fever.

When a woman named Mary called me back, I felt even more at ease. She had been my phlebotomist a few months earlier. I remembered Mary, but I was shocked that she also remembered me. I figured she saw dozens of patients every day.

Mary inquired, "How are you doing? Are your doctors any closer to finding a solution?"

I lamented, "I went to Temple and had lots of tests done without pinpointing a culprit. I am now seeing a pancreas specialist at Hopkins and of course he wants more tests done. My primary care physician thinks my pancreas duct may be blocked. I believe the duct is called Sphincter of Oddi or something like that."

Mary responded with true empathy, "I am actually having surgery in five days, this coming Wednesday, on my Sphincter of Oddi."

"What?!" I exclaimed. "I was told that Lancaster General Hospital would not perform this surgery."

"You are right. LGH has never performed this surgery before. I will be the first one to have it done in Lancaster."

Without thinking, I blurted out, "Aren't you nervous or concerned to be the first?"

Mary graciously replied, "The pain has been so horrible, I am willing to try anything to get relief." I could certainly relate to that feeling. Mary continued, "Plus, a surgeon from another hospital who specializes in this is going to be present to oversee the surgery."

"Oh wow! That sounds like an ideal setup. I am having a horrible time getting a doctor to schedule this procedure," I said. "Hopefully, the success of your surgery will pave the way for others to have this surgery in Lancaster." I was genuinely thankful for Mary's courage to be the first. I would be too worried to have an inexperienced doctor, but I supposed for any doctor to become skilled and achieve experience, some patient must be his or her first.

Typically I do not ask personal questions of friends, let alone acquaintances. However, questions regarding health just seemed to naturally pour out of my mouth now – perhaps since I was asked a plethora of questions every time I saw a doctor. Plus, I had never heard of anyone else having an issue with their Sphincter of Oddi. The last two questions I asked Mary provided answers that were miracles in my mind.

"Mary, if you don't mind me asking, what are your symptoms?"

"Horrible pain in my ribcage, abdomen, and back. It will come on suddenly and is so intense that I am forced to go the ER to receive any relief. I have had quite a few ER trips in the past four months. The pain is not always in the same place and comes without warning. When the pain subsides, I am left utterly exhausted and sore. The pain consumes me, and I have no quality of life. I have not been able to work for the past few months."

"Oh my goodness, I have the exact same symptoms."

Hearing her symptoms made me feel so much less isolated. I continued, "May I ask, Mary, why are you here working today?"

"I was going to lose my job if I did not work a few hours. I cannot afford to lose my job, so I am working for four hours a day just this week."

My jaw dropped. If I had been there a week earlier or later, Mary would not have been there. Even if I had been a few hours later, I would not have seen Mary. It was truly a miracle that I got paired with her. I could not wait to record this latest blessing in my journal.

I often looked over my gratitude journal when I would send my email updates to friends and family. I had sent out my first email update in October to friends as an excuse to reconnect and ask for prayers. I knew I needed prayers, and I also thought my message might open the door for me to help and pray for friends. I was surprised by the outpouring of emails and cards in response. I lacked the energy to respond to each message, so a mass email was the most energy-efficient way of communicating and updating friends and family. With so many individuals praying and sending their love, I felt responsible to keep them informed and share the answers to prayers.

Many times I received answers to prayer for events that were not even on my radar. For example, I had asked for extra prayers on Monday, January 9. This was the date of my sixth endoscopy. On our drive down to Johns Hopkins, a car swerved into our lane and, thanks be to God, Jack's fast reflexes prevented an accident. This was certainly a praise, even though safe travels had not been at the top of the concern list. I had been more concerned about my pain level.

I had specifically asked for prayer on January 9th because I could not eat, drink, or take pain medicine after midnight. I was extremely grateful and relieved not to have bad pain prior to the procedure.

However, I was disappointed that Jack could not go back with me as I was prepped. Usually Jack was allowed to stand or sit next to me up until the point that a nurse would wheel me away for a test or procedure. Jack was great at keeping me distracted with funny stories and jokes. Further, as he was the love of my life and my best friend, his presence provided comfort and peace.

Once the nurse showed me back to my bed, I understood why Jack had not been permitted to stay with me. There was absolutely no room. The large room was divided up with curtains into sections barely large enough to accommodate each hospital bed and monitors. The setup, with a dozen or more beds, reminded me of horse stalls. Some patients, like me, were being prepped, while others were recovering from their procedures.

Some nurses only meet their patients' "checklist" needs. My nurse's humor, however, helped to pass the hour and a half I had to wait before it was my turn to be put under anesthesia. I believe humor is needed by all, but especially by those in tense situations. I do not recall what this nurse said to make me laugh, but I remember that his wit took the edge off my anticipation.

I was pleasantly surprised not to be vomiting when the anesthesia wore off – as this was my most common reaction – and even more surprised to have some results. Two more items for the gratitude journal. I hadn't expected to receive any news until my follow-up appointment. However, Dr. Cole, who performed the endoscopy, reported that my pancreas looked fine, with the exception of it having fatty stuff in it. I was not sure what this meant, especially because I had been on a low fat diet for years. The good news was my pancreas would not need to be removed; but the discouraging news was that we still had no clear solution.

CHAPTER 10

PURPOSE IN THE PAIN

When I had been seeking to purchase a house, the number one criterion was a large living room. I wanted a space where friends and family could gather. I ended up purchasing a row home that was built in the late 1800s, with a spacious living room that could comfortably seat ten.

Now after being a homeowner for six years, I was spending most of my time in the bedroom instead. Our bedroom was small, and our queen-sized bed consumed most of the floor space. We had a dresser against the wall opposite the bed, and this was all the furniture that fit. I had my laptop next to the bed, we had a bathroom off of the bedroom, and I could lie down anytime I felt tired without having to go up or down any stairs. Stairs were now exhausting. Consequently, my favorite room in the house was quickly becoming the bedroom.

I sent most of my email updates from the comfort of my bed, with a warm electric blanket and plush down comforter. After writing an update, I always felt a sense of relief – along with some angst. I would typically read over my last mass email before starting my new one. My memory was so deficient that I could not remember what news I had already shared. Every time I went back and read my most recent update, the words surprised me. I would wonder how I managed to articulate and capture different events. It felt like I was reading someone else's words.

The day after my endoscopy, via an email update I asked my friends and family to pray for three things. First, for my future children – for their caregivers, family, and community. Second, for Jack who was not only an amazing caregiver, but also needed some care of his own. He had bronchitis. Third, for my healing and relief from pain. I concluded my update as I usually did, by asking how I could specifically pray for others. It was truly an honor and a joy to pray for others. I longed to also update friends with concrete answers and a solution to my health crisis, but my gratitude journal was helping me to focus on the blessings along the way.

On January 10th, I felt weary, but grateful after emailing an update. In my frail world, it felt like a huge accomplishment, primarily because it took all of my concentration and energy to recall the events and retrieve the words from by mushy brain. After hitting the send button, I lay back down to rest.

Two hours later, extreme pain jolted my body. I took my strong pain medicine – and waited, and waited, and waited. I tried watching Netflix to distract myself until the pain medicine took effect. However, the pain did not ease, but instead became more and more intense. The tears started to flow. I was exhausted and did not have the strength to battle the pain. I was scared. I wondered, *How long will the pain last? How long until the pain medicine will kick in?* I picked up my cell phone and called Jack at work, thinking that if I could just hear his voice, I would be okay. Thirty minutes later, we were on our way to the ER.

The ER trips were all starting to run together. I was starting to feel like a frequent flier, an expert in ER admissions. I had typed up a list with all of my prescriptions, allergies, doctors' contact information, and emergency contacts that I kept in my wallet. Jack would drive me to the entrance of the ER, get a wheelchair, and wheel me into the waiting room. I would be hunched over in pain. Next, Jack would go park the car. The nurse would wheel me back to a private room to collect some information and I would whip out my sheet of paper. This saved a lot of time and energy, as speaking was difficult to do while pain was ripping though my body. It literally took my breath away. I was starting to recognize nurses in the ER. However, if a nurse was new to me, Jack would always warn them that I react to the narcotic IV medicine when it first enters my body. I would thrash and moan for a few seconds and then fall asleep. The best way I knew how to describe it was a wave of intensity that would surge through my body. It was what I imagined it would feel like to be hit by lightning. I dreaded this phenomenon, but knew right after the wave, relief from pain would follow.

A few specifics stood out from this hospital trip. The wait was short: I entered "short wait at ER" later that day in my gratitude journal. And one of the ER doctors, Dr. Sport, I knew outside of the hospital. Many years ago, Dr. Sport had worked at the primary care doctor's office where I now saw Dr. Granger. Dr. Sport had seen me on New Year's Eve of 2007 when I woke up to muscle spasms in my neck. He had prescribed muscle relaxants. I was hesitant to take them, because of the stories of addiction I had recently heard on the news. However, Dr. Sport reassured me and also gave me stretches to do to help extend and strengthen the muscles. I had only needed one pill, and along with the help of the stretches, the issue had resolved. Given my earlier concerns about addiction to medication, it seemed ironic to now see him in the ER and to be requesting narcotic IV medicine.

Seeing him made me a tiny bit hopeful – that maybe he could again solve my health issues with some simple instructions. Instead, Dr. Sport advised me to find a pain management doctor, because I may face this pain for years! My, how this was *not* the answer I had hoped for. I felt like he had dropped a cement block on top of me. I had never fathomed this could be a long-term issue. I wondered if my gratitude journal, which had started out as a challenge and opportunity to be more appreciative, might become my lifeline.

I was admitted into a private room – triggering another line in the gratitude journal. Unfortunately, during my three days at the hospital, I continued to experience excruciating pain. When I was not sleeping, I was screaming. The doctors ended up tripling the dosage of pain medicine that they gave me through my IV, just to get me comfortable. Unfortunately, some of my nurses were a bit slow to understand and administer my medication, making the situation worse. Typically, I am rather patient with others; I once tutored a student who took three hours to learn the zero times tables. I would not label myself as demanding. However, when unbearable pain hit, it was exasperating to watch a nurse fiddle around with the computer, struggling to enter various fields, before she could give me the pain medicine. Even more challenging was the fact that my pain level would go from zero to ten within seconds. It didn't worsen gradually, so I couldn't give the nurse a thirty-minute warning before the pain got out of control.

Thankfully, my main doctor in the local hospital, Dr. Abet, was on the ball and gave Dr. Cole (my Johns Hopkins doctor) his personal cell number. They talked and came up with a game plan. Dr. Abet informed me, "If nothing is uncovered from the recent rounds of tests, then Dr. Cole's next step is to send a mini camera down into your organs." I felt like getting out a kazoo to celebrate. I thought, *Dr. Cole is not giving up. Hooray!*

After two long nights and three long days in the hospital, they discharged me, giving me a quadruple-strength prescription for my pain medicine so that I could better manage my pain at home. This was truly a gift, as I felt much more comfortable in my own home than in the hospital. At the hospital, with monitors beeping and measuring who-knows-what, and blood being drawn every few hours, I was never able to get quality rest. I felt like a lab rat and a child. I had to request help to go to the bathroom, and my urine amount was always measured and noted. The timing of meals was also decided by someone else.

In contrast, at home I could decide when I got up, as well as when and what I ate. I could sleep undisturbed for hours. My pajamas and bed at home were a million times more comfortable than the hospital gown and hospital bed! Yes, home was becoming sweeter and sweeter. It was my respite from the endless pricks of needles and tests.

I am not sure how Jack had the energy or creativity, but during this season he would intentionally, and in my eyes magically, transform a regular evening into a fun date night. I would have been content to just have meals and use my limited energy to tackle a chore or two. Instead, for something special, Jack would prepare a meal and either rent or stream a movie that I had not yet seen. Many times I would hardly have an appetite, so having something I could nibble on while we watched a movie was perfect. Even though we watched the movie in our living room, it felt like a date night. I could rest in my recliner if I became too tired to sit up. I truly had the best seat in the house.

Prior to this illness, I never would have allowed myself two date nights in a row. Instead I would have spent the time being productive. From a medical standpoint, my quality of life was declining – but when my pain was manageable, I was enjoying life more than I had in years. As captivating as the movies were, I would often find myself gazing over at my beloved husband. He never complained about lack of sleep from spending nights in the hospital or taking care of me at home. He worked hard at the church, but he always made me feel like his number one priority. I had so little to offer, yet Jack showered me with love and affection. When we married, I knew I had married an extraordinary man and I believed he would make an amazing caregiver. I had just assumed that at this time in our marriage, he would be a caregiver for our children and not for me. I wanted so badly to be a mother and for Jack to be a father. In large part, this was what propelled me forward and kept me fighting to find an answer – not to be content with narcotics minimizing pain but trapping me in a foggy state.

I was also spoiled by phone calls, emails, and snail mail notes that always seemed to arrive just when I needed a spirit boost. One particular call broke through the fogginess of my memory and saturated my brain. My dear friend Annie, who had given me the book *One Thousand Gifts* and had been my maid of honor, called to check in. I was quick to share all of the items of gratitude. I shared with Annie, "I am even beginning to see trials as blessings. The Lord is really helping to shift my perspective. My parents had generously paid for my sister, Jack, and me to join them on a seven-day cruise to celebrate my mom's sixtieth birthday. When we consulted with my primary care physician, Dr. Granger, he advised that we postpone the trip. Thankfully my parents had purchased travel insurance. As it worked out, I was in the hospital when we were scheduled to be on the cruise. Praise be to God for wisdom and provision!"

However, as a good friend, she then broke through the surface and asked, "How are you feeling?" Annie gave me permission to share the hard stuff that I was wrestling with.

I replied to Annie's simple question with, "I feel so loved and cared for, yet at the same time I feel alone."

Annie softly inquired, "How so?"

I lamented, "Jack can hold my hand, and nurses and doctors can treat my symptoms, but only I am feeling the intense pain. Not that I would want to transfer my pain to anyone, but I feel like there is no one that I can talk to who feels what I feel. I feel so isolated in my pain. I read in the book *One Thousand Gifts* about naming and Adam naming creatures and how important it is to specifically name things we are grateful for. Annie, I really wish I had a name for what I am going through. I want a name for this pain. Maybe then I could talk to someone who has had this before. I was blessed to talk to the nurse Mary, but I don't even know if we have the same thing – and it is not like I can call her up and ask her questions. I really want to talk to someone who has gone through this and is on the other side."

Annie gave encouraging sighs of agreement as I spoke. She paused and then said with genuine love, "There is someone who knows exactly what you are going through and knows all about suffering: Jesus."

A light bulb went on in my head. *Wow*, I thought. For some reason I had not made the connection. Jesus definitely knows what I am going through. I have known for years that my identity is in the Lord as a child of God, but now I am also able to identify with His suffering. This wisdom brought me a tremendous amount of comfort. I believe a person can appreciate many things without experiencing them. However, there is some deeper level of appreciation when experience replaces imagination. I thought, *Yes, I have appreciated Jesus' suffering on the cross, but now my depth of appreciation has grown.*

I always am asking about purpose. As a student in school I would frequently ask, "When will I use this? What is the purpose?" I have been hardwired to desire – and many times demand – a purpose. In my mind, if something does not have a purpose, it is a waste. This new understanding of Jesus' suffering helped to give my pain purpose.

A sense of purpose also arrived via another friend's wisdom. Alisa Bair, a published writer, talented musician, and dear friend, suggested to Jack that I start a blog. When Jack asked me what I thought about creating a blog, my knee-jerk reaction was, "No way! Blogs are for people who are good writers, are narcissistic, and/or are experts at something. Since I do not fall into the first two categories (I was a math major after all), and I do not believe the world revolves around me, I do not see any point in me writing a blog."

Jack listened to my logic and replied, "You are an expert at pain, and you always want to make a difference and help others. You could bring comfort to others who have chronic pain without a diagnosis." How could I argue with that? I started to become giddy thinking not only about how I could comfort people, but also about how my friends who lovingly supported me could use their unique and amazing words to comment and bring encouragement to readers. My technologically-gifted husband set up the blog, www.MourningIntoDancing.net, and I named the blog's followers "Companion dancers."

I wrote in the "About Me" section, "I've often heard that God only gives you as much as you can handle. I believe that God only gives you what your support group can handle. This blog is a place where I share my journey through a painful and undiagnosed chronic medical condition. It is a place to come to support and be supported. 'You have turned my mourning into joyful dancing. You have taken away my clothes of mourning and clothed me with joy, that I might sing praises to you and not be silent. O LORD my God, I will give you thanks forever!' (Psalm 30:11-12, NLT)."

As I set up the blog and read back through past email updates as I posted them, the Lord's creative blessings encouraged me as I began to see the interweaving of several themes – like humor, divine timing, and growing stronger in my faith.

A friend of my mom's emailed me a quote from Martin Luther King, Jr.: "Faith is taking the first step even when you don't see the staircase." Phone calls and notes like this helped me to have faith and hope even though I could not see what was ahead.

As I sat at home, propped in my comfortable bed, I continued to record blessings in anticipation of my next blog update. And in a way, without really knowing it, I was "banking" the blessings and simple comforts of home in preparation for my inevitable return to the hospital.

CHAPTER 11

CABIN FEVER

Four days after I was discharged from the local hospital, Jack and I got back in the car and headed to another hospital, Johns Hopkins. It was starting to feel like all we did was travel to and from hospitals. I jokingly shared with Jack that instead of being travel agents who have visited many exotic places, we could be hospital agents. I tried to keep things light because I was so nervous. Ever since that torturous test at Temple Hospital, I had become apprehensive about hospital tests. It also didn't help that I had to fast from all food, water, and pain medicine for my first test on this day.

My tension mounted as we passed a car on the highway that had flipped in the rainy conditions. The ambulance and fire trucks were just arriving at the scene. I said silent prayers of gratitude for safe travels and prayed for the driver and any passengers. I'm not sure if it was the bad weather, seeing the overturned vehicle, and/or lack of pain meds, food, and water – but I was not feeling well on the ride down. I was relieved when we pulled into the parking lot of Johns Hopkins after an hour and a half of sitting behind frantic windshield wipers.

My first test was a HIDA scan. Jack was not allowed to go back with me, which made me feel vulnerable. Jack was my advocate and knew me better than anyone. He always seemed to know just what to say to calm me down and to get medical attention fast. As I had to leave Jack behind, I could hear my mom's voice in my head, "Becky, now don't borrow trouble." I tried to reassure myself that I would be just fine.

The first step was to get an IV started and put some solution through it to make my ducts secrete any bile that might be in them. The nurse Lauren explained, "This is to help the doctors see the ducts more clearly with the machines." Lauren set a timer for ten minutes and then left me in a room by myself.

The thought of an IV – or any foreign object, for that matter – going into my vein made me queasy. As the nausea began to build, I reminded myself of Addie and Grayson. I needed to be brave and get this health issue resolved, so I could be strong and healthy when they arrived. But as the digital timer displayed the countdown, I felt worse and worse. When the timer finally went off, I thought I was going to black out.

Lauren arrived back in the room to shut off the beeping timer. Without me saying a word, she quickly called two men to move me to a stretcher, and she raised my feet and put ice on my neck and a wet compress on my forehead. The pain was so unbearable that my body felt like it was shutting down, and according to Lauren, the lack of color in my face confirmed what I was feeling. In an effort to keep me conscious, the doctor asked me what I did for a living. When I responded with "credit analyst," he then exclaimed, "Lauren, I told you not to show Rebecca your credit score.... Look what happens!" The humor definitely softened my nerves.

The test lasted an hour, and I was in horrible pain. While the test was going on, I was not allowed to move, which caused both of my arms to fall asleep. However, I hoped that because I was in pain, the machine would show the culprit.

I was very thankful when I was allowed pain medication before my second test. Jack got me some frozen yogurt from the hospital cafeteria, as he knew from experience that when I took pain medicine on an empty stomach, the medicine did not always stay down. I was just concerned about getting pain medicine in my system, but Jack was thinking comprehensively about my wellbeing.

The second test was an MRI. I had had MRIs in the past, but this one was not pleasant. I guess I should have known when they gave me ear plugs and large head phones (like the ones the airplane flaggers wear) that I was in for a treat. It sounded like a car alarm was going off and a concrete chiseler was at work. My face was only a few inches away from the claustrophobic tunnel's "ceiling," and I had to hold my breath for twenty to fifty seconds at a time – for *two hours*! I had to keep telling myself that there was plenty of air and I was not going to suffocate. The IV contrast also made me feel like I had gone to the bathroom in my pants. Needless to say, I was celebrating when it was time to be taken out of the MRI machine.

I had a week to wait between the tests and my follow-up appointment for the results. To distract myself, I once again concentrated on filling my gratitude journal. A few highlights: Jack and I went out for dinner on a date night, using a gift card that a friend had sent us. Another day, we awoke to four inches of snow, and when we came downstairs we discovered that someone had already shoveled our sidewalk. I was able to make it to church for the healing service, which was particularly powerful. I was able to catch up with some sweet friends in person for a little over an hour. And I received in the mail a CD entitled *Hidden In My Heart: A Lullaby Journey Through Scripture*.

Monday night, the 23rd of January, I went to bed excited and nervous. I was excited to get the test results back and to hear Dr. Cole's plan of action. Simultaneously, I felt nervous, as I wondered what Dr. Cole would say. I was confident that since I had felt so horrible during the HIDA scan, it would certainly have revealed to him the source of my pain.

Cherie, the wife of the senior pastor where Jack served, was also on my mind. She had battled cancer for a long time, and now she had no more treatment options. My heart ached for Cherie and her husband Randy. They were nearing retirement and should be making travel plans, not funeral plans. I knew that God did not work according to a reward system. However, I could not fathom why God would not provide healing for Cherie when she and her husband had sacrificed so much.

The thought of having something untreatable scared me to the core. I would not mind dying. But living with horrific, chronic pain was not something I felt I could endure. Many times when the pain was bad, I would actually pray that God would take me home to heaven. I tried to push these thoughts out of my mind as I drifted to sleep the night before my appointment.

At 1:00 a.m. I awoke suddenly to horrific pain. Instead of feeling like a Mack truck had hit me, it felt like an entire fleet of eighteen-wheelers had run me over. Instead of a few knives stabbing my abdomen, it felt like a good two dozen were stabbing and twisting all over my stomach and back. I took my strongest pain pill (equivalent to two IV injections in the hospital). Typically, this would knock out both me and the pain in under ten minutes. This time, however, by 2:40 a.m. the pain was not only still present, but getting worse. On a scale of one to ten, it was a fifteen! I took another strong pain pill. I had never taken this much pain medicine at one time. When the pain was so intense, I asked Jack to pray and to ask for forgiveness for me. Jack reminded me that this was not my fault and it was not punishment. However, I felt like I was being tortured. I practiced my mom's prayer mantra: "I love you, Lord; I trust you; I don't understand." After about another thirty minutes, the medication started to kick in.

Later that morning, Jack and I wearily readied ourselves for the trip back down to Hopkins. Thankfully, the Scripture Lullaby CD serenaded us, and I was able to sleep in the car. "What a contrast a week makes!" I thought as I rubbed my eyes. Last week we had arrived in the rain, I had no pain medicine in my system, and I was wide awake and nervous about tests. This week I had slept in the car, my body was saturated with pain medicine, and I was anxious for the test results.

Even though I was anxious, I was pretty weak from what felt like a beating in the night and the effects of the narcotics. We waited an hour and a half to see Dr. Cole. The entire time we waited, I prayed. I pleaded with God for insight and wisdom for Dr. Cole regarding the cause of my pain and a solution. I also prayed for Cherie and Randy. I prayed for comfort and peace to surround them, and for God's wholeness to fill Cherie. I prayed for Randy and Cherie to have quality time together.

The week of waiting for the test results seemed to pass much faster than the hour and a half we were sitting in Dr. Cole's waiting room. Finally the nurse called my name and escorted Jack and me to an exam room. When Dr. Cole knocked and then entered the room, I almost jumped off the exam table in anticipation.

Dr. Cole asked how I was doing as he flipped through my chart.

I replied, "Weak and weary. What did the test results reveal?"

In a monotone voice Dr. Cole stated, "Nothing. The tests did not show anything wrong."

"What?!" I exclaimed. "But before the HIDA scan when they gave me the injection, it totally mimicked the pain attacks I have been having."

Dr. Cole raised his eyebrow and paused. He said, "Think before you answer. Was the pain right before your HIDA scan similar or exactly the same as your pain attacks?"

I thought for a minute. My brain was mushy from narcotics, but I was positive the pain was exactly the same. I replied, "Exactly the same."

Dr. Cole finally agreed to now do an ERCP. He explained, "During the procedure I will put a stent in your pancreas, if I am able, and make an incision in your Sphincter of Oddi duct" (the duct my former gallbladder and pancreas share). Dr. Cole said all of this with no inflection in his voice and with no expression in his face. He flatly informed me, "If the ERCP does not work, then I am out of ideas and will have to call in other specialists." It felt like another jab to the gut.

Thankfully, the next day we had a follow-up appointment with my primary care physician, Dr. Granger. I arrived feeling pretty depressed, but Dr. Granger stated with encouragement and enthusiasm, "I am confident that the ERCP is going to solve everything. The replica of the pain from the HIDA injection makes me very optimistic. I think after this procedure, Becky, you may be pain free."

With both joy and frustration I thought, *One little incision that my husband and I have been asking for since the end of September is going to finally happen!* I left Dr. Granger's office feeling hesitantly happy; my hopes had been on a bit of a rollercoaster, and I felt somewhat guarded.

Once again, my patience was tested as I was forced to wait. It had been over a week and I still had not received a phone call from the hospital's scheduling department with a date and time for my ERCP. Then my insurance company denied coverage of my new pain medication prescription – one I had been ecstatic about because it was not a narcotic. I continued to receive paperwork from my disability insurance company, which I had to complete and fax in. I also experienced at least one bad pain attack each day for ten days in a row.

On Tuesday, January 31, I wrote the following on my blog and then ran out of steam: "I had a crash of feelings today. I feel exhausted despite over sixteen hours of sleep a day. I am discouraged and anxious. I want to know why this pain continues and what the purpose is. I want to be healed and move on. I feel stuck. I am with my husband, Jack, or my mom for long periods of time and have not really been around others for extended periods of time in over four months. I miss work and a schedule. My lack of energy and concentration make it hard for me to be on my computer for very long or to talk on the phone. I feel like I have cabin fever. Jack suggested that I try and process my feelings by writing; my words may help articulate how someone else is feeling." I wrote a poem entitled "Cabin Fever with a Twist." I posted the poem on my blog as well:

> *I have cabin fever, but it is warm outside and cold inside*
> *I am trying to take this in stride*
> *I have been so blessed, but I feel I am running out of all I've been supplied*

*The chains of work have been replaced with IVs and
pain
I try not to complain
I just don't know how to break free and fly away on
an airplane*

*I had an active brain that was saturated with lists —
now it feels like baby food mush
When I try and rush
My words get all jumbled and I am left with tears and
slush*

*My alert eyes have been exchanged with water faucets
that daily moisten my cheeks
This has gone on for over sixteen weeks
Fortunately there have been peaks*

*Time which I used to race, now ticks by so slowly with
no clear finish line in sight
I am blessed to be able to write
I process my feelings and recall miracles and pray for
others, which is a true delight*

*Food that provides energy and nourishment appears to
be a bomb now that triggers pain
I'd much rather be serving and have friends over to
entertain
Bake sweet treats and quiche Lorraine*

*Dancing is now only seen and not felt
However, I picture the day I can dance with my
children, and it makes my heart melt
Our dancing will be special and unique, obviously not
from a conveyor belt*

CABIN FEVER

Sleep is my comfort and escape from this limited life
A place away from a stabbing steak knife
This is all until I go under the surgeon's knife

Until then, I dream of energy, a clear mind, and a
warm home with my children and husband
That overflows with warmth and giggles and sunshine
covering the land
Where we can always lend a helping hand

I dream of a place where pain and sorrow are traded
for love and joy
A place where friends celebrate and community is rich,
and all enjoy
Every girl and every boy

I am blessed with sprinkles of my dream throughout
these blurry days
Email, cards, soothing songs, prayers – they all
transport me to my sunroom and out of the haze
Praise the Lord, for He opens windows in the waiting
room and brings in the rays

God heard my cries! Tuesday night, Jack transformed our living room into a spa/oasis by setting up candles all over and putting together a table fountain labeled Serenity. Wednesday I sat outside for twenty minutes and soaked in some sunshine, making some Vitamin D. I pretended I was in the Caribbean. (It was very mild in Lancaster – in the low 60s!)

Thursday morning I made it to a Beth Moore Bible study and was embraced by so many loving women. Their smiles and hugs helped me feel less isolated. Many, if not all, of these ladies knew what I was going through, were praying for me, and accepted me just as I was. Their actions and words expressed their genuine delight in my presence. I was humbled and baffled.

Guess what the Bible study was about: joy and anguish!

Beth Moore explained that joy and anguish can coexist, they can switch places, and anguish can even birth joy. This last point particularly empowered me. She backed up all of these points with Scripture and personal experience. I did not know exactly what God was birthing out of this pain, but I was hopeful about the birth of future children and possibly a new passion.

I had started to feel limited in my abilities. Now, instead of thinking about all the things I was unable to do, I decided to make a list of everything I could do: I can walk, I can do stairs, I can shower, I can pray, I can see, I can hear, I can touch, I can taste delicious fresh fruit that is out of season in Lancaster, I can communicate with friends and friends of friends, I can listen to encouraging music, I can read, I can write, I can speak, and I can love and be loved.

I was determined to focus on the positive and what I could do. I hoped that soon I would get a call with a date and time for my ERCP. I prayed that this procedure would eliminate the pain and allow me to return to work. However, I was trying my best to live in the present, so I could learn as much as possible from this season to help others and be a blessing.

CHAPTER 12

ROLLER COASTER DROP

For four months my life had been pretty unpredictable. As a type-A personality and a woman who liked to be in control and to plan, I struggled daily with my circumstances. But I thought I was handling the situation with a healthy, positive, and Christ-centered focus – or at least, that was what I was striving for. I certainly had my doubts and fears, but I was not giving up or letting discouragement consume me.

Logically, I believed that the more experience or exposure one had, the more proficient one became. With all of the unexpected twists and turns, I thought I was becoming more flexible. However, on February 3, 2012, I met a new limit on my adaptability when I was completely blindsided by a call from Johns Hopkins.

Dr. Cole's assistant Kayla called to inform me that the results of a test a few weeks ago had just come back positive. I was surprised, as I had assumed all of my tests results were back and had been reviewed during my last appointment at Hopkins. My first thought was, *Great, could this provide insight into my health issue?* But before I had a chance to ask my question, she informed me, "Now the ERCP is on hold. More tests need to be completed." My stomach turned with nausea. I felt like a marathon runner who was approaching the finish line – and then some wicked person had suddenly moved the finish line further away. Surely the call must be a malicious joke. This was not fair. I had followed all of the doctor's instructions. I had no control over when I had pain, and now the one option available to permanently relieve the pain was yanked out from underneath me. What was going on?

I got off of the phone and turned to Jack. I received the call on a Friday, so it was Jack's day off. Praise be to God that I did not receive the call when I was home alone. Based on my downcast expression, Jack knew something was wrong. I could barely form the words. Jack was as surprised and as devastated as I was.

Disjointed thoughts zoomed through my brain. *Why was I being punished? Why did I have to keep enduring pain? What was the harm in doing the ERCP and curing me of the pain? Did Dr. Cole take some warped pleasure in seeing patients endure pain?* Nothing made sense. I shared out of my anger and confusion, "I feel like I am drowning, and Dr. Cole is standing nearby with a life preserver and yawning without a care in the world." Jack held me close and did his best to reassure me that while he, too, did not understand Dr. Cole's decision, he was certain it was not out of hate or apathy.

I wanted to scream and have a temper tantrum, but I simply did not have the energy. We were both confused and overwhelmed. On autopilot, I called my mom to tell her the news. Thankfully she recognized that Jack and I needed help. My mom called Don Hackett and asked him to pray for us over the phone. Don was the minister who had married us and was Jack's mentor through seminary. He and his wife Rila were the ones present at Trader Joe's after our disappointing appointment at Temple.

Typically, Jack and I could come up with some positive words, but all I could say to Don over the phone was, "I cannot hold on any longer."

Don's compassionate and wise response was, "It is okay to let go. God will catch you." Don then sent an email to the list of friends I had been giving updates:

Hi Friends,
    Please pray for Becky and Jack. It has been a very discouraging and painful day. Here is what I am offering:

Dear Grace-filled God,
Please come alongside of Becky and Jack.
Surround them with your tender comfort and care.
Dispel all fear, pain, and discouragement.
Fill them with the light of your hope, complete
healing, and joy in Christ we pray. Amen.

Thank you for your faithful support of this great couple,
Don

Some days I could fill an entire page in my gratitude journal, but on this particular day I could only scrape together one praise – Don's phone call and prayer.

I had thought I was nearing the end of the waiting season, but now it appeared the clock had been reset and I was starting all over again. I was not even allowed to *schedule* the ERCP. At this point a date would have been helpful, but the decision was not up to me. Instead, Dr. Cole wanted to run genetic tests before proceeding. I was informed by Dr. Cole's assistant that this lab work would take several weeks to process. Waiting was one thing, but waiting while in pain seemed unbearable. I did not even know what Dr. Cole was checking for! What I did know was that if I had had veto power, I would have vetoed this plan.

I petitioned for prayers from friends and was open with them that Jack and I were both running on fumes. We trusted the Lord, but we needed prayers of comfort, peace, hope, healing, and joy. I also requested prayers of protection from fear and pain.

A ray of sunshine came three days later after an appointment with my local doctor in Lancaster, Dr. Granger. While Dr. Granger could not bring much insight to the situation, he did express his sympathy for the frustration and the waiting. He prescribed a new pain medicine for me to try in addition to the narcotics. This new medicine helped, although it made me extremely sleepy and made my brain feel like it was in a dense fog.

One honest concern that I vocalized to Dr. Granger was whether the pain medicine would damage my brain long-term. I needed a functioning brain to care for my future children, and there was no way I could pass the actuarial exams with a fried brain. I did not want my degree in mathematics to go to waste. Dr. Granger reassured me that none of the medicines I was on would have a permanent impact.

Dr. Granger also shared, "Chronic pain can make a person depressed, and narcotics tend to make individuals depressed, so it is okay if you feel depressed." I think I needed to hear that this was normal and to have permission to feel depressed. I was trying so hard to see the positive side, and there were certainly a lot of blessings. I was not discounting them. However, not having a date – or even a plan – to eliminate the pain was very overwhelming.

I ended my update on February 7, 2012, with the following prayer requests: "Even though I am very drowsy, I tend to be restless. Please pray that I could rest well. Also, please pray for Jack. He has been so amazing. He does not get angry when I wake him up in the middle of night screaming with pain or the repetition of my unanswerable questions. He is so strong and compassionate. However, I know all of this is taking a toll on him. I would greatly appreciate if you prayed for Jack, as well. As always, I love praying and do it often. Please let me know how I can pray for you."

Then on February 13, the day before Valentine's Day, I emailed out the following update:

Hi dearest friends,

What a week?! Last Wednesday, my next-door neighbor took me for physical therapy for my stomach. I was nervous, but it was a huge blessing. Afterwards my organs felt spread apart and open (not sure exactly how to describe it).

Thursday morning I woke up with horrible pain. Pain medicine was not working. Back to the ER. As usual, they took blood and got me comfortable with IV pain meds. For the FIRST TIME, the blood work came back with something: pancreatitis. Different tests have shown signs of pancreatitis, but never signs of current pancreatitis. Not sure what this means, but it is something. I had thought I would get my pain under control and then leave the ER on Thursday. This was my plan, but not God's. I was admitted into the hospital and am still at the hospital.

Also: FIRST TIME I had a roommate (I'm up to my fourth hospital admission now). FIRST TIME I had a catheter. FIRST TIME I have spent the night without my mom or Jack in the hospital.

Ready for the blessings?! Outstanding care of hospital staff, a good night's rest last night (the previous two nights I had been vomiting at night and having horrible abdominal pain), second roommate was really sweet, arrival of lots of beautiful flower cards from people not even realizing I was in the hospital (I have a shelf under the TV with the cards...I think of it as my flower garden of encouragement), fresh strawberries to eat with my meals (ecstatic to be eating solid food again after two days of no food or liquids), friends providing delicious meals for Jack (nothing better than seeing my amazing caregiver being taken care of), and many more blessings that my mushy brain is not recalling.

A huge MIRACLE happened on Friday. Jack went home for lunch and the mail had just dropped off the genetic blood work kit from Johns Hopkins. Jack quickly brought it back to the hospital, they took my blood (I didn't even wake up), and it was sent via FedEx with ten minutes to spare. Right under the wire.

Still in God's waiting room – waiting for results from the California lab (it is the only lab that processes this specific genetic test ordered by Dr. Cole) and a game plan to extinguish the pain.

I greatly appreciate your prayers. As always, delighted and honored to pray for you.

On eagle's wings,
Becky

Three days later, on February 16, I sent out another update entitled: "Good news: completely pain-free for several hours today."

Dearest prayer warriors,
*Praise be to God – I had a great day! I have had several consecutive hours of absolutely **pain-free living**! First time in approximately five months! After several bad days and nights, the doctors decided to put me on a morphine pump. I will not be staying on the morphine very long, but the doctors wanted to get the pain under control and provide me with some quality rest. I have slept for the better part of today and am still pretty sleepy.*
On Feb 13th my blood work arrived in California. Hallelujah! Can I get an amen? Jack called the lab, and it will take fourteen to twenty-eight business days to process the blood work. Needless to say, genetic testing takes a lot longer than other blood work that is processed within a few hours.
Areas I could use prayer – strength and endurance while I wait for the results (the pain and the delays have contributed to feelings of despair), pain management (figuring out how to keep the pain under control, so I can go home), digestion relief (the narcotics have stopped my GI track from moving), nutrition (they have put me back on a clear liquid diet for the past three days), and relief for my caregivers. This has been an exhausting journey, especially at times when I scream out in pain and I have to wait hours to get relief.

My eyelids feel like they have weights on them, so I will say good night. My prayers of thanksgiving go out for all God has done and for all of the support and encouragement that has surrounded Jack and me.

Love and deep gratitude,
Becky

On February 19 I sent the below email from my home.

Hi faithful friends,
    I feel wonderful! A dash giddy, a pinch of energetic, and a big bowl full of joyful. I was discharged this afternoon from the hospital. After eleven consecutive days in the hospital it feels wonderful not only to be home, but to be home without pain! Thanks be to God! This is a first since September. I wrote a little poem below to express my joy at being at home.

Free

I am FREE from hospital gowns with unsightly drafts and ties
I am FREE from liquid meals on trays that I despise

I am FREE from a hat in the commode
I am FREE from medical phrases that I try to decode

I am FREE from IVs with a pole companion
I am FREE from gaps in my memory the size of the Grand Canyon

I am FREE from a revolving door of doctors and some who are rough
I am FREE from being awoken hourly in the night by the squeeze of a blood pressure cuff

I am FREE from a bed that only holds one
I am FREE from one room to see the world and
setting sun

I am FREE from beginning my mornings with needles
in a good looking vein
Most of all, I am thankful to be FREE from the claws
of pain

Please do not mistake my newfound freedom to
reflect poorly on the hospital. I am grateful for their
service and feel blessed to have health insurance. While
the cause of the pain has yet to be discovered, a
temporary solution for the pain has been found. I have
long-lasting morphine pills that allow me to be pain-free
all day and night. Well, it has been an exciting day,
but now it is time to catch some Zs.

Thank you for your prayers. They certainly have
been heard and answered. Of course, I still need lots of
prayers for whatever is ahead. I will certainly keep you
posted on the genetic testing. Blessings and well wishes
to each of you.

Love and peace,
Becky

The morphine, more than any other pain medicine I had received up to this point, controlled my pain and erased my memory. The days were a blur and I was not lucid. I was so out of it that getting a catheter, having a roommate, and spending my first night in the hospital without my mom or Jack did not faze me. I felt physically and emotionally numb. It was a much-needed break from the pain, anxiety, depression, and discouragement.

CHAPTER 13

BATTLE

Even with groggy eyes from one of my numerous daytime naps, I knew as soon as I saw Jack that something was wrong. Jack's typical jubilant spirit was absent. My fun-loving husband looked so serious. I casually asked, "What's up?"

Jack sat down next to me on the bed and softly shared, "Cherie is now in heaven." Cherie was the wife of our senior pastor. I had asked for prayers for Randy and Cherie regularly in my updates to friends and family. She had battled cancer for many years, and I knew there was medically nothing more that could be done for her. Even knowing this, I was shocked. I had been hoping for a miracle. Randy was scheduled to retire in a few months.

Tears ran down my face as Jack held me close. I knew Cherie's suffering had ended, but my heart broke for Randy and their children. I had only been battling an illness for five months and I was exhausted. I could not imagine how one endures years of serious health issues.

I began to feel guilty for asking for prayers for myself. After all, my health issue was not fatal. I wondered if I was selfish for asking for prayers for my health, when others were facing much more devastating circumstances. My safety was not in danger, and I was surrounded by healthy loved ones. I thought of others who chose to endure round after round of chemotherapy and/or radiation. They suffered awful side effects, while I asked for narcotics daily and wanted to do anything to avoid pain, nausea, and vomiting. I had received multiple emails in which friends commented on how brave I was, but there was no courage in my situation. I was not choosing this pain, because if there was a choice, I would have passed. I wondered if people would pray for me if they thought I was a coward. I also thought of parents whose children had cancer. I daily prayed that our future children would be healthy.

Shortly after I shared my guilt with Jack, I was walloped with wave after wave of horrible pain. After liquid morphine (for break-through pain) in addition to my daily morphine pill, and a few hours of screaming, the pain subsided. I whispered to Jack, "Now I remember why I ask for prayers." I was grateful that this attack of pain did not cause vomiting.

Ever since I had been discharged from the hospital, I was averaging one bad attack of pain a day, with vomiting. I was willing to do just about anything to keep from having to return to the hospital. I knew food was a trigger for my pain, so I switched myself over to a liquid diet. This was a big step for me, because I loved food and especially loved chewing it. Early in our marriage when Jack had made several types of pureed soup for us, I had declared, "While I have teeth, I would like to use them!" I knew I ate pureed food as a baby, but I did not plan on consuming any more until I lost all of my teeth.

But as much as I loved chewing, I hated vomiting. So I made fruit smoothies with some yogurt for protein. I would have preferred milkshakes, but knew fat was another pain trigger. Between drinking my meals and taking morphine, I was very drowsy. I would sleep between sixteen and twenty hours a day. I typically had one hour of alertness per day.

On March 9, 2012, I used my one hour of alertness to update my friends and family.

> I had a nudge this morning from the Holy Spirit to write an update. It was confirmed when Jack said, "I think you should write a blog entry today."
>
> The biggest news is a beautiful, brave, and beloved friend met the creator of the universe yesterday evening. Cherie Riggs ran not a good, but an outstanding race, blessing all on her path and many to come. (Cherie was

involved with trial cancer drugs/treatments and thanks to her participation, some are now being approved and will help others battling cancer.) We are thankful that she is no longer suffering and is at a place with no tears.

However, there are a lot of tears here on earth. I continue to ask for prayers for Cherie's beloved husband, Randy. He is the head pastor of our church, an advocate for our community, a mentor, a friend, a father, a grandfather, and more. My prayer is that God would reveal greater depths of His infinite love and peace to Randy's heart and guide Randy's friends (including me) to know how to love and support Randy in helpful ways.

I am so thankful for each of you who do not even know the Riggs but are remembering them in your prayers. I cannot explain it, but I felt a real closeness with Cherie as a minister's wife whose strength came from the Lord and not her own body.

I have been anxious to get my lab results back from California. I asked Jack to call the lab. The response was, "Hopefully, by March 14ᵗʰ your blood work will be finished being processed. Good news: your insurance approved it." As disheartened as I am to wait some more, I am thankful for insurance to cover the cost.

I would be lying if I did not say I am weary. My heart aches for the Riggs family. My body aches from attacks of pain for the past 5.5 months. I am not as peppy, but my heart is still rejoicing that blessings are present even in the desert. Jack and I truly do not know how we could have made it this long without the prayers and community of love and support. Your prayers and love really do make a difference!

Blessings, love, and continued gratitude,
Becky

A week after the above update, I received news from the

lab in California that the results had been faxed to Dr. Cole at Johns Hopkins. I was anxious and excited. I felt the long wait was finally over. I emailed Dr. Cole's assistant to find out what the results were, and his assistant responded, "Rebecca, take a deep breath and relax. Dr. Cole *just* got back in the country. Once he tells me what's next, I will let you know."

I was glad our communication was through email, because I wanted to scream, "Relax!? I was supposed to get these results at the latest by Wednesday, and now it is Friday. Relax!? I have been in horrific pain for over five months going on six months and the pain has only gotten worse. Relax!? I never know when these attacks are coming or how long they will last. Relax!? My disability insurance wants to terminate coverage. Relax!? I am concerned about losing my job. Relax!? I have been on a liquid diet for over two weeks! Relax!?"

Relax was the last thing I wanted to hear. It was also the last thing I thought was appropriate to tell a patient. I certainly was in no physical or mental position to just relax and chill. It was not like I had just had a manicure and was told to relax while my nails dried. My strength was depleted and I felt like I had to go into battle not only with attacks of pain, but also justifying my illness to a disability company. I did not think I should also have to fight to get test results.

I waited as patiently as I could. After six hours of waiting, not to mention the past five weeks, I called the assistant and asked, "Is Dr. Cole in the office today? If not, when is he returning?" I thought maybe the results could be faxed to my primary care physician. The assistant informed me, "Dr. Cole has been in surgery all day, but did look over your lab results. He would like to meet with you face-to-face to go over different options. His schedule is booked solid for over a month, but I will try to get you an appointment to see Dr. Cole in two weeks."

I got off of the phone without a date to see Dr. Cole but felt at peace knowing there were options. After receiving this news, I once again updated friends and family. I also shared that I was struggling.

On March 16, 2012, I wrote:

I have felt like I was in Gethsemane for the past few days – I have felt rejected by God and crushed with guilt, fear, stress, and confusion. I trust there is purpose to the endurance of physical, emotional, and spiritual pain, but Jack and I are in a fragile and depleted place. It is challenging to stay positive. One of my favorite songs is "Blessed Be Your Name." One of the lyrics is, "You give and take away, but my heart will choose to say, blessed be your name." This is what Jack and I are choosing. We are thanking God even though we cannot yet see the blessings. Would you join us in thanking and praising God? He has provided us with an amazing community of love, support, and encouragement. God has also blessed us with medical care and provision for our every need. My prayer request this evening would be for restful sleep, eyes that see beyond the circumstances, and a peaceful heart and mind. Please remember Jack in your prayers, as he is strong for me, but weary, as well. Blessings to each of you.

Love and gratitude,
Becky

I continued to have an internal conflict about feeling blessed with prayers, but also feeling guilty about being so blessed. My situation was wringing me dry of strength and self-reliance. I knew I was in desperate need of prayer and healing. However, I had never thought for a minute that I had the worst circumstances. My heart broke for others, some I knew, and others I had heard about, who suffered from loss, abuse, or neglect. I could not imagine suffering without a strong support group. I thought I should be stronger. I also struggled to relax in the endless waiting and delays. I was anxious to meet with Dr. Cole and get a game plan. I was not sure how much longer I could endure being on a liquid diet.

CHAPTER 14

EMPTY

I put on an exaggerated smile to convince and reassure my mom that I would be fine. My mom had sacrificed her plans and trips for six months in order to take care of me, and now it was time for my mom and dad to fly out on a trip that had been planned long before my illness began. I promised my mom that I would take it easy and rest in her absence. I thought that my liquid diet would prevent ER trips. And to give my mom added peace of mind, my dear friend Annie from Chicago had agreed to fly out and stay at my house while my parents were away and Jack was working.

The day my parents flew out, I was not feeling well. However, I could not remember the last time I had felt truly well. I felt relief when my mom finally left for the airport; I really wanted her to have a respite from being my caregiver. Honestly, even I wanted a break from myself. Pain quickly replaced relief. I took morphine and waited and waited. I started vomiting, and my pain rapidly got out of control. Jack called Dr. Granger's office to see what to do. His office informed us to go directly to the local hospital. The doctor's office called ahead, so I was admitted without going through the ER.

After arriving at the hospital, I was promptly assigned to a room and given an IV and hospital gown. Jack and I were now accustomed to the drill. Within minutes of receiving intravenous pain medicine, I was asleep. When the fog lifted and I woke up, I wondered silently what had happened. I asked myself, *Why am I back in the hospital? I have not eaten anything in weeks. If I cannot keep liquids down, what hope do I have of staying out of the hospital?*

I also was frustrated with myself. My dear friend Annie was flying in the next day, and I was in the hospital. I asked my body, *Why could you not hold it together?* I wondered if I had gone to the hospital prematurely. With the pain medicine in my veins, I didn't feel too bad. However, as soon as the pain medicine wore off, I was certain that the hospital was where I needed to be.

Even in my weary and frustrated state, I could not stop smiling thinking of Annie's arrival. I had met Anne Elizabeth Michaels, my kindred spirit, in college. Remembering middle names was not a gift of mine. Honestly, if I remembered someone's first name, I thought I was doing well. However, this friend had the same first and middle name as my sister, just in reverse order; my sister was Elizabeth Anne. I also liked that my friend's nickname sounded just like her formal name with her middle initial: Annie and Anne E.

I had heard about Annie long before I knew her. We attended the same college and had mutual friends that kept telling both of us that we had to meet. However, we never had a single class together – as she was a history major and I was a math major. But one brave day, Annie stopped by my dorm room and asked if we could be friends. We actually shook hands on it!

Annie and I cemented our friendship the summer before our senior year during a four-week intensive leadership training, when we both were trying to discern where God was calling us to serve after college. Annie then continued to be present and encouraging at many pivotal moments in my life. She and I celebrated together the completion of our undergraduate theses and our graduation day. When I returned from New Mexico after teaching on a Navajo reservation and felt completely shattered and worthless, she reminded me of qualities and hope that I could not see.

Annie was the friend who had given me the book *One Thousand Gifts*. She was also my maid of honor on my wedding day. Right before I walked down the aisle, Annie asked me,

"How are you feeling?" I honestly responded with fear, "I don't know how I am going to hold the bouquet for the entire ceremony!" In my defense, the bouquet felt like a twenty-pound bowling ball. Annie reassured me that she would hold it for most of the service. Annie was not only physically present at so many crucial moments, but she was able to be in the moment. She accepted and embraced me during times of confusion, doubt, joy, tears, and quirky fears. After college, Annie and I tried to see each other once a year and talked weekly on the phone. Typically, when Annie and I would get together, we checked out thrift stores and did some baking, but mainly we hung out and talked.

When Annie's flight arrived for this visit, my sister and her fiancé picked up Annie from the airport. I had known that my typical hosting abilities would be limited, but I was rather bummed that I was confined by a hospital bed and IV pole.

Annie naturally brightened the hospital room with her presence. It certainly was not the ideal setting, but I would take any excuse to spend time with Annie. Over the years, one of the many gifts I appreciated about Annie was her ability to articulate a situation or feeling. She had a vocabulary I envied. Many times I was at a loss for words, but Annie could express herself – and my feelings as well – succinctly. There was something freeing and comforting in hearing words capture an experience and knowing that someone understood.

I loved that I did not have to hold back feelings or tears from Annie. However, I was quickly realizing that if I wanted my posts and updates to be authentic and helpful to others with chronic pain, I would also have to be honest on the blog. After Annie's visit I shared the following update.

> *Dearest faithful and **brave** followers,*
> *I added brave because where I am about to go is not pretty. Thank you for journeying alongside me through this unexpected and unpleasant season. These past two weeks have taken a drastic turn: the intensity of my pain has increased, while simultaneously my energy and*

hope have plummeted. The hardest part is that I thought the finish line was close (I met with Dr. Cole this past Tuesday after six days in the hospital and expected a clean, quick fix) and instead was met with the prospect of a long journey ahead. After six months of chronic pain, I am empty and have nothing left but tears. I no longer have the strength or the will to keep going. I have come to the place where I feel like the paralytic in the Bible and unless Jesus heals me, I will not live, but will just be. I have never been at this place before, where I am completely dependent on the Lord. I am learning how to REALLY ask for help. My dear friend Annie wrote the update below on Wednesday (3/28/12). My dear friend Sarah wrote a prayer Thursday (3/29/12). I am asking those who wish to pray for me and Jack to use the prayers below. I do not have strength to check my email, so all I ask is that you pray. Thank you from the bottom of my heart.

***This is Annie Michaels, Becky's friend from Chicago! I got to be with her this week. She is at home today and looking good, but since her energy is precious these days, I know it is sometimes hard for her to correspond with everyone she would like to. So I thought I would add a quick update to her blog for you all. Thank you for your continued prayer and support in all sorts of ways. It is so, so appreciated!

Becky has had a very full and long week. She was admitted to Lancaster General Hospital one week ago today, with the hope of letting her pancreas get some rest.

Notable events in this trip to the hospital included one crazy roommate who had the lights on all night and the TV blaring. It was rather obnoxious. Thankfully, after that experience, Becky was transferred to her own room that had a beautiful view of the city. As usual, a mix of characters were attending to her medical needs. The shining star amidst them all was her nurse named

Amy, who was divinely assigned to Becky's room for three of the days she was there, and was going to be moving to a new position in the hospital the next week (she will be working in the operating room instead). Anyway, Amy is the epitome of a gentle and competent nurse. She brightened the room whenever she was there, she was always a step ahead of her patients' needs, and no task was beneath her. We were all thankful for Amy's care, and we hope that she can be a role model for many young, new nurses in her field!

All in all, Becky was in the hospital for six days.

Becky was determined to get out of the hospital because she had a big appointment scheduled with Dr. Cole at Johns Hopkins yesterday (Tuesday). After making it through the maze of buildings, as well as being part of a fire drill while we were sitting in the waiting room (Everyone – doctors, security guards, visitors, and even a cart of lab rats – had to wait outside until it was over!), we got to see Dr. Cole.

Dr. Cole's news was that the next step is for Becky to get an ERCP. It is scheduled for April 9th. She will most likely be in the hospital for a few days following that procedure. That is the news for now.

Also, I just want to say something that she would never say about herself... Becky handles being in the hospital and having people poking her and waking her up all the time with the greatest grace. It is amazing that amidst the excruciating pain that she is in, she is kind and thankful towards all who come to her bedside. She is beautiful even in times of great weakness, and even in the most unfashionable of hospital gowns! (We were talking about how there has got to be a market for prettier hospital gown wear....any entrepreneurs out there want to go for that?) At any rate, I only hope I can exhibit that level of graciousness if I am ever confronted with such trials! Not that this is new information, but she's amazing!

Despite the delay for genetic testing, Dr. Cole had finally scheduled the ERCP. So why wasn't I more relieved, and why wasn't this the light at the end of the tunnel? Two days after my appointment with Dr. Cole at Hopkins, I had an appointment with my gastroparesis doctor at Hershey Hospital. I had been a patient of Dr. Slope's for several years, and she specialized in delayed stomach emptying. Her insight had been helpful in the past. However, it was very difficult to get an appointment with her, so I was typically only able to see Dr. Slope once a year. I was eager to hear Dr. Slope's perspective. The last time I had seen her was before I had ever spent a night in a hospital.

I am not sure what I expected Dr. Slope to say, but I never would have guessed her response. Dr. Slope flatly stated, "The ERCP will hopefully help your pain, but I do not believe it is going to eliminate your issues. I am not sure what is causing all of your symptoms, but a stent is not going to fix everything." Dr. Cole had shared a similar viewpoint two days earlier. Neither was confident that the ERCP was going to eradicate the pain.

Dr. Slope's words crushed my spirit. Maybe it was my longer history with her, or maybe I had expected her to be more compassionate – but her response delivered a very heavy blow. I am not sure which was worse, Dr. Cole's and Dr. Slope's opinions, or their lack of emotion. They did not seem sorry or sad for me. There was no sense of comfort, and no feeling that they were going to fight and do whatever they could to get me some permanent relief. I felt like my quality of life was of no concern to them. Maybe some doctors find this stoic wall essential to do their jobs well and not get burned out. Regardless, I was devastated.

After the appointment with Dr. Slope, Jack and I got in the car to drive home. I turned to Jack and said, "I cannot keep going. I feel so beaten down that I cannot get up. I just want to die. The ERCP has been my strand of hope that I have been clinging to, and if that is not going to end this horrible and intense pain, I do not want to live. I am tired of fighting to survive." As tears streamed down my face, I confessed, "Jack you don't deserve this. I am so sorry."

Jack felt beaten up and defeated as well. Jack replied, "I do not know what to say." One of many things that I appreciated about Jack was that he was honest. He tended to be optimistic and positive, but he never lied to me. He was tired of seeing me writhe in pain.

As we drove back home, Jack dialed Don Hackett's cell number. Don answered and Jack bluntly stated, "We have hit a new low and need help." Don invited us to come to the church and meet with him.

Jack navigated the car to the church. As Jack drove, my thoughts felt like dominos strategically placed so that once one was knocked over, none would be left standing. If my horrific pain could not be eradicated, I would not be able to get off narcotics. Narcotics and pain would prevent me from returning to work. Without my employment income, Jack and I could not aggressively pay down debt or afford to adopt. If I could not provide for or physically take care of children, what did I have to live for? Where was I to find hope? I had lost strength a ways back, so I could not even fake being hopeful.

Jack parked the car in the church parking lot. We were greeted with hugs from Don. He squeezed us close. Jack filled in Don on the details of the appointments. My brain was in such a fog that I could see their mouths moving, but did not know what they were saying. I was shocked that I was still breathing. I did not feel like I even had energy to inhale. Don asked if it would be okay if Sarah joined us in praying. Sarah was not only a church employee, but also a dear friend of both of ours. Jack and I nodded yes.

Sarah and Don prayed over us. They laid their hands on our shoulders. They begged and pleaded on our behalf for mercy, hope, and healing. I appreciated that Sarah wrote out part of her prayer and gave it to me. I could not absorb their words at that time, but I remembered and felt their passion. Their empathy strongly contrasted Dr. Cole's and Dr. Slope's apathy.

Prayer from Sarah:
God, with your infinite power, please, please,
PLEASE *re-draw the boundary lines around Becky*
so that they may fall in pleasant places. Freedom from
pain. A renewed body. **RESTORED HOPE.** *So*
that her lips can sing praises to you again…
In Jesus' name, amen.

In my update to friends, I not only included Sarah's prayer, but I also wrote one for Jack.

Dear loving and merciful Lord, please infuse Jack with
your strength, encouragement, comfort, and peace. May
Jack be cocooned in love and support by those around
him while he takes care of his hurting wife. In Jesus'
name, amen.

I left the church feeling loved, but still felt empty of hope. When we got home, the mail had been delivered. I tried my best to open all mail that looked formal and was addressed to me. I never knew when I would be required to submit more information to the disability insurance company.

I opened an envelope from our insurance company. It stated that they would not cover my most recent hospital stay. I had been in the hospital for six days. While I did not know the exact dollar amount, I was sure it would be an enormous amount of money. I thought to myself, *I am already paying a thousand dollars a month to have health insurance. Isn't the point of having insurance to cover large medical bills?!* The reason the health insurance gave for not covering this admission was because it was "unnecessary." Did the insurance company really think I went to the hospital for the fun of it? Our finances were tighter than they had ever been before, but I found worrying about money to be frivolous.

I noticed a shift in my concern for money. I was not overly worried about the cost of hospital stays and tests. I accepted that until I was well, I could not do much of anything to improve our balance sheet or cash flow. Thus, I did not waste my precious energy on worry.

Thankfully, Friday morning I received a call from Dr. Abet. He had been my gastroenterologist at Lancaster General Hospital during my most recent stay. He provided us with his personal cell phone number and was calling to follow up and see how I was doing. I appreciated Dr. Abet taking the initiative. I shared with Dr. Abet that my insurance company was threatening not to cover my latest hospital stay. I appreciated his words, "I'll take care of straightening out the insurance claim; you focus on resting. Please don't hesitate to call me." I was so thankful that Dr. Abet was willing to fight on my behalf.

In addition, Dr. Abet informed me that he had spoken to Dr. Cole. Dr. Abet was better able to explain the situation. "You have a gene mutation of your CFTR gene. One of the common mutations of CFTR is Cystic Fibrosis. While you thankfully do not have Cystic Fibrosis, your genetic mutation helps to explain the reason for your pancreatitis. Your mutation is rare, so there is not much additional information that can be deduced from your genetic test results. Hopefully, the ERCP will provide some relief and further information. Having an idea of what is causing your pancreatitis is good, but the fact remains you still have pancreatitis and that sucks. Right now, you have no quality of life." It may not sound impressive or major, but after Dr. Cole and Dr. Slope saying everything so matter-of-factly, it felt wonderful to have a doctor show emotion on the phone, be upset about my situation, and perceptively and compassionately express the awfulness of it.

I was grateful for each ray of light that entered my dark season. I continued to record blessings in my gratitude journal.

EASTER

Chocolate eggs, new spring dresses, baked ham, and flowers beginning to bloom – these were all things that I associated with Easter. To me, Easter was the best and biggest celebration of the year, because Jesus overcame death and bridged the gap between God and humans. I loved and appreciated that spring and Easter were seasons that occurred at the same time of year and represented similar themes. After a cold and dormant winter, it was always encouraging to see buds on trees and bulbs emerging from the cold ground.

On Easter Sunday, April 8, 2012, my family and I celebrated with a fresh perspective: the promise of new life and conquered death. We were ready to enter a new season. I was eager and nervous for the long-awaited ERCP (Endoscopic Retrograde Cholangio-Pancreatography) procedure scheduled the next day. We were honored and humbled to be surrounded by prayer warriors who met in my parents' living room and laid hands on Jack and myself. We had been blessed to be blanketed in prayer every step of the way and knew that now was no time to stop.

The next day at 11 a.m., my parents, my sister, my husband, and I traveled together to Johns Hopkins Hospital for my procedure scheduled for 2 p.m. The instructions were to arrive sixty minutes early. We allowed an extra cushion of time in case parking was an issue.

We all felt a mixture of excitement and concern. I tried to push out of my mind the thought that this procedure might not be successful, and instead I chose to be optimistic. If the procedure was successful, I would wake up pain free and be able to return to work. I had shed the belief that I was invincible during my teenage years. Nevertheless, I felt extra protection with prayer. I wondered if I had gone through this whole, long ordeal, specifically so that I could give God the glory in my next blog update. I was ready for a grand finale of miracles.

Jack and I knew the drive well, but this was my parents' and sister's first visit to Johns Hopkins. I was grateful to have the extra support not only for myself, but also for Jack. Unfortunately, there was a bad accident on the highway, and we had no choice but to sit and wait in the stopped traffic. As we sat and sat and the speedometer arrow rested at zero, it became clear I was not going to arrive in time for my scheduled surgery. I called the hospital to let them know of the delay. I was informed to still come but was not guaranteed that I would have the ERCP completed. My anxiety was beginning to overtake my hope. I had already waited more than six months, and the thought of yet another delay made my stomach turn with knots.

The normal hour and a half trip ended up taking us over three hours. When we arrived at the hospital and checked in, I was told that due to my tardiness I would have my ERCP performed after Dr. Cole's last scheduled procedure of the day. Yes, this did mean more waiting, but I was immensely relieved not to have to return on a different day. I once again sat in the same bleak waiting room that I had occupied before my endoscopy.

After two hours of fidgeting in a waiting room chair, I heard a nurse call my name. It was my turn. I knew from my previous endoscopy that there was little room in the prep area, because it was set up like horse stalls. But still I begged the nurse to allow my husband back with me. I was not sure if it was because I was one of the last patients of the day or if it was because I looked so panicked, but the nurse allowed it. Going without food before the procedure did not bother me as much as not being able to take any pain medicine or drink any water. I was parched and in pain, and the delay from the highway accident had consumed any reserved strength I had left. Jack made jokes, and we talked about what I would eat once the ERCP was completed. We dreamed together about soon having all this pain behind me. Dr. Cole had informed us that if I woke up from the procedure pain-free we would know the ERCP was a success, and our journey would be near its end. Our discussion distracted me as an IV was inserted and monitors were hooked up to my chest. I was able to hold Jack's hand up until they wheeled me into the operating room. Jack's presence was better than any medication to relieve my stress.

As the fog from the anesthesia began to wear off, my body made me instantly aware that I was in horrible pain. I began to moan. As soon as I had enough strength, I began to scream, "Help, help, someone please help me!"

A nurse quickly came over to my bed. She inquired, "What is wrong?"

I begged with urgency and panic, "I am in horrible pain. I am having a pancreatitis attack. I need morphine."

The nurse flatly stated, "You just came out of surgery, you cannot have any pain medicine."

I continued to scream, "No, I need something now. This pain is unbearable. I am going to die."

The nurse coldly told me, "Please stop screaming. You are disturbing those around you."

This was the first I realized my bed was in a row next to many other groggy patients recovering from anesthesia. There were no curtains between us. Several of them were still unconscious. I honestly did not care if my screaming bothered them. I needed help, and my voice was my best form of communication.

It was clear that this nurse could not be persuaded and was unwilling to get me pain medicine. Typically, I would give someone the benefit of the doubt. If someone cuts me off in traffic, I assume they have an emergency. If a customer service person at a store is snappy, I assume they are going through some sort of personal trial in their life. However, on this particular day, none of these thoughts ran through my head. I just thought this nurse lacked compassion and competence. After all, I was telling her the problem and what I needed.

I decided that if this nurse was not going to answer my request for pain medicine, I would ask for my husband. I was limited in my options, because I was writhing in pain, and I was hooked up to an IV. I was clearly not mobile. However, Jack was my knight in shining armor, and he could be my advocate. I thought Jack could ask questions and maybe better explain my health needs. Thankfully, she was willing to get Jack.

At 5:45 p.m., Jack was allowed back to see me. Seeing Jack helped relieve my anxiety but did not eliminate the pain. I explained to Jack that I was in the worst pain I had ever had and it was getting worse and worse. "I need help now," I exclaimed. Jack, with a calmer voice, asked the nurse in the endoscopy suite if I could get a morphine pump. Jack explained, "We've had success getting Becky comfortable with the patient-controlled pain medication option, and since she is so behind in her pain medication, this option is far easier than having to request pain medication from nurses each time Becky has another bout of pain." The nurse in the endoscopy suite explained that I was being admitted to a hospital room and I could receive pain medicine there.

I was wheeled down many corridors and in and out of different elevators, until I finally arrived at a hospital room that was already occupied by my roommate. Habitually, I would have been conscientious of my roommate's needs, but the pain was all-consuming. The only thing I was focused on was getting relief. My body continued to thrash in pain, and I clenched the hospital sheets in my hands and gritted my teeth. For hours, Jack begged nurses to please help, but was informed that there were no doctor's instructions for pain medicine. Jack was exhausted from a long day and a pitifully slow response time to answer a straightforward request. Eventually Jack's temper began to soar. He finally yelled, "Can you not see that my wife is in horrific pain? Can you not get a hold of a doctor? What use is it to be in a hospital if you can't get medical help?!"

A doctor appeared and informed Jack that if he did not calm

himself down, he would be escorted out. I was afraid Jack's outburst was going to hinder my medical care. I apologized to the doctor, "Please forgive my husband. He is upset that I am in pain and it is torture for him to see me suffer, especially when he knows a solution. Please, sir, I am in horrible pain. I am having a pancreatitis attack and I need pain medicine. Please won't you help me?"

At 8:45 p.m., after three excruciating hours, I was hooked up to a morphine pump that I could press every four minutes. If I pressed it before four minutes, no medicine would be released into my IV, to prevent overdosing. However, I was convinced that no morphine was being released at all: my pain was continuing.

Next, a technician came to wheel me away for a CT scan. I questioned whether he had the right patient. He confirmed all my information and said it had been requested. I did not remember Dr. Cole mentioning this as part of the ERCP post-procedure.

After the CT scan, the next thing I knew, I was having a tube inserted into my nose and told to swallow. It reminded me of the test at Temple Hospital. After a few minutes, I pleaded for the tube to be removed. It was then that I was informed that the CT scan revealed part of my small intestine had been perforated during the ERCP and that the air that had been pumped into my stomach for the procedure had leaked into my abdomen. There was a possibility that they would have to operate to fix the hole in the intestine. The morphine prevented my brain from comprehending the possibility of needing repair surgery. I just wanted this tube removed. I was informed that the "nasogastric tube," or NG tube, that went through my nose and into my stomach was suctioning out the bile and acid there, giving the intestine a better chance to heal on its own.

My mom spent the night in the hospital room holding my hands because, even in my sleep, I tried to pull out the NG tube. I felt like I was constantly being gagged by the plastic at the back of my throat. In addition, every time I swallowed, it hurt my throat. Each time a doctor came into my room, I begged, with tears running down my cheeks, to please remove the NG tube. A friend brought me a timer so I would not have to wait an extra second more than the required four minutes before pressing the button to release morphine. Different friends from Lancaster, as well as friends of friends I had never met before, stopped by my room to say a brief prayer and console my family.

All in all, it took three full days to get my pain under control. Thankfully, around that same time, the NG tube was removed and I was informed that my intestine did not require surgery. I should have felt relief from this news, but I was too discouraged. I had hit my lowest point. Now that my pain was under control, I was able to process all that had transpired – and I was left with fear and despair. I think what made it such a low point was that I had not anticipated it. I was aware of the possibility that the ERCP might not be a complete cure, but I was confident I would at least feel better. I was optimistic that my time of trial was wrapping up – when, in actuality, I still had a long road ahead.

I wanted out. I wanted to give up. I had hoped to be a mother, but that now seemed impossible, and I was certainly no benefit to my family or friends. (They would disagree, but this was how I felt.) I was a mess of pain, tears, and anguish. If I could have left myself, I would have. I was humbled at the outpouring of love from friends and family. I was baffled that individuals would spend their precious time with me. I clearly had nothing to offer but tears and moans. Throughout my life, I had secretly believed that people were nice to me because I was sweet and fun to be around. But during this season, I felt the opposite of sweet. I felt like vinegar or sulfur. Offensive. Awful. Making anyone want to run in the opposite direction. My empathy was growing for individuals who felt like they were at the bottom of a very deep pit. Others may have hit their rock bottom when a dream was shattered, or when they became aware that they were wrapped up in an unhealthy relationship or addiction.

I thought of the eight blessings that are referred to as the Beatitudes in Matthew, Chapter 5. The first three felt especially applicable: "Blessed are the poor in spirit, for theirs is the kingdom of heaven. Blessed are those who mourn, for they will be comforted. Blessed are the meek, for they will inherit the earth." (NRSV)

But Jesus had called those crushed in spirit, grieving, and weak blessed – and I felt anything but blessed. I wanted to be strong and self-sufficient. I desired to help others, not to be the recipient of help. However, I was learning that God's economy and kingdom were upside down.

When I hit rock bottom, several of my false beliefs were shattered: the belief that I was self-sufficient and in control, and the belief that productivity earned me value and worth. Before becoming sick, I would often tell Jack, "I make things happen," losing sight of the fact that God makes things happen. I also thought my productivity defined my value, when, actually, my sole value was rooted in being a child of God. I thought I deserved and was entitled to things, instead of realizing that everything was a gift from God and a blessing. I was truly starting to digest for the first time that God could do the impossible, and God did not need my help to accomplish it. Only by grace and love does God allow His children to participate in holy work.

While this may sound like a freeing epiphany, it was actually terrifying. It felt like the foundation of my life was a big sinkhole. As a child, I had thought my parents could fix anything; nothing was impossible for them. At some point I learned that they could not fix the world. However, still through most of my twenties, I thought they were my safety net. They certainly did everything they could to protect me from harm. I know that for many individuals, this façade is demolished much earlier. My husband, for example, lost his father at age eleven. He learned early on that his parents were not invincible.

Maybe I was a slow learner, maybe I had been well-insulated most of my life, or most likely, it had been a combination of the two. Regardless, I had been unaware that I operated under a set of false beliefs, that I had these huge blind spots, and that in reality no one could truly protect me. I thought that if individuals were unwell or hurt, all they had to do was get to a hospital. I thought once I was in a hospital, I would be safe. Obviously some people still died, but I assumed it was because they got to the hospital too late. I had heard many times, "They caught the cancer early enough," or "The cancer is too advanced, it went undetected for too long." There are of course definite benefits in turning to a hospital when one is seriously ill; hospitals have staff and equipment for diagnosing and treating many illnesses. Further, even my false foundation helped me to relax and, initially, be calm going into hospitals. I had thought, "Soon I will be feeling much better."

Yet now terror overwhelmed me in a hospital – one of the best hospitals in the world – as they struggled not only to diagnose my health issue, but even to merely keep me comfortable. I felt like I was being tortured. I would have happily given up any secrets or any amount of money to have the pain stop. I was not scared of my health issues being fatal. Truthfully, I was far more afraid that I would be in horrific pain for an extended period of time.

When you stub a toe, it really hurts, but the cause is obvious, and you know that the pain will go away soon. Similarly, with a stomach bug, you know that the vomiting will stop. Twenty-four hours may seem long, but relief is in sight.

It is hard to describe the layers of anguish associated with undiagnosed chronic pain. The pain was all-consuming. Not knowing the amount of time until I would receive relief was extremely daunting and distressing. Having morphine pumped into my veins every four minutes for days and *still* being consumed with pain was the greatest nightmare. If the most potent painkiller available was not able to combat my pain, I felt like there was no hope. Losing hope left me in the scariest and most frightening place.

I was becoming more thankful for my faith. No parents, no doctors, no amount of money, no cache of weapons can truly protect a person. We are all vulnerable. Maybe this seems elementary in concept, but to truly comprehend that I was vulnerable was difficult for me, especially because I had gone many years without being confronted with this truth.

The realization that my only safety net was in the Lord was hitting me hard. I was clinging to the truth that nothing could separate me from God's love. I felt like I was uncovering a new layer of understanding what it meant to confess Jesus Christ as my Lord and Savior. The good news of the Easter story was taking on a much deeper meaning for me that spring.

CHAPTER 16

CONFUSED

I had never been so scared before in my life. Sure, I had been nervous before. First day of high school and not knowing a soul in my class. Flying halfway around the world to attend a semester of college in Australia. Defending my thesis. Yes, all three of these events caused excess sweat and knots in my stomach. However, these seemed like paper cuts in comparison to the machete-like slashes I was now feeling.

I was physically and emotionally exhausted from seven days in the hospital at Johns Hopkins. As with most hospital stays, I got very little rest. I was constantly awakened to have my vitals checked, or by the shrill beeping of my IV bag alerting my nurse of an air bubble.

This stay was extra draining because I had expected to leave the hospital without pain and return to work. Instead, my pain had been exacerbated and my pain management care was inadequate. In addition, my doctors' listening skills were horrendous. I requested my daily prescription medications – each day. Each day a doctor gave the same response: "Oh yes, I will approve for you to take your regular medications." However, every time I asked the nurse to dispense the routine medication that my body was accustomed to receiving, I was informed that a doctor had not signed off on it. Each day I saw several doctors, but not once did Dr. Cole stop by my room.

One of the medications I had taken for years was for anxiety. My anxiety medication had warnings not to stop abruptly. Given that I had indeed stopped abruptly (and involuntarily), I wasn't sure whether my increased anxiety levels were from withdrawal, or from being in a hospital with horrific pain and lacking an action plan for healing. This hospital stay was also atypical because for seven days I had not been allowed to eat or drink anything, with the exception of popsicles. The hospital did not even have popsicles on the menu, so my parents had to go down to the gift shop and buy them for me. During previous hospital admissions in Lancaster, I was also not allowed to eat or drink anything for a few days after a pancreatitis attack. I was starting to become too familiar with this routine. By day seven, food seemed overdue.

The other "first" with this hospital stay was that I had two IVs. The one bag with saline solution was clear, and I had grown quite accustomed to it. The other IV had a milky white solution. The nurses referred to it as "TPN," which stood for Total Parenteral Nutrition. I did not know what was in TPN, but I did know my veins did not like it. Every few hours my veins would stop accepting the TPN, and they would have to change sites. My hands and arms were black and blue from all the different veins that the nurses had tried.

I assumed, now that my pancreas had rested for more than a few days, that I would get to go home and then would follow up with Dr. Cole to figure out the next step in this drawn-out game plan. I was feeling anxious and agitated. I had been cooped up for a week with nothing to look at but a brick wall – not exactly a great view. Thankfully, my nurses had been very attentive. I had become particularly fond of one nurse, Megan. She seemed to be the head nurse, and if anyone had questions they asked her. Megan picked up on my restlessness. She suggested that I get some fresh air, and when I returned she would help me take a shower.

She unhooked me from the TPN and got me a wheelchair. I sat in the wheelchair with a hand on my IV pole, and Jack pushed me down the hall to the elevators. From the elevators, we went out the front door. I felt like an escaped convict.

The sunlight felt like a long-lost friend. The air outside smelled wonderful, free of disinfectants. It felt like a long-awaited holiday. Jack had seen a garden while walking around the hospital. We went to cross the street to try and find it. A security guard started yelling at us and ran after us. We were harshly informed, "You are not allowed to cross the street." Did I really look that desperate to run from this place? Had I missed a no-trespassing sign? We were on the sidewalk. When had that become illegal?

Jack explained that we had gotten permission from my nurse to go outside and we were just going for a stroll. The security guard informed us that I could not leave the hospital property with hospital equipment. What was this security officer thinking? I was not about to take the IV pole and wheelchair home as mementos from my stay. I am sure my perplexed look clued the security officer to the reality that I was not tracking with his logic. He went on to say, "People will rip out your IV from your arm and sell it for money. It is unsafe to cross the street." Now my confused look was replaced with horror. Fabulous! I was ready to go back inside the hospital.

Jack wheeled me back to my room. The visit outside had been beneficial, but some of the refreshment had been depleted by the security guard's warning. I was ready for a shower. Showers always made me feel better.

I kept pressing the call button requesting my nurse to tape up my arm with a plastic covering. I knew that this was not an emergency, so I tried to be patient. For me, patient was waiting thirty minutes, and then I would press the call button again. By the third or fourth time, my voice conveyed some irritation. Megan had said she would help me take a shower when I got back. To me that was a promise.

Finally Megan appeared and apologized. She was swamped with discharges. I understood. She was probably working on my discharge paperwork, and I knew it required completing many forms. Megan said she did not want to hold me up any longer, so her assistant would help me bathe.

I was not thrilled with the idea of other people seeing me completely naked, especially when I was conscious. However, if someone had to see me in the nude, I preferred it to be the same person. Megan had helped me shower before. Plus,

Megan was closer in age to my mom. For some reason this made me feel less awkward. Now I was going to be bathed by someone who was younger than me.

My mom learned of this plan and suggested that Jack go get some dinner in the cafeteria while she helped me bathe. My dad's roommate from college lived in the Baltimore area and was coming over for dinner with his wife, so my mom would eat later with them. My mom and the aide helped me take a shower. Typically I love showers. I feel refreshed afterwards, and showering always improves my mood. This time, however, that was not the case. The showering part was fine – but the drying off did not go according to plan. There are two things I hate: one, being cold; and two, being wet. The aide failed to realize that hospital towels are only a smidgen larger than normal washcloths. Thus, when the shower ended, the dilemma was quickly realized. While I was shivering and wet, with half of an arm dry from one towel, the aide ran off to find more towels. I am not sure if the entire floor was out of towels or if the aide just had trouble locating them, but it took an awfully long time. Once I am cold, it takes me a while to warm up.

Megan then stopped in to see how I was doing, but I was cold and slightly grumpy. I asked her when I was going to be discharged. I could not wait to be back in my own bed and take a shower by myself, and without IVs and plastic bags. Megan said, "Oh gosh, honey, you have to get a PICC line in. You are going to be here for probably another week."

For the first time, Megan did not pick up on my body language. In her defense, this was towards the end of her shift, and she had been very busy with discharges. But I was in shock. I had thought I was going home. No one had specifically said I was going home, but I did not see any reason to keep me. If there had been talk of a PICC line, I had clearly missed it.

Megan asked if I needed anything. I flatly replied, "No." Megan was out the door when I started my meltdown. I started to cry. I asked my mom why I had to stay and why I was not allowed to eat anything. I was hungry. I started to cry so hard that I began vomiting.

Megan quickly returned to the room. She asked, "What is going on in here?" I blubbered between heaves, "I thought I was going home…. You were talking about all of the patients being discharged…. Why am I not being discharged? I want to go home." Megan felt terrible for the accidental pain I was blaming her for.

Megan sternly told me that I needed to calm myself down or else I was going to get myself sicker and have to stay longer. I tried to calm myself down, but it took my stomach a little longer to catch up with my head. Since I had not had anything to eat in seven days, I was vomiting stomach acid that burned my esophagus as it came up. I was certainly relieved when this ended.

Next I began to suffer from a phenomenon that I had never experienced before. My limbs started to jerk uncontrollably. I could not stay still. I tried to divert my attention with a movie, as that typically provided at least a partial distraction. But I was on the verge of hysteria. Megan quickly got a doctor. When the doctor entered, I pleaded, "Please knock me out. Please give me anesthesia, I can't take this. I am really freaked out! I need help."

The young female doctor said that she was going to give me a shot of Haldol (an anti-psychotic) and informed me, "You should feel better within minutes." The shot was injected into my butt. This was more than a tad embarrassing, but I was far beyond modesty and pride. I was desperate.

Nothing happened. I concluded that my IVs were causing the spastic movement of limbs. I begged Megan to remove my IVs. She and the aide in the room looked as terrified as I felt, which was not comforting. I am not sure what was going through their minds. Maybe they thought, "If it will calm her down, it is worth removing the IVs for a little while." Perhaps they reasoned, "She is blowing out IVs every few hours, so we will have to put new ones in soon anyway." Regardless, they removed the IVs from each of my arms.

The uncontrollable motions did not cease. A second shot

was administered to my gluteus maximus. The doctor warned, "Tomorrow your glutes are going to feel pretty sore, like you were on the stepper at the gym for hours."

Great, I thought, *something to look forward to.* Really I couldn't care less what was sore the next day – I just wanted this hellish experience to be over.

Fifteen more minutes passed and there was still no improvement. Time was passing at a very slow pace. Instead of feeling calm and sleepy, I was anxious and wired. These shots were having no effect.

I knew logically that nothing was crawling on my skin, yet it felt that way, and I could not stand to have anything touching me. I took off my hospital gown. I was desperate to get this electricity that kept shooting through my body to stop. My heart was pounding. I kept wondering, *Why is this happening?*

The doctor returned. I pleaded, "Please just take my good organs and donate them. I cannot take this." My request was ignored.

Another shot.

I attempted to focus on my breathing. Slow deep breaths in and out. Typically this would help slow my heart rate and calm me down – or at least give me something to concentrate on. After a few seconds and a flailing limb, I was back to horror.

Another shot.

Jack returned from dinner to find me lying naked in bed with doctors and nurses standing around. I asked Jack to climb in the hospital bed and hug me. I thought, *Maybe if he holds me tight, the surges would stop. Maybe it is like a hiccup and if the pattern could be interrupted, I would be back in control of my body, or at least my limbs.*

Nothing was working.

Megan said she would stay with me until this all ended. She stayed beyond her shift. This was clearly lasting longer than anyone anticipated.

The doctor came in and told me that she could not give any more shots without my heart being monitored. I had lost track of how many shots I had received. I now was going to be wheeled down to ICU. Jack helped me get my hospital gown back on.

I wanted to protest, *No, I liked my nurses and my single room. I feel comfortable here. I have been here a week and am not up for more changes!* I had never been in an ICU room. I asked if Jack could stay with me, and the doctor said yes.

I had a spinning feeling, like after you get off of a merry-go-round. I was at a hospital and I was getting worse. Even with doctors, nurses, my mom, and Jack in the room, I felt so alone. No one could help me.

I kept silently and sometimes not silently praying. I wanted God to take me home. I was done fighting. My pain was too intense, my hope was completely blown out. I loved my husband, family, and friends, and I wanted to be a mother, but I did not see the point or purpose in this moment. I had no strength to keep going. The tears were flowing. I kept racking my brain asking, *What did I do wrong? Where did I go wrong? Where is God?* This was worse than any hell I could have imagined.

My sweet nurse Megan who I had gotten to know over the past week was replaced by a rotund, all-business, not-warm-and-fuzzy nurse. She did not even fake a smile at me.

The new room I was wheeled into was frigid. The first thing the nurse did was wipe me down from head to toe with some sort of antiseptic cloth. Next I had heart monitors stuck all over. I started to shiver. Thankfully the jerking movement was becoming less frequent.

Now that I was cold and moist, I realized I had to go to the bathroom. I was given a bedpan. I tried to explain to the nurse, "My bladder will not release unless I am relaxed. Sometimes I have to turn the faucet on and hum. There is no way I can relax with my pelvis hoisted up on some piece of plastic."

This nurse did not seem to care about my dilemma. She sternly stated, "You should have said something before you were hooked up to all of this equipment."

After who knows how long of having the plastic bowl under me to no avail, someone brought a portable commode in the room. Thank goodness. After I was able to empty my bladder,

I felt tremendously better. The nurse informed me that a psychologist would be in the next day to see me. I was so embarrassed. I worried and wondered, *Am I going to be locked up in a mental hospital? Will these limb spasms become common occurrences?* My parents had not been able to join their friends for dinner. *What had they told them? Does everyone think I am crazy?*

I was not sure if I was going to be examined by a psychologist because of my jerking movements, or because I expressed that I did not want to live any more. Personally, I would be more worried about someone who would want to live in such hellish conditions. Of course, I kept those thoughts to myself. I started to feel groggy and drifted off to sleep around 3 a.m. Monday morning.

Monday evening, I woke up in a totally different room. Jack was still next to me. I was very confused. I had slept for almost twenty-four hours. I had been discharged to a regular hospital room, but not on the same floor. I was now in an area for more independent patients. I missed my old nurses, but I was delighted to need less care.

No psychologist ever came. A doctor at Johns Hopkins told me that I had experienced a bad anxiety attack the night before and that I needed to be seen by a counselor after I was discharged. I would later find out from my primary care physician and from a licensed psychologist that in fact I had not had an anxiety attack, and I did not need to worry about that happening again. Both attributed the uncontrollable jerking to the combined trauma of a procedure going terribly wrong, nothing to eat or drink for a week, vomiting, being told I was not being discharged anytime soon, and having all of my regular medication stopped for a week. Apparently this is why most of my medication came with warnings saying that you should not stop abruptly, and that you should consult with a doctor to slowly wean off of the medication. At the time, however, I thought the episode was my fault; I felt tremendous fear and shame.

I was told that on Wednesday I would be getting a PICC line. This would replace needing IVs and allow me to get nutrition without upsetting my pancreas. The PICC line would bypass my digestive track by delivering nutrition directly into my veins. A soft flexible tube, a little less than two feet in length, would be inserted in my right upper arm through a vein. Along with my other random and quirky fears, I do not like foreign objects in my body. The thought of a tube being in my vein for three months made me very nervous and anxious. I had the option to have it inserted in the hospital room or the Operating Room (OR). It had been decided that the OR would be the better option for me because I could be sedated. I think my doctors, family, and I were all worried that I would have another "panic attack," so Jack or my mom was with me at all times. As we waited, my parents and Jack tried to distract me with movies and TV shows, but I could not concentrate. My mind was obsessing about this piece of plastic that was about to be inserted into my arm.

Wednesday I waited all day to be taken to the OR. Some emergency surgeries came up, so my estimated time to get the PICC line kept being pushed back. Finally, a nurse came to my room and said it was time for me to be wheeled to the OR. As the nurse was getting me unhooked from monitors in my room, Jack's cell phone rang. It was a church in South Carolina calling to interview Jack about a full-time job opening. I heard Jack apologize into the phone, "I am sorry, but I cannot talk right now. They are wheeling my wife down to the OR."

I flailed my arms and whispered, "Take the call. I will be fine." Jack shook his head and said, "Thank you" before ending the call.

This was the second interview phone call that Jack had been unable to keep. I knew that a group of volunteers had gathered at the church in South Carolina to make this call. Jack was blowing off an entire committee! In this current economic environment, one does not cancel interviews. Now that I knew I was not going to be returning to work any time soon, and since Jack's current employment was temporary and part-time, I thought he needed to put his career first. The purpose of his current job was to give him the luxury of time (a year) to find a permanent position that would be the right fit for our family. Because of my serious health issues and so much time spent in hospitals, however, Jack had posted his profile (the equivalent of a resume), but he had not applied for a single job. I appreciated Jack's presence by my side, but I was thinking about how we were going to provide for a family. I was sure that Jack was doing everything wrong. I asked, "Jack, why didn't you take the call? You need a permanent job."

"My focus is on you right now and getting you better." Jack gave me a kiss and squeezed my hand before I was rolled away.

In the operating room, all sorts of monitors and equipment surrounded me. Individuals with masks scurried around the room. They put something in my IV to help relax me, but I was still awake. I politely interrupted a technician, "Excuse me, I am still awake. I requested to be asleep for this procedure." The anxiety in my voice gave away my concern.

I was quickly reassured, "You will be made comfortable." *Made comfortable!* I thought. *I want to be knocked out.*

Fortunately, the next thing I remembered was a surgeon's face hovering over me saying, "Rebecca, Rebecca, how are you feeling?"

With a groggy voice and fuzzy brain, I replied, "I am doing okay, I am awake. I don't want to be awake for the PICC line."

"The PICC line is in. You are all set. We were able to insert it in your right arm."

I felt a sense of relief. The procedure was over, and I had not had any limbs spasm out of control. I was also relieved that the PICC line was successful in my right arm. I had been warned that if they could not get it into my arm, that the second site option would be my neck. The idea of a tube sticking out of my neck concerned me more than my arm.

I was wheeled back to my room and I arrived with a smile. I was ecstatic to see Jack and to know another hurdle was behind me. I knew the PICC line was the last major item to be completed before I got to go home.

The next two days, the nurses monitored my PICC line to make sure that it was working properly. My favorite thing about the PICC line was that I did not have to be pricked for blood work. A valve from my PICC line could be used to collect a blood sample. I also did not have any more IVs. I started walking, which meant I did not have any more jabs to my thighs. (The shots to prevent blood clots were very painful.) I loved being needle- and shot-free.

I also received all of my nutrition via my PICC line. My mom referred to the white liquid as my "moo milk." I was not hungry, but I struggled with not being able to eat or drink anything. I missed the action of chewing and swallowing. However, I was willing to cooperate, because my discharge date was set for Saturday. I could not wait to be launched.

I updated friends and family and petitioned once again for prayers. Below is an excerpt from my update that I wrote at Johns Hopkins after my PICC line was inserted.

> *My main prayer request is that I would embrace each day rather than wish it away.*
>
> *Below is a prayer I wrote and ask if you are comfortable to pray this for Jack and me –*
>
> *Precious and merciful Savior, we praise you for your provision of outstanding nurses, friends to love on Becky and Jack from across the room and across the phone, competent doctors, and amazing technology. Lord, we praise you for the healing that has occurred and pray for continued healing in Becky's body. Please surround Becky with grace as she learns to embrace each day without eating, and may it help remind her and others of the manna you provided in the wilderness and how you, Lord, sustain us with sources uncommon to our society. Help Becky and Jack to abound with trust, gratitude, and joy. In Jesus' name, amen.*
>
> *I trust this pain has a reason. I know I want to use my experience with horrific pain to help comfort others in pain. I am not sure how, but for now I want to pray for those hurting in some form. If I can pray for you or a loved one, please know I am truly always delighted*

and promise to keep it confidential. Blessings and deep, deep gratitude.

Loads and buckets of love,
Becky

The following Friday I posted an update from the luxury of home.

Hi faithful friends and family,
Last Saturday (4/21) I was discharged from Johns Hopkins (after a thirteen day stay). As Jack wheeled me out of my hospital room and towards the car he asked me, "Don't you feel like the hall should be lined with patients and nurses cheering and applauding?" I think we have been watching too many movies :0) However, in my mind leaving the hospital was just as exciting as if there had been a pep rally.
I was so excited to leave Hopkins that I fell asleep during the ride home. We had a nurse come to our house Saturday evening to show Jack and me how to use my PICC line to get nutrition in me. Jack was amazing and is taking care of hooking me up every evening and disconnecting me every morning. It is painless, just tastes bad. The benefit of this process is it will help me gain weight and strength while allowing my GI tract to rest. Of course, I'd rather put on weight by eating cheeseburgers and milkshakes :0)
I slept most of the weekend and Monday. One highlight was taking a bath at my parents' home with the help of my mom and sister. (I cannot get my right arm wet because of the PICC line.) My mom and sister also washed my hair. Wow, did that feel great!
Tuesday through Thursday I rested at my parents' home. If I get up too quickly, I get lightheaded and everything goes black. Thus, I mainly stay in the recliner. My goal for right now is to listen to the Bible

on my iPod from Genesis to Revelation. My mom and I are listening together and writing down verses that speak to us in some new way.

Some praises: being home, kind nurses that come to our home, my blood work (taken twice this week) has been great, my bladder has been strong with getting lots of fluids at night, being able to sleep, watching a nine-month old giggle and army crawl on the floor, cards and emails of encouragement, amazing caregivers (primarily Jack and my mom), receiving a prayer shawl, and being blanketed in prayers.

I return to Hopkins this coming Tuesday (May 1) for a follow-up with Dr. Cole, along with a team of other doctors and surgeons to talk about removing my pancreas. I am the weakest I have ever been, which has been very challenging. I am learning to rest often. The phrase I am currently holding onto is "God's strength can be seen clearer in our weakness." Thank you for your continued prayers! My specific requests are for continued healing, wisdom for my family and the doctors, and blessings for my caregivers.

As always, I am delighted to hold up your prayer requests and/or praises in my daily chats with God.

Blessings and deep gratitude,
Becky

I felt a little guilty that my intention for the blog was to help others who were suffering from undiagnosed pain by giving encouragement and honesty, and I was falling short. I felt devoid of encouraging words for others, and I was keeping some facts secret.

I did not mention in my updates that a church in South Carolina was pursuing Jack. I knew my co-workers were following my blog, and I did not want to lose my job. Jack and I were also both secretly hoping that his current temporary employment would be made permanent. We loved where we lived. We had a diverse community with lots of friends and family nearby.

I always believed that God loved me and had my best interests in mind. However, I was starting to realize that God's perspective on what was best for me was not even in the same ballpark as mine. I trusted that God was in control, but was questioning if I still desired God's will for me since it seemed to include long-term suffering.

The church committee in South Carolina persisted and scheduled a third phone interview with Jack after we returned from Hopkins. It had been exactly one week since I had received my PICC line. When Jack received the phone call, I was lying down on our bed. No surprise, since this was where I spent most of my time. Jack sat down next to me.

The church's first question was, "Are you interested in this job?" Jack's honest reply was, "No." The position the church was seeking to fill was for a full time Director of Christian Education. Jack was interested in an ordained position. Jack said, "I don't want to waste your time. However, I don't believe ministry happens in a vacuum. I would love to hear what your church is doing and share what the church I am serving is up to." I could only hear Jack's side of the conversation. After sixty minutes, Jack hung up the phone, looked over at me, and said matter-of-factly, "Well, we will never hear from them again."

I felt some relief that Jack would not be traveling for an interview and ultimately that we would not be moving. I did not want to move to a new community and region of the country if I could not thrive. On the other hand, my medical expenses could not be sustained on my disability income and Jack's part-time income. I prayed for provision.

The PICC line was certainly a lot to adjust to, but not being able to eat food was so much harder. Anytime I turned on the TV, a commercial or show seemed to include eating. Even advertisements on the radio included food. It was awkward to be around family members who obviously needed to eat, but I could not participate. I got so mad one evening that I put food in my mouth and chewed it, just to chew and taste something good – and then I had to spit it out in the sink. Swallowing and digesting food would most likely cause a pancreatitis attack, sending me back to the hospital. It felt cruel to be absorbing four thousand calories a day and not be able to swallow any food.

I was terrified that I no longer had the ability to act or pretend to be okay. I struggled to dream. The future was no longer a source of hope. Since the ERCP had failed, I was not optimistic that removing my pancreas would be successful. Would there be a plan C, D, and E? Could I give up? I wondered if, figuratively, I was five hundred feet from relief or five hundred miles from relief. I also wondered if I would experience healing on earth or have to wait until heaven. I wondered if my next appointment with Dr. Cole would shed any light on my questions.

PART II:
DIAGNOSED PAIN –
AND A TERRIFYING PLAN

CHAPTER 17

MAY DAY

May 1 was a day filled with news. In addition to it being the start of a new month, I met a new doctor, had a new joy, a new hope, and a new challenge.

Less than a month after traveling to Johns Hopkins Hospital for my ERCP, my parents, Jack, and I once again made the hour and a half trek south. Thankfully this trip was smooth with no traffic complications. Even with some nervous, anxious energy, I felt strong and confident for the appointment. I was armed with my parents and Jack present, prepared questions, four note pads, and most importantly, heaps of prayer.

As we drove down, I thought, *What a difference seven months makes!* Seven months ago, I went to see Dr. Albert at Temple with no questions prepared, and I had anticipated that the doctor would solve my health issues quickly, competently, and completely. Now, I was aware that I needed to do research before the appointment, have questions prepared about different options and possible outcomes, and not expect quick resolutions. I truly felt armed for battle.

I had my best appointment with Dr. Cole. He spent a lot of time with my family and answered all of our questions. Of course, Dr. Cole never mentioned that he had been wrong or apologized for all the times he had been adamant that there was nothing wrong with my pancreas.

Jack inquired, "If your wife had the same medical conditions as Becky, would you recommend that your wife have the total pancreatectomy with islet cell transplantation?"

Dr. Cole responded, "I won't answer that question.

However, if your wife's case was in front of a board of doctors, I would recommend the total pancreatectomy." Dr. Cole's response reminded me of a politician's, but at least he acknowledged he was not answering the question.

I asked, "What is Hopkins' success rate with this surgery, and why, if I decide to have the surgery, should I have it at Hopkins?" My questions clearly let Dr. Cole know that we were doing our research and just because Johns Hopkins was world renowned, did not mean we were not going for a second opinion. Dr. Cole shared that the hospital had done less than ten of these specialized surgeries and I was welcome to get a second opinion.

Probably the most trivial of questions medically, but the one I was most excited about was, "Can I eat some food?"

Dr. Cole explained, "You are getting all of the nutrients you need through the PICC line in your arm. Therefore, you do not need to eat anything. But if you would like to eat small amounts of food that are low in fat, you can."

This was music to my ears! After three weeks of popsicles and every flavor of gum, I could not wait! As soon as the appointment was over with Dr. Cole, I ate a few animal crackers that I had stashed in my purse. Yes, I had been hopeful.

We next met with the coordinator and surgeon for the procedure Dr. Cole recommended. The coordinator told us what to expect. "The surgery to remove a pancreas and transplant cells from the pancreas into the liver takes eight to ten hours. The patient will then be in the ICU for approximately three days, and then will spend up to three weeks in the hospital. The recovery at home is two to three months."

I thought to myself, *I have spent over thirty days in the hospital this year and have had chronic pain for over seven months. This surgery doesn't sound pleasant, but it's manageable.*

The coordinator continued on looking directly at me, "Take your worst pain and multiply it by a million and this is how you will feel after the surgery. You will have a large incision down your abdomen. Patients post-surgery require more pain medicine than a trauma victim that was just hit by a car." Talk about crashing – I felt like I had just been in an accident. The coordinator's words felt like a strong blow to my gut. It made everything I had been through look like a small hill and now I was about to climb Mt. Kilimanjaro.

I tried to keep a calm façade as the coordinator stated, "We require all patients to be completely off of pain medicine prior to the surgery to prevent tolerance to the narcotics." I had no idea how I would wean myself off of pain medication. I was still taking breakthrough pain medicine every day, and it did not begin to control my pain. But I did not have time to process this, as the coordinator did not pause.

"Post-surgery, all patients are on insulin while in the hospital and go home on insulin. Two-thirds of patients do not require insulin after a few months. However, all patients eventually become diabetic and insulin dependent." Becoming diabetic was not a complete surprise. I had read on the internet that those without a pancreas require insulin. Checking my blood sugar and giving myself insulin were not skills I wanted to learn and add to my resume. I had always dreaded annual flu shots – and now I had to consider having insulin injections on a daily basis.

Next my parents, Jack and I returned to meet with Dr. Cole. He asked, "Do you have any questions?"

I asked, "Are there any other options besides the total pancreatectomy to control pain?"

Dr. Cole replied, "Pain medication."

I thought to myself, *Well, that is obviously not working!*

I was trying to digest all that we had learned, and I was horrified by the coordinator's description of the post-surgery pain. I thought it was interesting that Dr. Cole did not ask if I wanted to have the surgery. Instead Dr. Cole stated, "If you decide to move forward with the surgery, you will need to have some tests done to see if you are a candidate for surgery. I would recommend having these screening tests done if you are considering the surgery. If at any point you decide not to have the surgery, that is okay. You are not agreeing to have the surgery by having the screenings done. The earliest you could have the surgery would be in three months. We need to get your weight up and your strength."

Without Jack soliciting, Dr. Cole said, "If it were me, I would go ahead and schedule the screenings. Once again, completing these tests does not obligate you to the surgery." I agreed to schedule the pre-surgery test screenings. It seemed like a no-brainer to keep my options open.

After my family left Hopkins, we stopped at a Cheesecake Factory for lunch. I had a bite of my dad's mashed potatoes, a bite of Jack's salad, a few spoonfuls of my mom's soup, and several pieces of bread to go with my fruit smoothie. It tasted like the best meal in my entire life! I tried to drown my fears with the joy of eating. I was not sure whether it was psychological or physical, but I felt tremendously stronger and happier when I was able to eat food.

The decision about whether or not to have surgery seemed like a moot point for now. First I had to see if my body qualified for surgery. I was grateful that our lunch conversation was not about the possible surgery. Instead, our lunch conversation primarily focused on me being able to eat again, and my audible *mmmm*s.

The following day after Jack dropped me off at my parents' home and he headed to work, I confided my fears to my mom. I asked, "Mom, what did you think of the coordinator's description of the surgery?" Without waiting for an answer, I continued, "Do you think she was intentionally trying to scare me – because she was successful!"

My mom calmly responded, "I think the coordinator was trying to provide an accurate overview of what to expect. I don't believe her intentions were malicious."

In one breath I spewed out, "In some ways, I wished she had sugar-coated the truth. Now, I have three months to live in terror and anticipation. That is, if I have the surgery. I do not know if I want to have the surgery or if I will even qualify. However, I cannot keep living like this."

My mom had me sit in her lap on the couch, as she held me close. Tears poured from my eyes. I was so frightened and wondered if I was being a wimp.

After a few minutes, my mom looked me in the eyes and said with wisdom, "Becky, there is no question that the surgery won't be easy or pleasant. However, you have two choices. You can live in fear for the next three months and dread each day or you can choose to do something fun each day and enjoy the day. The choice is yours." The latter seemed much wiser and more appealing. My mom promised to help me to think of something fun to do each day. This was not to say, of course, that I was not still scared to my core.

To start, I asked my mom if she would teach me how to knit. For my first project I wanted to make a scarf for Jack. I thought possibly in the future, I could knit prayer shawls for others.

I was excited to start a new project and do something fun each day with my mom. My mom tossed out an array of ideas. Things we could do included getting my hair cut, having my nails painted, watching a movie, getting together with friends, etc.

I followed my mom's logic and certainly wanted to dwell on the positive. I continued to fill the pages of my gratitude journal. Unfortunately, I could not fully escape the feeling that a dark cloud was over my head. I kept thinking I had hit rock bottom – and then my situation and spirits would decline further. I was the most scared and depressed I had ever been in my life. I was in horrible pain and could not imagine how my pain could be more unbearable.

I combatted my wimpy fears by reading other people's description of pancreatitis online. It was helpful to read one sufferer's description that pancreatitis was ten times more painful than natural childbirth. I also read a man describe his pancreatitis pain as being worse than the pain he experienced when he was in a jeep that blew up.

Assuming the screening tests went well, my next big hurdle would be to get off of pain medicine. This seemed impossible.

However, I figured I would take one day at a time.

CHAPTER 18

ACUPUNCTURE

Many times I felt like Jack got the burden of my tears and unanswerable questions. Jack had recently learned how to hook up my TPN, add vitamin shots to my liquid nutrition, and properly flush my ports. All of this had to be done with great care to avoid infection. I knew Jack was also stressed with challenges at work. But I could not tell Jack – who had become an ordained pastor less than a year before – that I was doubting God's love and faithfulness.

I was losing hope of becoming a mother, but I wanted to at least be a helpful wife and to function. At this point, my family was helping to clean my house and make meals. I could do little for myself besides get dressed and go to the bathroom.

My mom always listened with empathy. She had had emergency surgery fourteen months earlier. The surgery had been major and had saved her life. She did not wait months anticipating the surgery, but she had dealt with the long recovery.

My mom saw me both literally and figuratively in my most vulnerable states. She bathed me and washed my hair. She took such tender care of me and did her best to restore dignity in my life. She never once complained about having to care for me. She kept her promise by working really hard to find something fun for us to do each day. I believe my mom would have had this surgery for me if she could have.

Therefore, it was out of tender and compassionate love that she encouraged me to check out acupuncture. My mom knew I needed to be off all pain medicine before I could have my pancreas removed. Every day when I would take my breakthrough pain medicine (morphine), my mom would ask, "Do you really need it?" I instantly became irritable and defensive, stating, "Of course I need it! I am in horrible pain." However, I knew my mom was just trying to help.

This was not the first time acupuncture had been suggested as a solution to my pain. Back in February during one of my hospital admissions, I had asked a pain management doctor for non-narcotic pain management options. He had recommended acupuncture. In fact, he had recommended I see the acupuncturist who had treated his daughter. However, I had ignored the recommendation back in February because I thought the ERCP would cure all of my pain.

Even with the personal testimony and recommendation, I was skeptical about how acupuncture could reduce pain. I had certainly been poked with enough needles in the hospital between IVs, blood work, and shots. Not once had the insertion of a needle relieved pain.

I resisted the idea for a while, but at this point, I felt like I had nothing to lose. I thought, *My body has been tortured through constant intense pain for over seven months, tests, an NG tube, and now I am being mentally tortured by the anticipation of major surgery. Why not have my body stuck with needles? My life cannot get worse.*

I called and made an appointment, thinking I had clearly lost all sanity and self-worth. On Tuesday, May 8, my mom drove me to my first acupuncture appointment. Between having to be bathed and driven everywhere, I felt like I had declined to child status.

The acupuncturist's office was only a few blocks from my home. She had converted the first floor of a large brick city home into an office and lived on the second floor. I was glad my mom was with me. I figured if it got too bad, she would intervene. In addition to feeling foolish for being twenty-nine years old and having my mom drive me to an appointment, I also felt embarrassed because I had on a bright yellow raincoat. There was a chance of rain, and I had to protect the PICC line in my right arm from getting wet. With the PICC line, I needed a coat with a little extra room in the sleeves, so my mom had lent me one of her raincoats. I felt like a big rubber ducky going into acupuncture.

When I opened the door, the first thing I thought was, *I am back in college.* The strong scent of incense almost made me gag. I walked into a waiting room. Someone called from down the hall, "Be with you in a minute." I took a seat. The waiting room was rather spare, with minimal furniture and decorations. A desk, a couch, and a coffee table. This waiting room was different than any other waiting room I had ever been in. Besides the aroma in the air, there was a Buddha figurine, bamboo plants, and framed Chinese writing.

I was nervous, but this feeling was overpowered by pain. I hunched over and could not sit up straight because of pain. My mom tried to fill the silence with ideas for my sister's upcoming bridal shower. She also talked about how I was going to look very chic in my matron of honor dress. My generous mom was having a seamstress design and make a dress that would cover my PICC line arm, but be sleeveless on the other side. I was grateful and excited about the asymmetrical dress, but at this moment all I cared about was relief from the pain and surviving the acupuncture appointment. I did not have high hopes for the appointment, but I figured afterwards I could at least say I tried it.

Suddenly a Chinese woman, who looked to be in her thirties, appeared. She had her hair pulled back in a bun and a white lab coat on. She declared, "I am Min. Come with me." She showed me back to a room. The room was empty with the exception of a massage table. The walls were covered with drawings of the body with Chinese characters.

Min asked, "What wrong with you?" I had to listen carefully, as English was clearly not her first language.

I explained, "I have chronic pancreatitis. Before I can have surgery, I need to be off of all pain medicine. I am looking for relief from pain, so I can get off of pain medicine."

She pointed to my arm, "What this?"

I replied, "It is a PICC line. This is how I get nutrition."

Min muttered, "Not good. Not good. People should eat.

Pain medicine problem."

She took my pulse from my wrist. "Pulse fast. You nervous?"

I nodded my head yes.

Next she instructed me to take my shirt off and lie on my stomach. I secretly wished I was about to get a massage. Min started at my neck and pressed her fingers along my spine and asked, "Hurt? Pain?"

I replied, "Yes."

I sensed a prick. She continued to move her fingers down each side of my spine, pressing every inch or so. There was not one place she pressed that did not hurt. It felt like I had a bruise everywhere she pressed. I experienced a little prick with each needle, but then did not feel anything.

"Any needle hurt?" Min asked in broken English.

I replied honestly, "No. I cannot feel any of them."

"Good. Lie still. Be back."

After fifteen minutes or so, Min returned to the room and twisted the needles and then once again asked, "Needle okay?"

I replied, "Needles fine." Again Min left the room.

Maybe all of my time in hospitals had gotten me accustomed to lying without moving for stretches of time. Prior to my illness, I always had a mental to-do list scrolling through my mind. However, these days all I did was rest. I did not have energy to make lists, let alone to cross items off a list. Thus, I just lay on the massage table with needles sticking out of my back and thought about nothing.

When Min returned, she removed the needles from my back and instructed me to flip onto my back. She pressed along my arms and legs once again asking, "Pain? Hurt?" In this position I could see where she was pressing. There were clearly no bruises, but everywhere Min pressed hurt. As a result, every place she pressed got a needle. After she was done inserting five or six needles in each arm and leg, Min left the room.

I had more trouble relaxing in this position because I could see the needles. I looked like a voodoo doll or pincushion. I tried my best to close my eyes and imagine lying on a towel at the beach.

When Min returned, she once again twisted the needles and checked to make sure no needles were causing pain. She commented, "Your heart beat too fast. You need relax."

I thought I was doing pretty well, all things considered.

It was not until Min took the needles out and I went to leave that I realized I could stand up straight and I had no pain. My pancreatitis pain always originated in my torso, so I didn't understand how needles in my arms and legs had helped to relieve pain. I had not been planning to make a second appointment right away, but with these results, I was hooked.

I asked Min how often I needed to come. She replied, "In Chinese hospital, patient get acupuncture three times a day. You need at least three times a week."

I felt like an infomercial with the unbelievable before and after pictures. I arrived hunched over and now could stand up straight. However, I was more excited about the lack of pain than the improved posture.

I went ahead and scheduled two more appointments for the week. I was quite aware that my insurance did not cover acupuncture and that my husband and I had a negative cash flow. It was not unusual for me to go four to six months without getting a haircut, and now I was going to plunk down a couple of hundred dollars a week to be pricked with needles. Prior to my first acupuncture experience, I would have lumped acupuncture into the same category as massage and manicures – a luxury. But now, while I was still mindful of our finances, I was beginning to place my wellbeing above the dollar sign.

CHAPTER 19

JANAE

In high school, if I had been able to trade places with anyone, it would have been with Janae. She had thick, naturally curly brown hair that went in all different directions. Her hair was so wild it looked good. I had always hated my thin, limp hair that was straight but had a few stubborn sections that would flip out. Janae's hair was the first thing one noticed about her, and it made her stand out. However, Janae's smile was also a focal point. She always had a big, genuine smile on her face, and she had a contagious laugh. Janae was gorgeous – but she was popular because of her kindness. She was genuinely nice to everyone, and everyone loved her.

I had stayed in sporadic touch with Janae after high school. She kept me informed about a friend's cancer treatment when I was studying abroad in Australia. We would see one another at mutual friends' weddings. However, my real admiration for Janae bloomed in 2010. Janae found out early in her pregnancy that the fetus's skull was not developing properly. Her doctors recommended that she abort the baby. Instead, Janae asked for prayers and carried the baby to full term. She decorated a nursery and purchased a car seat. She trusted that God would provide. I prayed so hard and sent Janae brief e-mails to let her know that I was praying. Unfortunately, Janae's firstborn, Aliyah Joy, was stillborn. At Aliyah's funeral, Janae praised and worshiped God. I could not fathom her strength and faith.

After Aliyah's death, I unconsciously avoided Janae. I just did not know what to say. Life was busy, and time passed. However, I included Janae on my email updates about my health. Janae repeatedly asked if she could come over and pray with me. I had been wary of hosting company because I never knew when my pain would flare up or if I would have uncontrollable diarrhea. However, Janae persisted in asking. In part, I was worn down by her asking – but the bigger factor in my accepting her invitation to visit had been her vulnerability and transparency with her first pregnancy. If anyone understood pain and confusion, it was Janae.

On May 15 Janae came over to my parents' house. She was almost nine months pregnant with her second daughter. Janae plopped herself on the couch. She wasted no time and directly asked, "Becky, what do you need?"

I blurted out with tears in my eyes, "A full-time job for Jack." I had no idea when I would be able to return to work, and our savings were drying up faster than water in Phoenix. My disability income and Jack's part-time salary did not cover our bills.

Not wasting a second, Janae grabbed my hand and started boldly praying. She began with, "Lord, I ask that you provide a full-time, ordained position for Jack TODAY!"

She continued, but I did not hear anything else after this. My mind was going in a hundred different directions. I thought, *Poor Janae. She does not understand how the Presbyterian Church operates. A committee has to be formed, then they must read through a lot of applications, interview candidates, go to their session (the governing body of the church) with the committee's recommendation, and then the church members have to vote.* I thought it was a sweet prayer request, but Janae did not know what she was asking. She was asking for a miracle. Then it hit me: maybe I was not praying with enough faith. After all, we only need faith the size of a mustard seed to move mountains.

Before falling asleep for a nap that afternoon, I said a silent prayer requesting a full-time job for Jack. We were hoping the position at the church where Jack was currently serving would be turned into a full-time position. I fell asleep with hope for the future.

As usual, Jack picked me up at my parents' home after he was done at work. I shared that it was nice to see Janae and that I had forgotten she had also had a PICC line in high school. I honestly do not recall whether I chickened out or forgot, but I did not tell Jack about Janae's bold prayer.

After dinner, Jack's cell phone rang. He looked confused as he spoke, but I gathered it was the church in South Carolina. *What?* I thought. Jack had told them very clearly that he was not interested. *What could they want now?*

It turned out that they wanted exactly what Jack wanted. The committee was so impressed after speaking with Jack back in April that they went back to their session and requested that the job be changed to an ordained position. The committee's request was accepted. This may seem small, but changing a position from non-ordained to ordained requires a lot of steps, and there are many regulations about ordained positions, including the salary.

They asked Jack if he would be willing to fly down to Beaufort, South Carolina, for an in-person interview. They also requested that I join him.

Jack said yes. When he hung up the phone in total amazement, I shared Janae's prayer spoken just hours earlier in the day. My sister later shared that earlier in the day she had also prayed for Jack to be provided with full-time employment.

After so many delays and so much pain, I could not believe something was moving quickly and in the right direction. I wondered how I would fly with a PICC line and what we would do if I had to have surgery at Hopkins in the fall. However, I figured that if God could orchestrate all the other details, then God would also take care of my health needs.

Looking back on this time much later, I saw how like Sarah in the Bible, I thought I had figured out how God was going to answer the prayer. I had figured that the church in South Carolina would offer Jack a job, and then his current church in Lancaster would be motivated to offer him a full-time position so he would stay. I had no idea that God was going to work out things far better than I could have ever imagined.

CHAPTER 20

TURNED A CORNER

On May 23 I posted the following update.

Hello my dearest faithful friends and family,
I am delighted and thankful to share good news. I have long anticipated sending this email :0)
I began acupuncture two weeks ago, and I feel like a new person. I have had 6 sessions so far and feel better after each one. The pain has decreased so much that I have been able to significantly reduce the amount of my daily pain medication (slowly of course and with my doctor's permission), and I have not had to use my breakthrough narcotic medicine in a week. (Prior to acupuncture, I needed breakthrough pain medication, on average, once a day.) Woohoo!
This is such an answer to many prayers. Praise God for His faithfulness. I feel SO wonderful that I forget all that my body has been through. Thus, I have to remember to pace myself and that I still need to rest. I would ask for prayers as I step down off of my narcotics. With each decrease, I feel a bit yucky for a day or so. However, the tradeoff is totally worth it. I have more energy and more brain clarity with each decrease.
I saw my family doctor yesterday and he is enthusiastic about my progress. I have been able to put on ten pounds and overall just look healthier and happier. My family doctor's recommendation is still to continue forward with the steps for surgery. I have more tests scheduled at Hopkins the end of June and then

meet with Dr. Cole on July 3rd to go over the test results. Dr. Cole was very clear that I can at any point decide not to have surgery. I would also greatly appreciate prayers for discernment and wisdom in this department.

I cannot begin to capture or describe how wonderful it feels to really live again – to go days without horrible pain, and to eat food without fear of going to the hospital. The Lord's healing has helped me to enjoy and appreciate life again. I am also learning to live one day at a time, enjoying the treasures sprinkled throughout each day. My current mantra is, "God is in control, and God is trustworthy." This helps me to combat fear and "what if" thoughts.

I know this journey is not over, but I anticipate my updates to be less frequent as I feel a tremendous corner has been turned. I greatly appreciate the dedication of your prayers and words of encouragement. I am a true believer in the power of prayer.

As always, it is my true delight and honor to lift up any prayer requests that are weighing on your heart.

Jubilant thanks,
Becky

I was not taking a minute of pain-free living for granted. While I continued to rely on my mom to help me bathe, I did not feel like an emotional burden any more. I was smiling, laughing, giggling, and beginning to dream about the future once again.

CHAPTER 21

SQUEEZED

On Thursday, May 24, I heard the most powerful and life-changing message. It was delivered by Priscilla Shirer in her DVD series on Jonah. I watched the video along with a dozen or so ladies at our weekly Bible Study. Priscilla opened her talk by asking if we felt squeezed. Energy squeezed? Financially squeezed? Spiritually squeezed? Emotionally squeezed? With each question, Priscilla picked up a slice of fruit and squeezed it over a pitcher. She then proceeded to say, "Only after we are squeezed can we be poured out to be a blessing to the Lord and others."

While making this profound statement, she poured the fresh-squeezed juice into a glass. The message continued on with many more powerful observations from the book of Jonah, including, "I am thankful I serve a God that gives us second chances and doesn't place us on the shelf when we are disloyal." And, "It is easy for us to impersonate obedience." (This one refers to when Jonah arose and went, but not in the direction the Lord had instructed.) I felt like God was talking directly to me through Priscilla. I certainly had felt squeezed, and the idea of blessings pouring forth from this season was encouraging.

I felt so encouraged that I began anticipating the blessings. I believed that the blessings primarily meant my future children and being able to provide for them. Now that Jack had an upcoming interview at the church in South Carolina, I was optimistic that Jack would receive an offer from the church in Lancaster, Pennsylvania. After all, my family and doctors were here. We knew no one in Beaufort, South Carolina.

I continued getting acupuncture treatments, and after each one I felt better. With the advice of my primary care physician, I was able to wean off of morphine and had not needed any breakthrough pain medicine in over a week. It looked probable that I could get off of all pain medicine and not be in pain. If this were the case, I would not need to have surgery. The mere idea of keeping my pancreas provided mounds of joy, energy, and hope. I thought, "Maybe I can return to work soon."

My sister was getting married in less than two months. I was so excited for her. I saw her marriage as a blessing from God and certainly worthy of celebration. I knew my sister wanted to start a family. I wondered if maybe Jack and I would soon receive a referral from Ethiopia for our future children. Maybe my children and my sister's would be close in age. I had no idea how God was going to use my illness to bless others, but I certainly had numerous ideas about how God could bless me and my family. As I sat in Bible Study, listening to Priscilla's discussion, the hope balloon inside me was swelling. I could not wait to share Priscilla's squeezing analogy with Jack. I just knew blessings were coming.

A few hours after I shared the analogy with Jack and while my spirits were still soaring, I received a call from Human Resources (HR) at my workplace. They were calling to let me know that my employment with the bank was officially terminated. Since I had been out on short-term disability for over six months, I would be switching over to long-term disability. However, she explained, so far my disability claim had not been approved. If I wanted to keep my health insurance, I would now have to pay the COBRA (continuing health insurance coverage) amount. The HR lady continued on with formalities, like that I would need to return my badge and pick up my personal items at the office. She was very thoughtful in expressing that I was not fired and that my termination was bank policy, not a reflection on my past performance. She encouraged me to be in touch once I was physically able to return to work, but made it clear that there were no guarantees of future employment.

I felt like all of the air had been removed from the room. I managed to get out, "Yes...sure...I understand...thank you." I had known that my job could not be left open indefinitely, but the formality of the termination did more than sting. I felt like a wild beast had taken a bite out of my abdomen. I felt a swirl of emotions, from anger to embarrassment.

I lamented in my head, *I am twenty-nine years old, I graduated with honors in mathematics from a prestigious college, I stayed with the same company for five years, I am a hard worker, I am ethical.... This should not be happening!* I knew my employer was not at fault, but I was angry and frustrated that my health had deteriorated to a point where I had lost my employment. Further, I had not only lost my job, but also lost the health benefits that covered both me and my husband.

I felt embarrassed that Jack had married a sinking ship. I was embarrassed that my parents had paid for me to get a solid education, and now I was unemployed. Even before my illness, I had struggled with self-esteem and self-worth. Then the long-term disability coverage company started shredding me to pieces. Not only did they require me to complete a small rainforest worth of paperwork, but they constantly belittled me over the phone with comments like, "Don't you want to work?" "Are you even trying to get well?" "You are awfully young to need disability."

I knew I had a serious health issue, but the jabs still stuck, and I felt guilty for not working. I would ask myself, *Why can I not pull it together? Why can I not overpower the pain and fatigue?*

God was gracious, and Jack was standing right next to me when I received the call from HR. Before I could manage to form words, the tears poured out. I turned to my husband and choked out, "Unemployed." Without missing a beat, Jack opened up my Jonah workbook and pointed to the quote, "Only after we are squeezed can we be poured out to be a blessing to the Lord and others."

Wow, in those words, God had provided me with something to trust and hold fast to for this unexpected blow. When I had heard Priscilla's message that morning, I thought the major squeezing had already occurred. I had not anticipating more significant squeezing.

CHAPTER 22

CALLED

Two days after finding out that my employment was terminated, I hosted a bridal shower for my sister at my parents' home. My sister's upcoming wedding served as a great diversion from the slowly dawning reality that my life was not going to return to "normal" anytime soon.

The morning of the shower I awoke in horrible pain and could not get out of bed. Thankfully, the pain lifted at 4 p.m., which was divine timing – because the shower started at 4:30.

I was delighted that the event included lots of laughter and that my sister felt special. At 6:30, Jack arrived to pick me up. I was having so much fun that I did not want to go. Jack had to remind me that I needed to get home to be hooked up to my TPN at 7:00, so I could get unhooked twelve hours later. I could not believe I had forgotten. For two hours, I had felt normal and giddy.

When I got home, a package was waiting for me. I did not recognize the return address; it was from a woman in North Carolina. Inside, a bunch of papers were folded in half and taped shut. On the outside of the papers, a note read, "Please listen to CD before opening." The message intrigued me. I felt like I was a detective in a movie, about to receive some clues.

After Jack had my TPN flowing into my arm, he went to retrieve our CD player and brought it downstairs to me. I sat in the recliner and listened to a voice that sounded like Carol Burnett introduce herself as Rhonda and share a story that she had never shared with others.

My Aunt Becky, the family friend for whom I was named, had asked her niece Rhonda to pray for me. Rhonda felt God impress on her that she should not only pray for me, but also share her story. Rhonda had never met me before, yet she was willing to share a very personal experience with me. Rhonda explained that she had had a very painful health condition that was incurable. She had gone for many painful treatments, taken lots of different medication, and at best only received temporary relief. Like me, Rhonda was a pastor's wife. She had prayed for relief many times. The illness went on for years and interfered with her daily life. Rhonda understood chronic pain.

One day, Rhonda felt the Lord say to open her Bible to Isaiah 53:5, which declares, "But he was wounded for our transgressions, crushed for our iniquities; upon him was the punishment that made us whole, and by his bruises we are **healed**." (NRSV) Rhonda knew this verse, but this was the first time that she realized the word "healed" was in past tense. Rhonda decided to claim the truth that she was healed, regardless of how she felt. She took all of her prescription pain medicine and threw them out. She had her husband help her find different Bible passages that spoke about healing and she wrote them out. She then wrote her favorite ones on index cards. She surrounded herself with these Scriptures and would read them on her way to work and on her way home. She and her husband took a trip to Alaska and she took the cards with her. She had pain every day of the vacation, but she continued to declare that she was healed by Jesus' wounds. One day, Rhonda realized she had no pain – and the pain never returned. No doctor could explain it. Rhonda's voice sounded choked up at times as she recalled the series of events.

After listening to this humble and inspiring CD, I was in awe. I could not believe that Rhonda had not only shared a personal story with me, but also took the time to share it via CD. Rhonda had no way of knowing that it was difficult for me to concentrate on written words, but that I loved listening to CDs. Inside the folded pieces of paper were index cards with her favorite healing scripture verses. Reading through the verses, I was encouraged. One after another reinforced that Jesus was in the ministry of healing. The ironic thing was that the same exact verse God had used to tell Rhonda she was healed was the verse I had chosen for my Lenten devotional a few months earlier. Just as with Rhonda, the past tense of "healed" had not previously clicked for me.

I could not abruptly stop taking my pain medicine, but I was taking less and less. With each decrease, however, I experienced worse and worse withdrawal symptoms – from pain to leg cramps, nausea, diarrhea, and insomnia. I looked on the Internet to see if anyone else had dealt with morphine withdrawal and what helped. I discovered that my symptoms were very common, but most people vomit as well. For the first time I felt blessed by the PICC line, because I did not have to eat anything! The only answers for relief that I found online were time, fluids, and sleep. However, the acupuncture treatments also helped me with the withdrawal symptoms. As awful as the withdrawal was, I was ecstatic to be getting off of pain medicine. These Scripture verses were like added ammunition in my arsenal.

Ten days after I began claiming I was healed, my right upper arm started to feel funny. It felt sore, and the skin felt tight like it was going to burst. I thought maybe the most recent dressing around my port was irritating my skin. I called Pam, the nurse who changed my dressing twice a week, and asked if she would be willing to stop by and take a look. She had a full afternoon, but said in the evening she would stop by my house. Thankfully, Pam measured my arm each visit. The measuring tape quickly revealed that my arm was swollen. Pam told Jack and me that she thought I had a blood clot and that I needed to go to the emergency room. This was the first time in over eight months that I found myself in the hospital for something other than abdominal pain.

An ultrasound at the emergency room confirmed that I had a blood clot. Thankfully the blood clot was not in the vein with the PICC line, so the PICC line site did not need to be changed. Unfortunately, I needed to take a Coumadin pill and get Lovenox shots in my thighs twice a day to thin my blood. These shots were the most painful shots I ever had. I would scream with each one, and a black and blue welt would appear shortly after the injection. Poor Jack had to administer the shots. I think he dreaded them as much as I did.

Thankfully, I only had to receive the shots for a few days until my blood clotting ratio was in the desired range, and then I could just take a pill once a day. I was a little nervous, because I knew I had to now be on blood thinners for three months, and I could not have surgery while on blood thinners. This meant that the earliest I could have surgery would be in September, rather than July. However, I was hoping my pain would stay manageable and I would not need surgery – so the blood clot did not appear to be a major setback.

I continued to go to acupuncture, decrease my pain medicine, and experience intense withdrawal. Six days after the blood clot, I was getting ready for bed and called for Jack. I felt like I was going to vomit and pass out. He came running and noticed that ten inches of my PICC line had slid out of my arm.

As usual, Jack had a calm head and helped me lie on my back on the bathroom floor with my feet raised and a cold washcloth on my forehead. Jack called the emergency number for my PICC line nurse. Jack explained the situation and was told I needed to go to the emergency room.

Two trips in one week was not the type of record I was reaching towards. Fortunately, I was in and out of the emergency room in just 45 minutes – with the entire PICC line removed. Unfortunately, I was informed that my doctor at Hopkins would need to be contacted to see where he would like the new PICC line site to be.

The next day, I emailed Dr. Cole at Hopkins updating him on my blood clot and my PICC line sliding out. His response indicated I had the choice of getting a new PICC line in my left arm or a PEG-J feeding tube in my stomach. I would not have minded getting a PICC line in my left arm, except that my matron of honor dress had been made to cover my right arm and was sleeveless on the left side. I explained the dilemma to my husband who sincerely responded, "Why don't you just turn your dress around?"

I exclaimed, "Does the front of me look like the back of me?! I can't just flip my dress around!"

I usually am not overly vain. I was aware that the wedding day was my sister's day. However, I was self-conscious about people seeing two tubes with nozzles emerging from my arm. First of all, I thought, no one wants to see this; I certainly do not like looking at them. Second, I do not want photos of this. The custom dress had solved the problem. But now they wanted to put the tubes on the other side.

I decided to do some research online about the PEG-J, and I found out that the patient must pour stuff into a tube that goes into the stomach. The idea of the PEG-J scared me and caused me anxiety.

I decided to be bold and relay to my doctor at Hopkins that I would prefer to not have either. I wanted to try eating and to see if I could maintain my weight. If I was not successful, after my sister's wedding I would get a second PICC line. Dr. Cole agreed to my request.

The following two weeks I had more tests done at Hopkins, including ingesting radioactive material in preparation for a surgery I hoped I would never have. Between the side effects of these tests, and insomnia from morphine withdrawal, I was feeling tired and weak.

On July 3rd Jack drove me back to Hopkins for my follow-up appointment. Dr. Cole began the appointment with the test results. I was informed that I was not pre-diabetic, my liver was strong, and my stomach was emptying. The result that shocked me the most was that my stomach was emptying. I had failed this test on numerous occasions in the past. The tests also showed that I continued to have pancreatitis. Based on all of the test results, I was an ideal candidate for the total pancreatectomy with auto islet transplant, and Dr. Cole was ready to schedule my surgery.

Poor Dr. Cole must have been confused when I then asked, "Do I have to have the surgery? I do not think I need the surgery." I felt like the definition of a discontented person who wants one thing and then as soon as it is offered does not want it any more. However, Dr. Cole did not realize the progress I had made. The last time Dr. Cole had seen me I was with my parents, had a PICC line, was in horrible pain while taking narcotics, and wanted surgery as soon as possible. Now, I had no PICC line, was not in pain, was off all narcotics, and was maintaining my weight.

Dr. Cole said he had never seen a patient improve so drastically, and I attributed it to prayers and acupuncture. Dr. Cole requested the acupuncturist's contact information for other patients.

I felt like I had won the lottery when Dr. Cole said I did not need to have surgery. He informed me that I would not be causing harm to leave my pancreas in. The only reason for removing the pancreas was to eliminate the pain caused with pancreatitis attacks. The fact that the hospital tests had shown that I still had pancreatitis during the past two weeks reinforced that the acupuncture was effective even with the condition continuing to exist.

I was in shock. I was afraid I was dreaming. My outlook on life seemed so much brighter, and the dark cloud that had been hanging over my head was gone. I cannot begin to describe in words the extreme joy that overtook me. I truly felt healed. I could not wait to share my good news with friends and family and to let Rhonda know as well.

The following was part of my blog update on July 3rd:

> *I cannot begin to capture in words how relieved I am to not have to have horrible surgery that would split my abdomen in half, require a feeding tube, require me to give myself insulin shots, and spend more weeks in the hospital. Instead, I get to eat and taste normal food and focus on getting stronger at home. All of the praise and glory belongs to the Lord — for He is indeed faithful! Jack and I were carried many times during this trial via your encouraging words and prayers. We cannot begin to express our gratitude.*

Ten days after the great news at Hopkins, Jack and I boarded an airplane to fly to Savannah, Georgia, for Jack's interview. I had to chuckle at how worried I had been about flying with a PICC line. God had taken care of my PICC line in a unique way. The trip was a whirlwind. We were in Beaufort, South Carolina, for less than twenty-four hours. I thought the area was beautiful, the town was small and quaint, and the people I met were certainly nice. However, I really did not want to move far away from my friends and family, and I loved the church that Jack was currently serving at in Lancaster.

We did not have much time to process the trip because of preparations for my sister's wedding. I was able to give my toast, eat, and dance at my sister's wedding reception. Many of the guests were friends of the family and had been prayer warriors for me. I was ecstatic that they could visibly see their prayers answered. If someone did not know me, they never would have guessed that I had been sick for the past ten months.

A few days after my sister's wedding, Jack received a call with an offer for a full-time ordained associate pastor position at Sea Island Presbyterian Church in Beaufort, South Carolina. Now, we really had to make some tough decisions. During the past year, so many decisions had been made for me by doctors. This time, Jack and I had to make a choice that would impact our future and our future children.

Randy, the senior pastor at the church where Jack currently worked, had retired in June. The associate pastor, Don, was filling in as an interim. The church was in limbo as a committee searched for a new senior pastor. Jack shared with Don and others the news of the job offer in South Carolina. The personnel committee and session both said that they could not offer Jack a full-time position or a permanent position at this time, but possibly down the road. This was devastating news.

I had very specific ideas about how God should bless us, and my plan included a full-time position for Jack in Lancaster. I thought I knew best, and I could not fathom why God was not following my logic. I had figured out that Jack's part-time position had been divine because I was sick and needed Jack. Now that I was well, Jack could work full-time and we could work on paying down debt and preparing for our future children. Lancaster seemed like the ideal place to raise a family, with my parents just ten minutes away and Jack's family only a few hours away. Plus, we lived in a diverse community. In Beaufort we knew absolutely no one. In the back of my head, I also wondered if I would have a flare-up with my pancreas in the future – and I preferred not to meet any new doctors.

Jack and I had been meeting with a counselor since 2010. The seminary had recommended counseling for couples, as ministry is very hard on marriages. The counseling had helped us communicate better, and during the past year had helped me through anxiety with my illness. Now, we came to our counselor needing help discerning whether to accept the job in South Carolina or stay put. We weighed the pros and cons. I made list after list of all of the potential benefits and challenges of each location. After a counseling session and lots of prayer, Jack and I came to the same conclusion. God was calling us to move to South Carolina. God had answered our prayer request and had orchestrated all of the details. We felt called to trust God once again.

CHAPTER 23

WRONG TURNS

Sunday, August 5, after Jack preached at all three worship services and had led Vacation Bible School the prior week, we got in the car to drive to South Carolina. Jack was understandably exhausted, so I took the wheel for several hours. Typically Jack did the driving in our marriage. However, now that I was completely off of narcotics I could drive. Driving around Baltimore and Washington, D.C., had never been my favorite stretches of road, and I was extra nervous after almost a year without driving. It seemed like role reversal for me to be clutching the wheel while Jack slept peacefully in the passenger seat.

We broke up the twelve-hour drive over two days and arrived in Beaufort, South Carolina, on Monday evening. Jack attended a few meetings at the church, and that week we had dinner with different families from the church almost every evening. Large groups of people, especially new people, overwhelm me. Thus, meeting a few people at a time was ideal and helped Jack and me get to know our new church family.

Beaufort and Lancaster seemed to have little in common. Beaufort was surrounded by water and palm trees and had sandy soil and flat terrain. On the other hand, Lancaster was several hours from the Atlantic Ocean, the oldest inland city in the United States, and had rich soil, rolling hills, and deciduous trees. We had lived in the city, with a grocery store at the end of our block and tons of art galleries and cafés within walking distance. One of the things we appreciated about Lancaster was the art culture and diverse population. But the majority of streets in Beaufort lacked sidewalks, and we needed a car to travel to any stores or restaurants. From Lancaster, we could easily take a train to New York City, Philadelphia, Baltimore, or Washington, D.C. With these large cities surrounding Lancaster, my hometown seemed like a small city; around sixty thousand people lived within the city limits, and over half a million lived in the county. Beaufort's city population was less than thirteen thousand.

During our week in Beaufort, our schedule was fairly open, but we had one major goal: to find a place to live. On Wednesday, the other associate pastor, Heather, drove us around to some different neighborhoods. We looked at apartments and houses to rent. We were surprised by the high rent and limited options. We would have preferred to purchase a house, but were not sure how long it would take to sell our home in Pennsylvania.

A realtor and member of the church, Greg, called us on Thursday to let us know about a rental property that had just become available. He showed us the property first, but warned that if we did not sign a lease right away, someone else would. We asked if we could have until the next morning to make our decision, as we had a few more homes to look at. Our visits to each of the other places confirmed that the one Greg had shown us was our best option.

It was also our four-year wedding anniversary, and Jack had a surprise planned for me. He had made reservations at our favorite restaurant on Hilton Head Island. It seemed bizarre to be looking for a home near where we had vacationed. I never would have guessed a year ago that this would be where and how we would be spending our anniversary.

Friday morning we signed a twelve-month lease, gave a deposit, and felt at peace with our decision. We went back over to the house to take some measurements. It felt like everything was falling into place. I was most looking forward to the warmer climate that would come with this move, but there were other benefits as well. After living in a row home for almost six years, I was excited not to be sharing walls with neighbors. I also was excited about the two-car garage and driveway. In Lancaster City, I had to park on the street, and there were no reserved spaces. I enthusiastically squealed to Jack, "I know where I will be parking each night." The house was also all on one level; no more taking laundry up and down two flights of steps. The rental house had three bedrooms and a fourth potential bedroom over the garage. It was important to us to have room for our family to visit and to have bedrooms for our future children. It had been a year since we had completed our adoption paperwork, and we had not yet received a referral from Ethiopia. I trusted that at the right time, we would receive our children.

Friday night at the hotel, my head hit the pillow thinking about our new home and getting to see dear friends the next day. But in the middle of the night, intense abdominal pain jolted me awake. I knew the pain all too well. I got out of bed and took the breakthrough pain medicine that I carried in my purse. A few minutes later instead of feeling relief, I began vomiting all over the side of the hotel bed. After throwing up, I started to feel a little better, although I was terribly tired. I was also distraught that I had gotten last night's dinner on the bed sheets.

Jack graciously called down to the front desk and asked if we could get a new set of sheets and explained that I had gotten sick. A young male arrived at our door with yellow rubber gloves, cleaning supplies, and clean sheets. I wanted the employee to know it was not due to excessive drinking. I could not believe how I still obsessed about what other people thought of me. I had Jack give the employee a generous tip, but I still felt embarrassed, and I apologized repeatedly. I curled up in the clean sheets and tried to go back to sleep. I dozed a little and then the strong nausea came back. This time I ran to the bathroom and successfully hurled my guts into the toilet. After vomiting multiple times, the pain was not diminishing. I knew we needed to go to the emergency room.

The sign outside of the hospital stated that the emergency room was under construction and to use a different entrance. There were no wheelchairs, so I hobbled into the lobby stooped over with my arms wrapped around my abdomen while Jack helped to steady me. We entered the makeshift lobby and went to sign in. The receptionist asked for my name and health issue. This was standard. She proceeded to ask for my date of birth, social security number, insurance information, and all of my current prescriptions. I was horrified when I was asked all of my personal information right out in the open. I was used to being led into a side room to answer questions and provide information. I figured HIPPA must not apply here. Fortunately, at eight in the morning on a Saturday, few patients were present. I had actually never seen such a deserted emergency room. It appeared only two families were waiting. I thought to myself, "Good, I should have an IV in no time and we can still keep our plans to visit Beth and Colin."

Jack and I sat, and sat, and sat. The chairs in the waiting room reminded me of the ones at airports. They had metal armrests on either side. I was in horrible pain, and the chairs were not conducive to resting comfortably in the fetal position.

Families and individuals trickled into the emergency room, but no one was escorted back by a nurse or hospital employee. I kept staring at my watch and groaning. Minutes seemed like hours. I tried to be patient. I knew exactly what the problem was and what I needed. If I could have given myself an IV, I would have. After an hour, I asked Jack to check at the front desk to see how long they anticipated the wait to be. I wanted to make sure they had not forgotten about me. Jack came back and said they were just waiting for discharge paperwork to be completed. Another hour passed. I asked Jack to see if I could just get an IV before a room freed up. Jack was informed that soon I would be taken back. After three long and excruciating hours, I told Jack, "We are leaving. I would be more comfortable in the hotel room." When Jack went up to tell the hospital employees that we were leaving, they said a room had just become available.

We were shown through a maze of hallways and up an elevator. I was then shown a hospital room. I was instructed to sit on a chair, because fresh sheets needed to be put on the bed. At this point, I really could have cared less if the sheets were clean. I just wanted to be horizontal and to have an IV. No one seemed to be in a rush or moving very quickly. I had heard different church members joke about how Beaufort is not only the low country, but the slow country. A slower pace of life seemed healthier and appealing – but not in a hospital. I wanted to snap my fingers and tell people to move it. Everything seemed to be moving at a snail's pace. I wondered if this community put out fires with buckets of water. Nothing seemed efficient.

Finally a nurse inserted an IV and a doctor entered my room and asked, "What seems to be the problem?"

I wanted to scream, "Idiots are running this place!"

I explained, "I have chronic pancreatitis and had been approved as a candidate to have a total pancreatectomy. I recently was getting relief from acupuncture, but had a bad flare-up this morning. I tried taking my breakthrough pain medicine, but threw it up."

The doctor agreed to provide pain medicine. Within seconds of it entering my arm, I was conked out. Once the fog lifted, I was ready to leave the hospital. Jack asked if I still wanted to try and see our friends who lived an hour away. I told him I did not have the strength and to please take me back to the hotel. I was not surprised that it took several hours from when we requested to be discharged until the paperwork was completed.

As we waited, I got more and more upset. I suppressed my fear and anger until we got into the car, then I erupted in tears. "I thought I was done with pancreatitis attacks! I am not sure whether to be more scared of having another pancreatitis attack or having to return to that hospital! I don't want to have surgery, but I also never want to go back to that hospital! Jack, we cannot move here."

Jack tried to calm me down and encourage me that maybe this was a fluke flare-up. However, I was not buying his logic. He reminded me that we had just signed a twelve-month lease and we could not afford the lease and our mortgage without taking the pastor position in South Carolina. I secretly wondered, *Where is God? Why would God do this to us? I thought I was healed. I feel tricked and trapped.*

Sunday morning we woke up, packed up our car, and headed to the new church Jack had just agreed to pastor. We went to both services, and many individuals came up to introduce themselves. I tried my best to smile and remember names. After the service, the senior pastor and his wife invited us to lunch. History and doctors had taught me to let my pancreas rest after an attack by not eating or drinking anything. Thus, at the restaurant I ordered nothing and drank nothing. Once again, I worried about what others would think.

After lunch, Jack and I got in the car to drive north.

I was struggling to have a spirit of gratitude. My gratitude journal forced me to seek and record the blessings. I was grateful for the hotel employee who cleaned up my vomit and our friends' understanding that we could not get together. I truly was grateful. However, I felt like I was battling fear mixed with anger. I was afraid that I was not healed and that I would suffer from future pancreatitis attacks. I was afraid to move somewhere that I felt the medical care was unsatisfactory. I was angry with myself that I was allowing fear to creep in. I was angry with God for allowing these hurdles that shook me to my core. I was trying to trust in God's provision and love, but I felt weak and like a failure.

All of a sudden, a loud car horn honk woke me up. Jack was pounding on the horn and screaming. I opened my eyes just in time to see a truck pulling a trailer cross into our lane and collide with my side of the car. I heard a crunching and scraping sound. I called 911 and quickly realized I had no idea where we were. Looking around, I noticed we were on an interstate. Thankfully our GPS provided our coordinates and a police officer arrived within minutes. I thought to myself, *We must be close to home. People are responding quickly.* In fact, we were less than two hours from home.

Miraculously, no one was injured. The police confirmed

that the other driver was at fault.

If my stomach had not already been in knots, it was now. I felt like a switch had flipped and now one catastrophe after the next was happening. All I could think was, *Where did we go wrong?*

CHAPTER 24

STRUGGLES WITH BOXES AND TEARS

A few weeks later, I was standing in my living room surrounded by nothing but boxes. I felt like there was not enough air in the room. I had once had the wind knocked out of me while playing football with my cousins, but this feeling was a new phenomenon. I had not been punched and I was not under water. A moving company was in my home, boxing up everything. I had been so busy getting the house ready to be sold and meeting with doctors, that the reality that I was truly leaving my beloved house, neighborhood, and family had not sunk in until now.

I did not have a car, because the insurance company had determined that my car was totaled. But I needed to get out. I called my friend's mom and asked if she would take me to my parents' house while my mom oversaw the packers and answered their questions. It was so nice to return to my parents' home. It felt comforting to be back in a house with pictures on the walls. My parents' house had been a constant my entire life. They had bought the house when my mother was pregnant with me. I went up to my childhood bedroom and flopped down on the bed. I wondered if we were making the right decision to move south. Jack and I definitely felt called to move and serve this church in South Carolina, but my anxiety seemed to be consuming my body. I cried until I fell asleep.

Crying was something I did a lot these days. After the car accident, my pancreas continued to flare up and my body was not as receptive to the acupuncture. I went on a gluten-free diet to try and help with digestion, since gluten caused bloating and I was willing to do anything to help my body feel a little better. I cried at all of my doctors' appointments. I had told them all how well I was doing, and now I had to return and share the news that the pain had resumed and I needed pain medicine once again. It felt like complete defeat and humiliation. I did not write any blog updates. I was so embarrassed for my premature celebration.

I also felt like I was up against a countdown clock. I had less than a month before moving to get in to see my doctors. The doctor I was going to miss the most was Dr. Granger, my primary care physician. He was sympathetic and helped to explain the test results that my specialists spouted off in medical lingo. Dr. Granger had not given up on me. Jack and I asked Dr. Granger for a recommendation for a primary care physician in Beaufort, but he did not know anyone. Jack then called every medical practice he could find on the internet that was located within a fifty-mile radius of our soon-to-be new location. None of the medical doctors were taking new patients. Many of the office staff said I could be seen by a physician's assistant or a nurse practitioner. Jack tried to explain that my medical condition was complicated and it was imperative that I have a medical doctor to oversee my health. Finally, we found a medical doctor that was new to the area and was accepting new patients. I requested that Dr. Granger's office send my medical records to this new office. This felt like a huge accomplishment. Jack also stumbled upon a teaching hospital in Charleston called Medical University of South Carolina (MUSC). They had a pancreas surgeon, so Jack went ahead and scheduled an appointment there as well.

Dr. Cole did not have much insight. He stated that I was still a candidate for the total pancreatectomy. If I decided to have this surgery at Johns Hopkins, I would need to live with my parents for at least three months while I recovered. There would be no way Jack could take the time off to be with me while he was just starting a new job. I really did not want this surgery, and I definitely did not want to be apart from my comforting and hilarious husband for months.

Two days before we moved we also had our final visit to the adoption agency. The social worker we had been connected with over the past two years was on maternity leave, so we met someone who was new to us. We explained that we were moving to South Carolina. One of the reasons we had selected this agency was because they had offices all over the country. We needed to find out what the process would be to transfer our file to South Carolina. We also knew that Ethiopia had recently been delaying adoptions because of human trafficking, so we were hoping to learn good news about this situation resolving.

When we met with the social worker, she informed us that all Ethiopian government employees that processed adoptions had been fired due to human trafficking concerns. Now our adoption agency was no longer allowing families to start the adoption process with Ethiopia. We were told that it may be years before our request was processed and in the meantime, we would have to have all of our paperwork updated annually to keep clearances from expiring.

This news was entirely unexpected. The paperwork included updates from our employers, our doctors, our bank, etc. – all of which was changing. I did not have the energy or strength to resubmit all of the paperwork, nor did we have extra funds to pay for all of these updates without any certainty that we would ever be able to adopt.

I left the agency feeling like I had lost my children. It may seem extreme or dramatic, but I had pictured my babies and prayed for them at least once a day for the past two years. My future children were my inspiration and drive to get off pain medicine and keep fighting to find a solution to my health issues. I felt like my purpose and hope had been yanked out from underneath me. My heart felt like it was ripped out. I felt like Job in the Bible. My dream of Ethiopian children, my house, my friends, family, doctors, and everything familiar was gone. I soon would need a GPS to get out of my neighborhood and to the closest grocery store.

All I really wanted to do was crawl under my bed and hide

from the world, my responsibilities, and my health. Of course this was not an option. I had to keep putting one foot in front of the other and checking things off a list. There were so many minor details, like getting renters' insurance and having the electric, water, and cable turned on at our new home.

Since my car had been totaled, Jack and my dad drove down to South Carolina in Jack's car on September 24th. My mom and I then flew into the Charleston airport on the 26th. I was surprised and delighted when Jack picked us up at the airport in my brand new car. I had never had a new car in my life.

My parents continued to make sacrifices for me. My dad flew back to Pennsylvania, and my mom stayed to help us get settled. We spent a night in a hotel in Beaufort and woke the next morning to meet the movers at our new home.

The closest I have come to meeting an angel on earth was in the form of my new neighbor and church member, Denise Bono. She stopped over at our house right after the moving truck parked in front of our house. She brought over a case of bottled water, a roll of paper towels, a trash can, and trash bags, and she invited us over to their home for dinner that night. She did not stay long, but she wanted to welcome us.

After all of the boxes were unloaded and the movers had left, it was nice to know we did not have far to go for dinner. My mom, Jack, and I took showers and headed over to the Bono family's home two doors over. It felt wonderful to enter a house devoid of boxes. The aroma of home-cooked food filled our nostrils. Five beautiful and sweet girls ranging in age from ten to fifteen welcomed us. Like honored guests, we were told to fill our plates first. Denise had found out that I was on a gluten-free diet and had made the entire meal gluten-free, including gluten-free brownies. Everything was delicious. It felt wonderful to eat off of real plates and sit at a table.

Denise did not work outside the home due to health issues. She informed me that she would take me out in her minivan and show me the shortcuts around town – as Denise confessed that when she had first moved to Beaufort, she drove around in circles and got frustrated. She made us a list of phone numbers and information, from pest control to radio stations. She gave us the inside information on her favorite places to shop and where to get what. She also let us know about the convenience center where we could take trash, cardboard, and recyclable items seven days a week for free. This was huge news, because our garage was filled with flattened boxes. I think God knew that I felt overwhelmed in this new place and blessed me with an instant friend.

As we left, Denise reassured my mom that she would take care of me like a daughter. This of course helped put my mom's heart at ease. That evening I slept in my own bed for the first time in a week. I went to sleep without crying.

CHAPTER 25

SURPRISES

It was startling to wake up in my own bed, with my sheets, but in a room I did not recognize. I felt like I was staring up at a mountain that I needed to cross over: there were still boxes everywhere. We broke up the day of unpacking by getting our new driver's licenses. With the license, I felt like everything was official. Now I really lived in South Carolina.

Jack and my mom continued to work hard at unpacking. I, however, really wanted pictures on the wall. Blank walls made me think of hospitals – and I had trouble relaxing with blank walls. At my request, before all of the boxes were unpacked, Jack hung pictures meticulously in our new rental home, using a level and tape measure to make sure everything was hung just so.

As much as I appreciated his attention to detail, part of me was already dreading having to move again. I wished we were unpacking in a home we owned. We did not plan to rent indefinitely, so most likely in a year or so we would be moving again. This thought also paralyzed me and made it harder for me to truly invest myself in this home.

Miraculously by Monday, just five days after moving, we had opened all of the boxes. I hated moving. I was grateful that my mom was willing and able to help significantly with the move. I joked that she could be a professional mover and help people get quickly settled in their new homes. My mom said with humor, love, and seriousness, "I only did this because I love you. I would not do this for others."

On Tuesday, Jack and I took my mom back to the airport for her flight home. The following day, I finally wrote a blog update. It had been three months since my last one. I always procrastinated when it came to sharing hard news. I had been hoping by this point to be looking for new employment, not new doctors.

Before Jack officially started at the church, he had a little over a week to get settled in Beaufort. The church members welcomed us both with open arms. I had never been very good with remembering names, but with around seven hundred new names to learn, I really felt out of my league. I tried to study the church photo directory to learn names every day while I ate breakfast and lunch by myself. Jack was constantly meeting new people, and many of them were eager to share their thoughts and ideas.

This was the first time in our marriage that Jack had a full-time job and I did not. Naturally, he would come home in the evenings exhausted and ready for some solitude. I, on the other hand, had waited all day to have someone to speak to. But there were plenty of projects to keep me busy around the house. On good days, I would have a few hours of pep and my pain was minimal. On bad days, I would barely have the strength to make it back and forth between the bed and the bathroom.

Denise, my new neighbor and friend, lived up to her promises. She showed me the shortcuts and took me with her on errands. We tried to walk outside to get a little fresh air and exercise. We were in a similar boat, never knowing how our bodies would behave on any given day. As a result, we typically got together about once a week. I was certainly grateful for this friendship. However, it was still a new friendship, and I did not feel comfortable confiding to a church member that I was homesick.

After a month in Beaufort, I had an appointment at MUSC, the teaching hospital in Charleston. I was very nervous to meet a new doctor, and I did not have much energy for more rounds of tests. However, I did my best to muster up some optimism that this appointment would provide some insight into my next steps. I prayed for direction, wisdom, and hope.

On Friday, October 26, God far exceeded these requests.

The staff at MUSC was compassionate, competent, and organized. The care of the physicians, nurses, PAs, residents, and even registration employees was evident in their words, actions, and body language. We never waited more than twenty minutes between appointments. Staff walked us from one office to the next, and one nurse even gave us a hug. Dr. Adams, the pancreas specialist and surgeon, was open to different options. He continued on to say, "Ultimately there is only one permanent solution, and it will provide you with greatly improved quality of life."

"Quality of life" was what my heart yearned for. Unlike Dr. Cole at Hopkins, Dr. Adams seemed more aware of my quality of life – or lack thereof. He showed compassion and shared honestly about success stories and hurdles. Every week it became more evident that my quality of life was decreasing, and the harder I fought to be strong, the weaker I became. Dr. Adams did not pressure Jack or me into making a decision.

I did not want to have surgeries that would only provide me with temporary relief. I wanted to be well so I could return to work, take care of others, be a good friend, be a helper for my husband, and eventually be an active mother. Even though we would not be adopting from Ethiopia, I had not given up all hope of adopting in the future. I figured when the time was right, we would assess our situation and the circumstances in other countries, and we would start our paperwork all over again.

Even with the hope of significantly improved quality of life, it was a struggle to decide to have the total pancreatectomy. I was still haunted by the description of the recovery given at Hopkins. At MUSC, I was informed that post-surgery I would be a diabetic and be in the hospital ten to thirty days. The expected recovery time at home was six months. If I had the surgery in January, by July I would be feeling pretty good. In some ways July seemed like a long way off, but knowing there was an end to excessive pain and exhaustion was a huge source of hope.

Once again, I felt like God was providing and things were

falling into place. Three days later, I had an appointment with my new primary care physician. My appointment at MUSC had gone so well that I was not too nervous to meet my new PCP. My new PCP's office was less than a mile from the church. Jack graciously went with me to the appointment. I arrived early and completed all of the paperwork. But there was no way I could have been prepared or anticipated the introduction and words that would spew from the doctor.

Dr. Ogrite entered the room without shaking my hand or introducing himself. Instead, he started by declaring, "It is totally inappropriate for you to be here!" My first thought was, *He must have me confused with someone else. I am a rule-follower.*

He then informed me, "You are on way too much medication and have a drug problem. There is no way I would refill any of your prescriptions." The bizarre thing was I did not need any of my prescriptions filled at that time, nor had I asked him to fill any prescriptions. I had merely listed my medications as requested by the office paperwork.

My body was so weak from over a year of battling pain that this unexpected stress shattered my fragile nerves. With tears streaming down my face, I explained, "I have chronic pancreatitis and am planning on having a total pancreatectomy in January at MUSC. I am not here to request refills. I am here because we moved last month from Pennsylvania to South Carolina and I need a new PCP to oversee my care. When I made the appointment, I explained that my disability insurance company required that I be seen by a doctor each month and that a doctor sign off that I have been seen."

Dr. Ogrite flatly stated, "It is absurd to ask me on your first visit to complete disability paperwork." He continued, "You need to make a follow-up appointment to give me time to review your medical records before I will sign anything." Dr. Ogrite left the room as wildly as he had entered. I made an appointment for a week later and paid my copay.

I was so thankful Jack was with me. As soon as we got in the car, Jack angrily declared, "We are not returning to him! It is clear that he does not care about getting to know your health background or helping you prepare for surgery. He should not be a doctor."

I cried, "But who am I going to see? I need a PCP, and I need my disability paperwork signed."

Jack shared with the senior pastor about our unpleasant experience and dilemma. The very next day they had set up an appointment for me with a PCP who was a member of our new church family. Thankfully, they had informed Dr. Kessel of my situation. He stated that he was happy to take me on as a patient, completed my paperwork, and even asked how I was feeling emotionally about moving and preparing for the surgery. This doctor went above and beyond.

I still was not sure how I felt about living in a small town, but I was finding some advantages. I was eager and excited for Jack to preach at our new church. Jack has a deep, booming voice and speaks with such expression. I could not wait for our church family to realize what a gem they had hired. However, I did not anticipate that Jack's sermon to would relate to me.

On October 3, 2012, I posted:

> *Jack preached this past Sunday for the first time at our new church home. His message focused on wounds and scars and our three choices: 1) stay stuck in the past and shackled to fear; 2) pretend everything is perfect and project an airbrushed image; OR 3) view our scars and trials as gifts and opportunities to relate to others, and as tools in our ministry as we follow Jesus and place our trust in the LORD. The third option is ideal and what I am striving for. I am not a saint and certainly fall into option 1 or 2 frequently. God has placed some amazing role models in my life over the years who have revealed their scars to me. While we do not have the same scars, being able to relate is very helpful and healing for me.*
>
> *Thus, as much as I would like to focus on the good days, I want to be authentic, and that includes sharing the challenges. Right now I am trying to stay as comfortable as possible on pain medicine. As mentioned*

before, the challenge with the pain medicine is that it makes me very drowsy and my brain foggy. Having no energy and mush for a brain is difficult when trying to meet new people and get settled in a new home and community. As a result I tend to stay home and feel pretty isolated and alone. I have also started to have a lot of pain with eating, causing my appetite to plummet. The pain escalates my anxiety, causing me to worry about how intense the pain will become and how long it will last.

I ask for continued prayer for the Lord's healing, strength, and peace. I feel fragile and empty, so I greatly appreciate prayers that truly sustain me. My other major prayer request would be for my husband, Jack. He has a full-time job as a minister in a new community AND is taking care of me. It breaks my heart that I cannot take care of him, and then I feel like a huge added weight. Please pray for strength and comfort to surround him.

My struggles and challenges seem teeny tiny in comparison to the obstacles facing those affected by Hurricane Sandy. My heart and prayers go out to those impacted. I often feel guilty, because I easily become self-focused with my own pain and challenges. I feel quite needy with very little to offer. Many days I lack the energy to return phone calls or e-mails. I do not have much, but what I have I give freely. 1) I keep a prayer list and pray many times throughout the day. I am constantly aware of my dependence on the Lord for strength. I am always honored to pray alongside of you or even pray for something when you do not have the strength to pray for it yourself. 2) I will try and be as honest and open as possible about my journey. God deserves all the glory. If my experience can be utilized to bless others, I am all for it.

The thought of helping others through my vulnerability kept me grounded in accountability. It forced me to look for blessings and look beyond my current circumstances. Praying for others played a huge role. It provided a purpose in my life and it was something I could do for others. Praying was also a positive constant in my life when so much around me was new and different.

CHAPTER 26

WAITING

My surgery date at MUSC was set for January 10, 2013, and my mom offered to stay in South Carolina with me for up to two months while I recovered. Waiting has never been a gift of mine. My natural response in situations where I have had to wait was to either try and take care of whatever it was myself (instead of waiting) or do something else to occupy my time.

To help pass the time and make the eight to ten hours I was alone all day not seem so overwhelming, I made a schedule for myself, outlining my day in fifteen-minute increments. The schedule included eating meals, devotions, prayer time, knitting, showering, taking naps, sending e-mails, stretching, making meals, and one mini-project like laundry or dusting. Having a routine really helped split up the day and prevented me from doing something for too long and wearing myself out. For example, I knew that after I showered I needed to take a nap. I tried to have one task each day that would get me out of the house if I felt up to it – for example, going to the convenience center to drop off our trash, going to the grocery store, or going to the bank. These little outings helped me to avoid cabin fever. Of course, some days I would spend the entire day in bed with pain and fatigue. On the other hand, on a really good day I would go to the church office and help fold bulletins.

I also found that taking breaks to watch Netflix helped me rest when I could not sleep and gave me something to talk about. With the pain medication, reading continued to be a challenge because I could not focus and remember what words I had just read. At a friend's suggestion, I started watching documentaries. My favorite was on Dietrich Bonhoeffer. Learning about other people's trials helped me avoid throwing pity parties for myself.

Unfortunately, the dreaded day came when I had a bad pancreatitis attack at our new home. Fortunately, it was in the evening and Jack was home. I started screaming as the pain tore through my body. Jack stayed calm and reminded me to keep taking deep breaths. He fetched my pain medicine and some water. The pain medicine seemed to take a long time to take effect, so I tried to distract myself with a show on Netflix. Once the pain medicine kicked in, I fell asleep out of exhaustion; the intense pain consumed tremendous amounts of energy. I slept and slept. I only woke up when the pain medicine started to wear off. Then I would take more pain medicine and drift back to sleep. The last thing I wanted to do was return to the local hospital where I had had such a bad experience in August.

After three days of not eating and taking only minimal sips of liquids, I realized that my pain was not getting better, and I could not handle the continuous intense pain. I called MUSC and left a message for the nurse coordinator, Betsy. It was her day off, but she still returned my call and told me to come to the emergency room at MUSC. She would let them know I was coming. Betsy advised me that I may need to stay for several days, so she encouraged me to pack accordingly. I put my iPod, gratitude journal, and a few pairs of underwear in a bag. As I was packing, Jack informed me, "I will not be able to stay with you up in Charleston due to my work obligations." I understood.

The hour and a half car ride was not pleasant along a bumpy road that was under construction. When we arrived, we entered the building I had been in before for my initial appointment and Jack asked for directions. Betsy had said to go to the cardiology ER. We were told to go down the hall to the end and then make a left. We followed the hallway and came to a large room with several nurses typing away at computer screens behind a high counter. I stood hunched over while Jack went up to the counter and said, "Excuse me. My wife, Rebecca Miller, is a patient of Dr. Adams. She is having a pancreatitis attack, and we were instructed to come to the cardiology ER."

The nurse walked around the counter and showed us to a room. He immediately put an IV in my arm, and the IV fluids started to make my dehydrated body feel better. I then had the strength to speak. I confessed to the nurse, "I am sorry. I think there was a mix-up. I am supposed to be in the ER."

The nurse reassured me that I was in the ER. I asked with confusion, "Where is the waiting room?" They did not have a waiting room. They just took patients immediately, the nurse explained.

Wow! Not only was the speed of care impressive, but my room was also nice. Most of my experiences in ERs had included a bed with a curtain around it. This room not only had walls, but cabinets for items and a personal restroom. With the exception of the hospital bed and monitors, the room looked a lot like a hotel room.

A doctor came in promptly and asked a few questions like, "When did the attack begin? Where is the pain?" and then had pain medicine administered. There was no pushing on my abdomen or questioning the validity of my pain. As usual, the pain medicine made me jump and jerk for a few seconds and then I was comfortable – and asleep within minutes.

When I woke up I felt much better. The doctor ordered one more round of IV pain medicine and then informed me that I could go home. Jack and I were only at the ER for a few hours before I was discharged to go home. I had been prepared to spend several nights at the hospital by myself, but ended up not needing to. This was a huge praise.

I returned to MUSC in mid-December for my pre-surgery tests. I really appreciated that all of my appointments were scheduled on the same day, so I did not have to make trips back and forth to Charleston. I kept finding more and more ways that MUSC was considerate of their patients.

My first test was blood work. Jack and I arrived early and

had brought our Christmas letters and cards to assemble. I had to fast for this test, so I was grateful for something to keep me occupied and focused. When the nurse came to get me, I told Jack I was fine to go back by myself.

The small room was decorated for Christmas, with tinsel on the door and holiday decals on the windows. My nurse seemed in a chipper mood. She pointed to a chair and pleasantly asked me to take a seat. I sat down in the hard, blue chair and rolled up my sleeve. I had been told years ago that keeping my arm warm made it easier to draw blood. The nurse quickly tied a tight band around my upper arm, causing my veins to rise.

The nurse commented, "You have great veins."

I said, "Thank you. If you don't mind, I get a little queasy, so I won't watch."

The nurse replied, "No problem." She began humming as she picked up vials and started putting labels on them.

I wondered, *Are those all for me? No way, they cannot all be for me.* Rather than get myself anxious unnecessarily, I decided to ask, "How many vials am I having drawn?"

The nurse pleasantly responded, "Sixteen." I tried not to let my terror show, but acting was also not a gift of mine. The nurse continued on, clearly seeing my panic as the color drained from my face, "Don't worry. I am going to take them over a two-hour period. I am only going to draw eight vials right now."

This really did not make me feel much better. I tried looking out the window and taking deep breaths while the blood was drawn and as I heard the snap after each vial was filled. I returned to Jack feeling a little woozy.

After the blood work was completed, Jack and I met with someone from the anesthesia team. We went over all of the medicine I took on a regular basis and when I would need to stop taking each medicine prior to surgery. I was afraid they would have me stop taking my pain medicine weeks before surgery, like Hopkins had required. Instead, I was informed to keep taking the pain medicine – and the anesthesiologist even recommended that I take a pain pill the morning of the surgery.

I wanted to make sure I heard correctly, so I asked, "You are serious? I can take Dilaudid the morning of my surgery?"

She replied, "No reason to arrive at the hospital in pain." I certainly was not going to argue with that logic. I was informed that I would be given an epidural. The anesthesiologist inquired, "Have you ever had one before?"

I replied softly, "No." I associated epidurals with giving birth, and neither sounded pleasant.

Perhaps the anesthesiologist could see a little panic in my face, or maybe it was just that I was sixteen vials short of blood. Regardless, she reassured me, "The epidural will keep you very comfortable. I can also have you get some medicine via IV before the epidural to relax you if you like."

"Oh, that would be great!" I exclaimed.

The anesthesiologist continued on, "Do you have any questions for me?"

I shared, "I am really concerned about my pain post-surgery. I have heard it is horrible. Will I be allowed IV pain medicine when I wake up?"

"Oh goodness, you will be on a morphine pump. Our goal is to keep you comfortable. If needed, we will give you liquid Tylenol."

"Liquid Tylenol?" I repeated, wondering if I had heard correctly.

"Yes, that is even stronger than morphine. Any other questions or concerns?"

"Yes, when will I be able to go back on my regular medicine? I had a really bad reaction when I was taken off all of them for a week."

"You will be back on your regular medication within twenty-four hours of surgery. You should never stop taking some of these medications cold turkey."

Hmmm, I thought, *someone should tell Johns Hopkins that.* I was now convinced that Johns Hopkins had made a serious medical mistake by stopping all of my regular medications for a week. If I could be back on my medicine after this major surgery, there had been no reason for the delay after the ERCP.

I was still nervous about the scheduled surgery at MUSC, but I was feeling less anxious about the recovery. I was confident that I would receive quality care at MUSC.

We did not have much time before the next scheduled appointment that day, to meet with a psychiatrist. However, I was in desperate need of some fluids and food. We stopped by the hospital cafeteria. While I felt weak, I also felt nauseous. I took a few bites and was afraid of vomiting, so I stopped eating.

I was not sure what to expect for the psychological evaluation. I was told it was required by insurance because my surgery fell under the umbrella of a transplant. It was also a part of MUSC's desire to provide total care. I slurped a few more sips of lemonade before Jack and I proceeded to yet another building.

The psychology building was staffed with a guard. We had to provide our names and who we were seeing. Next we were given badges. I wondered if we were entering a mental institution. Images from the movie *The Changeling* with Angelina Jolie entered my mind. I was relieved when we got off the elevator and it looked like a normal doctor's office. I was given a stack of papers to fill out. I completed them and returned them to the receptionist.

I was called back by a gal who looked to be around my age. She was an intern. She was very sweet, but I felt like a lab rat. She showed me a card with multiple pictures and asked which one did not belong or which would be next in the sequence. She showed me a picture with a bunch of items, and I had thirty seconds or a minute to look at it. Next she would turn the picture face down and ask me to tell her as many items as I could remember. She also read to me a list of random nouns; five minutes later she asked if different items were on the list or not. This went on for well over an hour.

By the end, my head hurt. I was in physical pain and was feeling like I might pass out. I knew that passing this evaluation was required for being approved for surgery. Tears started rolling down my cheeks as I begged, "Please pass me. I really am not stupid. I had sixteen vials of blood taken and am not feeling very well."

The woman sitting across from me chuckled, "Honey, your IQ is in the ninety-fifth percentile. No need to worry."

Oh, thank goodness. I returned to Jack feeling ragged, but happy to know even with all of the pain medicine making my brain mush, I had not become dumb.

During the day of tests, MUSC even gave me the e-mail address of someone who had the surgery four years ago with the same surgeon. Her name was Lisa, and I e-mailed her a list of my questions. She said she would be happy to talk on the phone. I gave her my number, and the next day she called. I felt more relief from hearing her experience than anything a doctor could have said. Lisa was so sweet and said no question was too personal. She reassured me that her pain was kept under control after the surgery. I asked her what the feeding tube was like, and she told me that she did not have a feeding tube after surgery. This was another difference between Hopkins and MUSC; MUSC did not use a PEG-J post-surgery. Lisa stated over and over again that the recovery was long. She stayed with her sister for three months.

I asked, "Do you have any regrets about having the surgery?"

Lisa quickly responded, "I would make the same decision again in a heartbeat. I have no regrets. It has tremendously improved my quality of life."

"Are you able to work?" I asked.

"No. I was a teacher for over twenty years and while my quality of life is much improved, I am not able to work."

This was a bit discouraging to hear, but I thought, *Clearly she is older and maybe has other health issues.* I found out she was on an insulin pump and that she highly recommended the pump if needed.

Her call was the best Christmas gift. I was really starting to feel at peace about this surgery and believed the reason why Jack was offered a job in South Carolina was so that I would have my surgery at MUSC.

CHAPTER 27

FINAL MONTH

The month of December really flew. Some evenings, Jack and I would go look at Christmas lights. We baked cookies and had different families from the church over after dinner for milk and cookies. It was a great way to get to know church members in an intimate setting.

On December 10, 2012, exactly one month before my surgery was scheduled to happen, I shared all of the blessings that had transpired and listed my five prayer requests.

1) To stay healthy, so I can be as strong as possible prior to surgery. This requires prioritizing and pacing myself, which is not my natural gift.

2) Wisdom for the doctors, surgeons, nurses, etc., who will be a part of my healing process.

3) Lots of islet cells. The more islet cells that can be extracted from my pancreas and transplanted into my liver, the less likely I will be insulin dependent (aka diabetic).

4) Support for my caregivers, especially my dad, my mom, and Jack. I am a screamer and don't like foreign tubes in my body.

5) Lastly for peace. Peace before the surgery and peace through the recovery. My hope is to glorify God through this season, and having the Lord's peace is a key ingredient.

Jack and I both have birthdays in December. Jack's birthday happened to fall on a Sunday. Jack's friend from college, Beth, along with her two sons, Duncan and Jeffrey, joined us after church for lunch and to watch a parade downtown. I coordinated with my neighbor and friend, Denise, to have a cake made. That evening we had a Christmas concert at our church. At the very end, the director of music announced it was Jack's birthday and asked everyone to sing happy birthday –and then celebrate in the fellowship hall with cake. Jack is an extrovert, so I knew having a hundred or so people celebrate with him was a high. I was so glad I had pulled off this surprise.

Ten days later was my thirtieth birthday. I was very clear with Jack that I did not want a party. But the church office Christmas party actually fell on my birthday. A gentleman from the church hosted a Christmas luncheon for the entire church staff and their spouses. He made the entire meal gluten-free for me, including chocolate lava cake. The evening of my birthday, a couple from the church also invited us over to their house for dinner.

Food was not the only blessing: I received over *one hundred* birthday cards in the mail. Some of them were from people I did not even know. They all said that they were thinking about me and/or praying for me. I held the stack of cards in my hands and loved the visual of the prayers that were being lifted up on my behalf.

Of course, the most special card came from my beloved husband who wrote out thirty things that he loved about me and thirty "honey-do" coupons. He also had me go on a scavenger hunt through the house, following rhyming clues, which ended with a certificate to an inn in Charleston for Christmas night and a tour of the oldest landscaped gardens in the United States. I felt incredibly loved and special.

Two days later, Jack said he wanted to take me out for a birthday lunch, just the two of us. When we arrived, I saw my neighbor Denise with three other ladies. They shouted, "Surprise!" Jack started to back away.

I asked, "Where are you going?"

He gently responded, "This lunch is for you and your girl friends. It has all been taken care of."

I could not believe that Jack had found a way to surprise me and not stress me out. Jack was not one for planning or paying attention to detail. However, he had even planned ahead so that I could have my favorite sandwich made on a gluten-free wrap. All four ladies were from the church, and I felt budding friendships with them. I was so touched that with four days until Christmas, they would take time out of their busy schedules to have lunch with me. I still missed my friends and family, but this was the first time I felt like I was going to be okay in this community.

The blessings did not stop pouring. Astoundingly, I received a check in the mail from a prayer warrior to cover my surgery expense. My surgery was estimated to cost over $115,000 – and between insurance and this generous gift from an individual, it was paid in full.

God was gracious and allowed me to enjoy Christmas with minimal pain. Our church participated in something called the Advent Conspiracy. The tag line was, "Christmas is not your birthday." The congregation was challenged to match however much they spent on Christmas gifts for friends and family with gifts for Jesus (giving to "the least of these"). Our congregation encouraged members to give funds to the local food bank, or to an organization that provides clean water around the world, or to another organization that benefits "the least of these." I am humbled to say this was my first Christmas where my focus was on giving to the least of these. This Christmas was the most low-stress and joy-filled, making it my favorite Christmas yet.

My parents flew in for Christmas. It was a low-key time, just the four of us. My mom brought gifts. A friend of hers, whom I had never met, had made me two pillowcases. The lady had not realized until she returned home from the fabric store that the name of the pattern was "Heavenly Peace." The giver also did not realize that pillowcases have a special place in my heart. When Jack and I were first married and he would have to be away, he would spray a pillowcase with his cologne, so that while I slept it would seem like he was there. I planned to take the pillowcases with me to the hospital. I liked the idea of resting my head on Heavenly Peace and holding Heavenly Peace in my arms. (I knew from my mom's surgery that holding a pillow against one's abdomen after surgery helps to reduce the pain when one sneezes or coughs.) Only God knew all of these details.

In the month of December I recorded over 400 praises in my gratitude journal. This is not to say that December did not include heartache and pain. They were present, but God's presence was never absent. In December I read in a devotional, *The Cup of Our Life*, that sorrow and joy are sisters in the same house. (This devotional calmed me down and centered me on my most anxious days – no small feat! I highly recommend it.)

The next major blessing came disguised as a trial. Right after my parents left, Jack got the stomach flu. He was vomiting and had a fever. Our dear friends from Lancaster, the Hacketts (Don, Rila, and their son Colin), were supposed to stay at our house for Jack's installation service (a Sunday morning worship service similar to an ordination service, making the accepted call of a pastor to serve a church official). Don and Rila had been mentors to Jack and me for years and had supported and encouraged us – from low points in our life when hope felt completely absent, to our most joyous day when Don married us. There was something tremendously special about having people from our past supporting and launching us into our future ministry.

I frantically used disinfectant wipes on all countertops, doorknobs, and light switches. The last thing I wanted was for the Hacketts to get sick. Plus, my immune system was not at full capacity with all of my health issues – and if I had any flu symptoms, my surgery would be postponed. Anyone who has anticipated major surgery knows there is a lot of mental preparation. At this point, I could not imagine a delay.

Unfortunately, Jack continued to get worse, so I found a

hotel for our guests to stay in. Jack felt so bad that I went by myself to pick up the Hacketts from the airport, and I prepared the meals by myself. This consumed all of my energy, which was a gift, because I did not have time to think about my fast-approaching surgery. Looking back, I saw that I had specifically asked for prayer requests to stay healthy, and this prayer was directly answered. I never had any flu symptoms.

We did not choose the installation date, but God made it possible for me to be present and gave me an additional distraction before surgery. I had been so busy focusing on the birthdays, Christmas, and Jack's installation, that only during the installation service did the reality hit: my surgery was only four days away. But what better place than in church to fall apart? My Lancaster church family (represented by the Hacketts) and my new church family embraced me in my brokenness.

Sunday evening Don and Rila gave Jack and me yet another tremendous gift – in addition to having already traveled from Pennsylvania, been flexible with Jack's health, preached, and played music at the service. Don and Rila asked us four simple questions:

1) How can we pray for you?

2) What Scripture has spoken to you recently?

3) What are your future hopes and dreams that we could pray for? (This question was particularly hard, because for the past year pain and illness had shattered many of our hopes and dreams.)

4) What would be helpful?

These questions really made me think. As a response to these thought-provoking questions. I sent a final blog update prior to surgery on Tuesday, January 8, with two requests.

*1) **Prayer** – prayers for healing; for minimal pain; for strength and courage (right now I feel terrified); for support for my caregivers; for the doctors, nurses, and staff who will be caring for me; and my greatest request* *is that God would be glorified through this surgery and recovery. (FYI - The surgery is scheduled to begin at 8 AM this Thursday (Jan 10th) and last between 8 and 10 hours.)*

*2) **Cards of encouragement** – I would love to hear answers to prayers in your life and where you have seen God at work. For example, a friend shared a story of needing bookcases and finding beautiful ones, but she could not afford them. On her way exiting the store, the same model bookcases were on clearance because of a small imperfection. Or a lyric from a song that touched you; a friend shared the line from a song that went something like "when times are dry our roots run deep." Also sharing Scripture or a quote and how it has touched you. Hearing how you are encouraged (in whatever form that takes) encourages me. Snail mail is the most helpful. E-mail overwhelms me right now.*

I am told that the next three months are going to be rough and in six months I should be well enough to look for employment. Hallelujah!

Jack will be posting updates here on this blog. We look forward to sharing how God is answering prayers. Thank you from the bottom of my heart for your prayers.

Blessings and love to you in this new year,
Becky

I was ready to have this long-anticipated surgery over, but I was terrified of the recovery. My biggest fear was having an unsuccessful surgery that resulted in worse pain long-term plus would leave me a diabetic. I wished that I could hit a fast-forward button to see what the future held.

CHAPTER 28

SURGERY EVE

On Wednesday, January 9, Jack and I loaded our car and drove an hour and a half north to Charleston. I had my "Heavenly Peace" pillowcases, my iPod, and a care package from Denise and her daughters. My parents flew into the Charleston airport and rented a car. We planned to meet them at a group of outlet stores near the airport.

Jack and I casually meandered around different stores having after-Christmas sales while we waited for my parents. We picked up a few items for birthday and Christmas gifts. I caved to Jack's request to go in a bookstore. As I was aimlessly walking up and down rows of books, I received a phone call. The woman on the other end of the line introduced herself as Nancy Kessel, a member of our church. I could vaguely form a picture in my head from the church directory, but I could not remember ever personally meeting her. She was the wife of Dr. Kessel, my wonderful primary care physician.

She continued, "I was calling to let you know that I will be praying for you tomorrow. I also wanted to let you know that I am a brittle diabetic. If you have any questions or problems when you return home, please feel free to give me a call." I thanked her and appreciated the call. My two biggest concerns post-surgery were managing the pain and managing my blood sugar levels – although I was trying my best not to think about either.

Once my parents arrived at the outlet stores, they asked where I would like to eat. There was a restaurant close by that had a great gluten-free menu. In some ways, I felt like I was a person on death row having my last meal. I did not know the next time I would be able to eat food, so I wanted to make it a good meal. I had shrimp and salad.

After dinner, I thought we would go back to the hotel and call it an early night. I figured my parents were tired from traveling, and I knew we had an extremely early morning ahead. Instead, my mom surprised me and said she had some coupons and wanted to get me some new outfits at one of her favorite stores, Chicos. I thanked my mom, but told her, "I do not need any more clothes." Most of my clothes in my closet were hand-me-downs from my sister or clothes my mom had bought me. I truly was content with my wardrobe.

My mom insisted and added that the store was having a big sale. My mom continued on, "If nothing else, would you not help me look for some new clothes?" This did the trick. I agreed we could go see what was on sale.

The Chicos's sales lady asked as we entered the store, "Can I help you find anything?"

My mom piped up right away, "I would like to get some new tops for my daughter."

I had thought we were there to help my mom look at clothes! But I realized there was no point in trying to argue.

The sales lady took us all around the store and filled up her arms with possible tops. I was not allowed to look at any of the prices when making a decision about whether or not I wished to try on something. These were my mom's rules. My mom knew that if I saw the prices, I would not try anything on.

Jack and my dad were good sports and sat themselves down on comfortable chairs near the dressing rooms. I tried on an assortment of tops. Naturally, some fit well and some did not. When all was said and done, about five or six tops looked and felt nice on. As I prepared to narrow down my selection to one or two, my mom declared, "We will take all of them!"

I was mortified. I tried to say to my mom that I should be the one buying the gifts. After all, they had flown to me and were coming to take care of me and support Jack.

My mom said, "Nonsense. I want to do this for you. You

should have some new clothes to look forward to wearing."

I had always enjoyed shopping for new clothes, but after college I could never justify the expense. Now I started thinking about wearing these new clothes to my new job and wondered where I might work in the future.

Our hotel room was spacious and inviting. I really just wanted to stay at the hotel for ten to thirty days instead of at the hospital. But I set the alarm for 4 a.m. and got ready for bed. I checked my phone and saw that I had quite a few text messages from friends and family saying that they were praying. I also had a message from Rhonda to please give her a call. I called Rhonda, and she told me that she had been praying for me and felt very clearly from the Lord that I was to write down a word for each day and to keep the list. Rhonda had no idea what the list was to be used for, or when I was to stop adding to the list, but she trusted God would reveal these answers to me in due time. She and others had commented that they felt my time in the desert was coming to a close and soon I would be in the "Promised Land." I clung to this image as I drifted off to sleep.

CHAPTER 29

THE BIG DAY

Surgery Update #1 from Jack at 8:07 AM on 1/10/13

It seems hard to believe that we are already well into January, and that Christmas Day was over two weeks ago. The weeks leading up to Christmas constitute a season called "Advent." For many Christians, Advent is a time to prepare for Christmas. It reminds us of the time when people were waiting for a Savior, hoping for God's physical presence in their midst. It was a painful time, marked by persecution and exile. Many images associated with Advent, including the lighting of the Advent candles, signify the movement from darkness and despair to light and hope.

As Becky, her parents, and I were praying together this morning, Becky's mom reflected that this painful season — the past few years, and this past year in particular — has been Becky's Advent. She has been waiting, oftentimes experiencing deep darkness and despair because of her pain. Today is Becky's Christmas Day — the day she has been waiting for with hopeful expectation of God's healing miracle. Today is the day where we mark the dawning of a new light in Becky's life. Beginning today, Becky will be able to experience life without the torture of chronic pancreatitis and the pain associated with it.

However, as in the Christian journey, there is no promise that the road going forward will be easy and without its challenges. We are realistic about the painful three- to six-month recovery from this surgery. We understand that Becky is trading in an unmanageable disease for a manageable one, as she will go from having chronic pancreatitis to having diabetes. We know that our lives will change, and Becky will have days of limited energy.

Yet, also like the Christian journey, we aren't walking this path alone. We have found tremendous care and a wonderful facility at the Medical University of South Carolina (MUSC). Our doctors, nurses, and technicians have all gone above and beyond to show compassion, care, and competence as we've explored this procedure as an option. We are thankful to be surrounded by loving family – both near and far – who have been nothing but supportive. As I write this, I am sitting with Becky's parents, Sue and Ed, who are committed to being here to help me and Becky as she recovers.

We are also exceedingly blessed by our church families. The congregation of Sea Island Presbyterian Church where I am currently serving as an Associate Pastor could not be more loving and supportive. Even though we have only been here for a few months, they have claimed us as their own, and we feel like they are our extended family. We are also lovingly prayed for and supported by our former church families from First Presbyterian Church in Lancaster, Pennsylvania, and St. James Presbyterian Church in Mechanicsburg, Pennsylvania. The people who make up these fellowships have continued to bless us with cards, e-mails, calls, and prayers during our transitions and continue to hold us close in their hearts as we undergo this trial.

It is just about 8 a.m. as I write this. Becky's procedure began about twenty minutes ago. It's going to be a long day. The surgery is estimated to last eight to ten hours. They are currently working on removing Becky's pancreas, spleen, and part of her stomach. Following this part of the procedure, Becky's pancreas will be taken to a lab in order to harvest her islet cells. Becky will be moved to a surgical ICU room where she will remain unconscious. After the islet cells are harvested, Becky will go back into the operating room so they can transplant the cells into her liver, which will eventually begin to produce insulin and glucagon to help her body regulate sugar. We are indeed "fearfully and wonderfully made" (Psalm 139:14). We are so thankful for the science, technology, and skill that God has given that is making this day possible.

As I said above, this is the dawning of a new light in Becky's life as she realizes the potential to begin living a more normal life free from the bondage of physical pain. The journey here has been difficult, and we thank you all for the part you played in making it bearable. The journey ahead will have its own challenges, and we praise God because we know you are all gifts that will help us make it through. Thank you all. Keep your prayers coming.

Surgery Update #2 from Jack at 8:44 AM on 1/10/13

The transplant coordinator, Betsy, just met with us. The surgery is going well so far. Dr. Adams has estimated that he should have the pancreas removed by 9:20 a.m. He is seeing a lot of damage to the pancreas. Betsy said that, based on the amount of damage, it is evident that Becky has suffered a great deal.

They anticipate moving her to ICU around 10:30 a.m. Betsy told us that at that time we will meet with Dr. Adams to find out how things went with the pancreatectomy. After we consult with him, we will be able to go back to ICU to see Becky! That is an unexpected surprise and blessing. She will still be asleep, but we can talk to her.

Once the islet cells have been isolated, Becky will be moved to a radiology suite where they will complete the procedure. (That part should take about an hour.) Betsy estimates that Becky should be awake and off the ventilator around 8 p.m., but we'll know more as the day progresses.

Surgery Update # 3 from Jack at 9:42 AM on 1/10/13

Becky's pancreas is out and off to the lab! Betsy just came out to let us know that Becky is now pancreas-free. She also affirmed that having this surgery was indeed the right decision. This part of the operation should be finished in about an hour. She'll be moved to the ICU then and we should be able to see her in about two hours. So far things are going very well, praise God!

Praying for 150,000: Surgery Update #4 from Jack at 11:12 AM on 1/10/13

Becky is out of surgery and on her way to the ICU. We just met with Dr. Adams. He said everything went very well, praise God, and that she had "a good anatomy" for this surgery. The doctor said there were no complications and she didn't need any blood.

We will move to another waiting room until they let us go back and see her. Now we are praying for 150,000 – that's the number of islet cells they will need to transplant that will give her the best chance at not being an insulin-dependent diabetic long-term. Thanks for your continued prayers – and praises!

Surgery Update #5 from Jack at 3:31 PM on 1/10/13

Becky is currently receiving her transplanted cells. We haven't heard how many they were able to harvest, but we are anxious to find out.

Becky's parents and I were able to go back to the ICU around noon and spend about an hour with her. She was unconscious the entire time and breathing with the help of a ventilator, but we could talk to her and be near her. She looked good, and the nurses and doctors attending to her confirmed how well she is doing. It was wonderful to have that time with her, especially because it helped alleviate any fears we might have had about how she was doing or feeling. We feel very reassured at MUSC's commitment to keep Becky comfortable and manage her pain during her recovery.

The Youngs and I were able to grab some lunch. I think the food is giving us a little energy as we hit those late afternoon doldrums. We've also been bolstered by brief visits from Pastor Steve and Pastor Ashley. Your prayers on our behalf are also keeping us going. Thank you. I look forward to updating you soon with the results of the transplant.

Surgery is Officially OVER: Surgery Update #6 from Jack at 4:56 PM on 1/10/13

Betsy just let us know that Becky's eyelet cell transplant is complete and she is back in the ICU. Her surgery is OVER!

They counted the harvested cells twice. The first count came out to 130,000 cells. The second count came out to 170,000. They believe that, taking the average, Becky probably received 150,000 cells! Praise God! That was the number Dr. Adams told us to hope for! Betsy is now back checking on Becky, and we may be able to see her soon.

As the anesthesia wore off, but before I could open my eyes, I began saying "Thank you, Jesus!" over and over again. One of the hospital staff asked another, "What is she saying?" That person replied, "I think she is praying." I was not just praying, I was praising God! I had never before come out of a surgery or a procedure without pain. My abdomen was completely numb. I had been warned by Johns Hopkins about the extreme pain post-surgery. I figured MUSC did not mention the post-surgery pain in such graphic detail, because they did not want to traumatize their patients. I had never imagined zero pain being a possibility right after surgery.

Not long after I opened my eyes, Jack and my parents were present. I felt like shouting, "We made it!" The surgery was behind me and I felt good. I was of course groggy and numb, but was elated nonetheless. The scariest obstacle that I had ever faced in my life was behind me.

I told my family with a humongous grin, "No pain! I have no pain!" They seemed as excited as I was. They informed me that my surgery went well and that lots of islet cells were harvested. I could not comprehend everything they said, but I knew things were good.

I could not believe I had two nurses in my room. One was focusing on my pain level and kept asking me how I was doing. If I started to feel a little pain, she adjusted things and I would again feel great within minutes. I felt like royalty.

A little before 7 p.m., Jack and my parents said that they would see me in the morning. There were no visitors allowed from 7 a.m. to 8 a.m. and from 7 p.m. to 8 p.m. This was the time when the shifts changed, and nurses and doctors would pass along reports and updates to the new shift of medical employees.

A little after 8 p.m., a new nurse introduced herself and said she would be taking care of me. The first thing I noticed was that she was not sitting in my room like the other nurse had. I started feeling pain on the right side of my abdomen and panicked. I yelled for the nurse, and she quickly appeared. The nurse said she would give me some pain medicine. However, after a few minutes I did not feel relief. I cried out again in pain. The nurse came back in and calmly told me, "I cannot give you any more pain medicine right now."

I realized at this point that I had no control. I could not move. I was in a corset-like apparatus to keep my epidural from moving and my incision from opening. In addition, I had an NG tube up my nose and down my throat, a catheter, and tubes coming out of my neck, arms, and abdomen. I was not tied to the bed, but there was no way I could get out. My head and neck were all I could move on my own. I felt trapped and helpless.

I started becoming paranoid. I became convinced that the nurse was trying to kill me. I felt my only chance of survival was to get my husband present, because he would be my advocate.

I asked the nurse kindly, "Would you call my husband? I need him."

The nurse disappeared. I was sure she could tell I was agitated. I started doubting the nurse's competence.

I was truly shocked to see my husband appear in my room a few minutes later. Jack had just returned to the hotel from dinner when he received the call from the nurse that I wanted to see him.

As soon as Jack arrived, I whispered to him, "The nurse is trying to kill me. I am in pain and she does not care. She is not even staying in my room." My words sounded crazy even to me. I was worried that Jack would not believe me. I continued my petition, "Please, Jack, do not leave. I beg you to stay with me. I am so scared."

Jack knew me well enough to know I was not joking. I was truly scared that I was going to die. Jack was also aware that the night nurses sat outside the rooms to minimize disturbances while patients slept. I had a glass wall, so the nurse could easily see me and monitor me. My range of vision was limited, so I could not see her. However, instead of arguing with me and trying to convince me of reality, Jack held my hand and said, "Do not worry. I am here now, and I will make sure you are well taken care of. Nothing is going to happen to you."

I instantly felt relaxed. I sent up silent prayers, thanking God for the advocate I had in Jack. I prayed for anyone who was suffering and feeling vulnerable and did not have an advocate. My mind went immediately to those in nursing homes who are paralyzed. My mind started to wonder what would have happened had Jack not come. I felt my hand being squeezed and was brought back to the reality that my loyal husband was with me. Jack gently whispered, "Take deep breaths. Everything is going to be okay. Rest, sweetheart."

Jack spent the entire night with me in the ICU. He had not slept the previous two nights and was drained from a full day of surgery updates. Visitors were not supposed to sleep in the ICU. However, the nurses accommodated us and brought a reclining chair for Jack, along with some pillows and blankets. I am sure Jack would have much preferred to sleep at the hotel, but he did not complain.

When the sun rose, Jack was still with me and I was alive. Jack wearily said, "I am going back to the hotel, but your parents will be over soon. Anything I can do for you before I leave?"

I replied, "No, my love. Thanks for staying with me. You saved my life. I'll see you later. I love you." And then I drifted back to sleep.

Wonderful News: Surgery Update #7 from Jack on 1/11/13

Becky had a pretty rough night. Her epidural shifted and she wasn't receiving any pain relief in her right side. They adjusted her epidural a couple of times and they were finally able to get her back to her baseline around 2 a.m.

While Becky continues to be uncomfortable, we are rejoicing in some very good things that are happening. She has been off the insulin drip since 5:30 a.m. and has been maintaining blood sugar levels ranging from 108-110 every time they check it. This is amazing news! This means that the transplanted islet cells are taking to their new home and beginning to work! This is a huge praise.

They also removed Becky's NG (nasal gastric) tube around 3 p.m. This tube ran down her nose and into her stomach to help drain her stomach to allow healing in her stomach. Becky finds these tubes extremely uncomfortable and annoying (and who can blame her?). When they told her they were going to remove it, she got a sudden burst of energy and her face lit up. I don't think she would have been happier if they told her she just won the lottery! They have ordered ice chips for her, and they plan on starting her on a clear liquid diet soon.

We continue to be impressed with the level of care that Becky is receiving here. Her nurses and doctors have been wonderfully attentive and compassionate. With all of Becky's progress, she is no longer considered an ICU patient. (She is now considered a step-down patient.)

We are continuing to pray for Becky's comfort and pain relief as she recovers, but we are praising God for how wonderful she is doing less than twenty-four hours after the surgery. God is good… all the time.

CHAPTER 30

RECOVERING AT THE HOSPITAL

Milestones on the Road to Recovery: Update from Jack sent 1/12/13

Today was another long, but great, day. We celebrated a lot of milestones on Becky's road to recovery.

She had a relatively restful night, getting about three solid hours of sleep and dozing off and on the rest of the night. Hospitals are not great places to get rest to begin with, especially when they are checking your blood pressure and blood sugars every hour. When we arrived at the hospital this morning, Becky was sitting up in bed with a big smile on her face. She looked very good, and her heart rate and fluid output had normalized. However, she was still in a good deal of discomfort.

The pain medications were helping her, but they were also making her very drowsy. Her breathing was shallow and slow. Because her doctors and nurses were afraid of Becky coming down with pneumonia, we were tasked with being Becky's breathing coaches and cheerleaders. For several hours we sat by her bed watching her monitors and encouraging her to take deep breaths. While we were cheering her on, the pain team came in and fixed her epidural again. It was a big ordeal and tired Becky out.

However, the day was just beginning. Becky saw her first visitor today when Pastor Heather from Sea Island stopped by. Shortly after Heather's visit, Becky's nurse, Amy, made Becky get up and out of bed! She was able to take several steps to a chair, and they were able to get her comfortable and situated in an upright position. Amy wanted her to stay in the chair for at least two hours, but Becky was able to remain there for three!

In addition to sitting, Becky was served two meals from the diabetic diet. She enjoyed some sugar-free popsicles and Jell-O, along with apple juice and lemonade. It really perked her up. It was also relatively kind on her islets, as her blood sugars didn't spike to astronomical numbers; this is another great sign that Becky may not need insulin long-term. Before she returned to bed, Becky got a sponge bath and her hair washed. You can only imagine how good that felt to her.

Just before we left her tonight, they were transitioning her from her pain pump to a combination of oral and IV pain killers. No doubt this will lead to some additional discomfort, but with Becky's breathing troubles and the doctor's desire to get Becky more mobile tomorrow, it is the best thing to do.

After we left Becky before the shift change, Sue, Ed, and I went to a great restaurant that specializes in southern food. We had a very nice meal and a time to relax. We are trying to take care of ourselves in the midst of being present with Becky, and overall, we are all doing fine. Thank you to those of you who have offered words of care and concern for our well-being. God is definitely providing for us from an unfathomable well of energy. We are able to find things to sustain us and celebrate every day. In fact, two days so far.

Ultimately, we keep trying to encourage Becky, and we appreciate you joining us in your prayers for Becky's encouragement and strength. She is doing remarkably well for someone who has just undergone this type of major surgery, but she still has a long road ahead of her. Thank you all for walking beside her on the journey. Keep your prayers coming.

Two days after my surgery, through the fog of sleep and pain medication, I remember Jack and my mom encouraging me to take deep breaths. They would breathe in and out with me. A monitor kept showing my oxygen level was low. I was aware that I could not get additional pain medicine if my breathing was too shallow. Therefore, I tried with all of my strength to take deep breaths. I was grateful to my two cheerleaders, because taking deep breaths felt like running a marathon. When my oxygen level would begin to rise, Jack and my mom would cheer, "Way to go! Nice work! Awesome! Keep it up! You can do it!"

I also remember the pain. When the epidural was working, my abdomen area was completely numb. However, when the epidural got out of place, I would feel tremendous pain. In order to adjust or fix my epidural, the doctors and nurses had to roll me to one side. Unfortunately, any movement caused excruciating pain. The process to get me on my side included pulling the sheets under me and gently pushing my one shoulder and hip away from the bed. Even though this was done with utmost care, I would scream and moan. I initially wondered if it was worth getting the epidural adjusted, because the pain escalated before it receded. But this was just one example of how hard it was to see the big picture and long-term benefits.

Another Great Day: Update from Jack sent 1/13/13

Today has been a day of celebrations. We started this morning celebrating Becky's mother's birthday. Sue started her day with a special breakfast, followed by spending time with Becky, and finished it off with a nice dinner out with Ed in downtown Charleston.

We also had a lot to celebrate with Becky's progress on the road to recovery today. Becky spent some more time sitting in a chair this morning. Later, she was able to walk to the bathroom, twice. They've reduced her epidural medication, and they are planning on removing the epidural tomorrow. But perhaps the biggest celebration of the day was that Becky was transferred out of the ICU this afternoon. She is now settled into a regular room.

As always, we thank you for your continued prayers, and we invite you to join with us in praising God and celebrating all the little things that quickly add up to BIG things. May the days ahead be full of celebrations for us all.

The third day of my recovery felt momentous because my catheter was removed. This was a huge celebration for me. It was a step closer to freedom and independence. I also felt victorious when the nurse got me out of bed and I was able to take a few steps and sit upright for a while. In order to walk, I shuffled my feet. Movement was painful, but I knew the more I moved, the sooner I could leave the hospital.

More Good News from Charleston: Update from Jack sent 1/14/13

We just received a very good report from Dr. Adams. According to him, Becky is doing very well. He told us to expect her to come home this week! Given that today is Day Four, we are in utter amazement at God's handiwork as we are beginning to talk about Becky being discharged!

Moving towards this goal, they removed Becky's epidural this morning. Her pain has increased slightly, and she definitely notices a difference without it, but the worst of the pain is behind her, and the oral medications seem to be helping keep her relatively comfortable most of the time. She is currently receiving an infusion of magnesium through her IV, but once that is completed, they will temporarily disconnect her so she can take her first walk down the hallway. They are also planning on removing a drain that they inserted to help promote healing around the incision, and in the next couple of days they will remove Becky's staples. Once they confirm that her digestive tract is indeed ready to process solid foods, there won't be anything substantial preventing her from going home.

Regarding that, and not to be crude, but we have an unusual prayer request. Becky needs to be able to pass gas. As Dr. Wright, one of the docs on the surgical team, said, we aren't looking for a girly fart, but a big old manly fart. I've given Becky plenty of encouragement through example, but she needs a little more prodding. Part of it is facing the pain that will come with that kind of exertion, and part of it is the trauma that her gut has experienced, but we are confident that it will happen soon.

We also ask that you continue to pray for pain relief and comfort. We are so amazed at the progress she has made thus far and so proud of Becky being what Dr. Adams called, "a superstar patient." We thank you all for your prayers and encouragement, and we praise God for all this provision – miracles are happening every day! With all of this progress happening, it makes it a little easier for me to return home this evening as I prepare to go back to work tomorrow. Becky's dad, Ed, will also be flying home tonight so that he can return to work as well. Becky's mom, Sue, will remain with her in Charleston. I plan on returning Thursday afternoon – hopefully just in time to get her packed up and on the road to home. I will be in regular contact with Becky and Sue and will continue to post updates to the blog.

A Down and Up Day: Update from Jack sent 1/15/13

Becky had a down and up day today. She had a rough night sleep-wise and started the morning feeling a little run down. She was also experiencing a lot of pain today, but nothing out of the ordinary considering everything she's experienced.

Becky's doctor changed her orders this afternoon so that she was once again considered NPO (nothing by mouth). This meant no more food or liquid until she was able to move her bowels. Becky felt like this was a step backwards.

Today was also very busy in her room. She received a lot of education today from the surgical team, the endocrinologist, the diabetic educator, the dietitian, and the pain doctor. While a lot of the information was extremely helpful, some of it was very scary (especially when they talk about rare, but extreme, complications). The combination of having so many people visiting with Becky and absorbing all the information they had to share made Becky extremely exhausted.

After a nap this afternoon, though, she rebounded. She took a nice long walk down two hallways and was surprised when they wound up back at her room. She was also able to take her first shower. She told me that she was finally starting to feel like a human again. However, she is still very groggy, and not being able to drink anything has left her throat feeling very sore and scratchy as she still recovers from the ventilator and NG tube.

Even in the midst of today's setbacks, God remains faithful, and we are continuing to recognize answers to prayers and reasons to give thanks. After a lot of painful effort, Becky was able to pass some gas and move her bowels a little.

Thank you all for your prayers. I have appreciated hearing from so many in e-mails, Facebook comments, and here on the blog. I am able to share them with Becky at different times, and it means so much to her that so many are sending their love and prayers. Please know that you are all tremendous blessings during this time, and we are encouraged by your care, concern, and love. Blessings to you all.

I think it was five days after my operation, but I do not remember for sure, when Lisa, the woman who was so kind to share her surgery experience and recovery with me over the phone, stopped by my hospital room. She lived several hours away from MUSC, but she was there for a follow-up appointment with Dr. Adams. She tapped gently on the door, and I said, "Come in." Like in a game show, I had no idea what was behind the door. She introduced herself as Lisa, and as soon as I heard her voice I recognized it from our phone call. I was delighted to meet her in person. She had not mentioned that she would be at MUSC during my recovery time. Thus, her presence was a complete surprise.

Lisa was absolutely stunning. She could have been a model with her petite frame and long, flowing hair. I thought to myself, *I hope I look that good when I fully recover.* Her exterior beauty matched her interior beauty. She was just as sweet and warm as could be. Lisa told me that she and her entire Sunday school class were praying for me. She asked how I was feeling. I was honest and said I felt pretty nauseous, but I was thankful the surgery was behind me and my pain was well-managed. I thanked her profusely again for how her words had given me peace and hope. My mom, who was with me during the visit, piggybacked on my gratitude saying, "Lisa, I cannot thank you enough for the gift you have given my daughter." My mom gave Lisa a big hug on my behalf.

Another unexpected visitor came to my room in the form of a four-legged friend. My sister and I had co-owned a dog in Lancaster and when I moved to South Carolina, she kept Chettie. I certainly missed Chettie, but I knew he was being well cared for. When a volunteer came to the hospital with her well-trained dog and went from room to room, I could not help but smile. The dog kissed my hands, and I petted his soft fur coat. The dog's visit immediately lifted my spirits and distracted me from the fact that I was not able to eat.

I was mortified, however, when I found out that Jack had asked people to pray that I would pass gas. I later found out from a friend that her pre-teen son, who is also a preacher's kid, said it was his favorite prayer request ever.

Pain Management Resources: Update from Sue (Becky's mom) sent 1/16/13

I felt led this morning to write before returning to the hospital. Jayne, the pain management nurse, has been fantastic and spent over an hour with us yesterday. She herself was a wonderful source of information and she also recommended different resources. I know many of you who are reading this deal with chronic pain, and so I hope this will help. First, she recommended a TED Talk explaining that pain can be a disease and not just a symptom. When Becky and I watched it this Monday night we felt it was enlightening. You can watch the video by searching YouTube for Dr. Elliott Krane. She also recommended a book that you can get from Amazon for about $15 entitled Managing Pain Before It Manages You *by Dr. Margaret Caudill. She also suggested the web site www.painaction.com. I pray these resources will be a help for you or those you love. I know that we are all on a journey together and I can't thank you enough for all the prayers.*

Love,
Sue

A Great Day with Wonderful News: Update from Jack sent 1/16/13

Today has been a wonderful day. I talked to Becky early this morning, and she sounded wonderful and energized. She had a restful night and was feeling refreshed. She still had some pain, but was managing very well. Becky wanted to eat, but wasn't sure when they would allow her to have food.

The answer came around 4:30 p.m. Becky called me to tell me that the surgical team had just come in to visit with her and gave her their plan of action. First, she could eat real food for dinner tonight. Second, she would have her staples removed on Friday. Third, they tested the islet cells and learned that they are functioning just as they should. Finally, they were planning on discharging her on Friday! This is all incredible news.

Becky was so excited about the prospect of eating real food again that I think she wanted to order one of everything off the menu. She planned out her next three meals. When she finally got her tray, she started with the vanilla wafers. She also ate some corn muffin and a little bit of a quesadilla. Becky was told to take eating slow, but it sure felt good to eat again. However, a week without food caught up with her very soon, and she needed some pain and nausea medicine shortly after eating. We know it will get better soon, but it is still hard to be so hungry and not be able to eat much.

Even with eating food, Becky's blood sugar continues to remain in the normal range, and she hasn't needed insulin today. Her strength is also continuing to return to her, and she took a couple of long walks with her mother today.

Needless to say, this is all thrilling news and we are rejoicing. It has been good to get back to work for a couple of days, but I miss being with Becky and am looking forward to going back tomorrow. It is wonderful to know that she will be coming home with me on Friday. She still has a long recovery ahead of her, but we all feel a lot more confident and encouraged that Becky is going to make it through her recovery with flying colors.

With Digs Like This, Who Could Leave? Update from Jack sent 1/17/13

It seems we got our hopes up a little too soon. Becky has been struggling to eat and keep food down. As a result, she won't be coming home tomorrow as we had expected. While this is not the best news, we know that being in the hospital is the best thing for Becky right now.

Becky couldn't wait to try everything on the menu, but she couldn't keep her breakfast or lunch down today. That meant that her dinner consisted of a couple of lemon wedges for her water. Even though she has been sick several times today, her spirits are still good and she looks wonderful. She has continued to walk the hallways, and she is getting faster and stronger with every lap. Her blood sugars continue to be in the normal range for the most part, although she did need some insulin earlier today. Becky was able to inject herself for the first time. She said it didn't even hurt.

Tomorrow we will meet with a few more educators who will help us understand how Becky's lifestyle will change. As excited as Becky is about food, the doctors have told us that it might be a while before Becky is really able to eat more than a small snack or meal at any one time.

We are so thankful for all the amazing healing that Becky has experienced over the past week. It seems natural to be discouraged by this bump in Becky's healing journey, but she has been doing so well overall that we remain convinced that Becky will be feeling better and back at home very soon. Please continue to pray for Becky to be able to eat food without experiencing pain and without vomiting, and also for her nausea to go away.

I was deeply discouraged and frustrated when I could not hold my food down. I was hungry and wanted to enjoy food again. Vomiting is never pleasant, but it was especially awful with eighteen staples holding my abdomen together. I was disappointed that my discharge date was postponed. However, I did not want to leave the hospital until I knew I could keep food down. In addition, I knew that Lisa, who had the same surgery several years before me, had to return to MUSC several days after she was discharged. The last thing I wanted to do was have to ride in the car for an hour and a half back to MUSC while feeling sick. Therefore, I was at peace about staying until I felt my body was ready to go home.

Onward and Upward: Update from Jack sent 1/18/13

While Becky didn't get discharged today as we had initially hoped, she is continuing to improve in big ways. It was great to be here to encourage her throughout the day, which proved to be a very full one.

Becky ordered herself some diet ice cream and Jell-O for breakfast this morning, but after taking her morning pills, she didn't feel up to eating anything. The nurse was very nice and put the ice cream in the freezer. Becky got some of it down for lunch, in addition to a Club cracker. While it doesn't sound like much, it was truly wonderful that she was able to keep it down and not feel overwhelmingly nauseous.

Becky ran her mother and I ragged circling the halls. Unfortunately, the temperature in Charleston dropped about 20 degrees overnight, and in only 60 degree weather we decided not to venture outside. That didn't stop us from enjoying the beautiful panoramic views of the Ashley River marina, the blue skies, and the bright sunshine from the windows in the hallway.

Our day wasn't all walking and eating, though, and at times Becky's room felt like Grand Central Station. We met with the diabetic educator and then a diabetic dietician. Thankfully, Becky can eat just about anything she wants, although we will need to be diligent in counting carbohydrates and portion sizes.

Becky's surgeon, Dr. Adams, also came by after being out of town for a few days. He seemed pleased with Becky's progress and felt she would be able to leave soon. In addition to this good news, Becky's staples were removed.

A couple of members of our church family also stopped in for a brief visit this afternoon. Before they left, they offered these words from the Apostle Paul's letter to the church in Rome: "In the same way, the Spirit helps us in our weakness. We do not know what we ought to pray for, but the Spirit himself intercedes for us with groans that words cannot express. And he who searches our hearts knows the mind of the Spirit, because the Spirit intercedes for the saints in accordance with God's will. And we know that in all things God works for the good of those who love him, who have been called according to his purpose" (Romans 8:26-28).

Becky and I want to offer these words as our hope and prayer for all of you who are reading this. Most of you have experienced those groaning prayers, and many people have offered them on Becky's behalf over this past year. God indeed continues to show us how all things are working out for good. May this hope and promise sustain you as it has sustained us.

The sight of the staples protruding from my abdomen made me queasy. At least once a day, the surgeon or someone on his staff would inspect the incision to make sure everything was healing properly. The incision stretched from the base of my sternum to right above my belly button. The staples had been inserted while I was unconscious, but I unfortunately had to be awake for their removal. I dreaded the process to remove the staples, but I was certainly looking forward to their absence.

A young male resident came to my room to remove the staples, and Dr. Wright oversaw the process. Once again, I felt like my modesty flew out the window. Jack held my hand, and my mom read devotions. I was trying to focus on my breathing, but it was difficult having someone in my personal space pulling pieces of metal out of my body. I tried to tell myself that although I felt very exposed, that this resident was like a mechanic fixing a car. He was focused on parts. Overall it went quickly and was not as painful as I thought it might be. I only had one staple that was stubborn and required a little wiggling to get loose. I believe that the resident was as happy to be done with the staples as I was. I figured it was probably rather stressful to have four people watching and working on a conscious human being who was clearly nervous. I was thankful that, like my pancreas, the staples would not grow or come back.

I am definitely a routine gal. By my ninth day after surgery, my morning routine was to be awakened around 5 a.m. to have blood drawn. When the phlebotomist would come in, I would be asleep and sometimes I would only wake up as the last vial was taken. Typically, I was groggy and disoriented. They would usually say something like, "Have a nice day!" and I would mumble something back along the same lines. By 6 a.m. I was fully awake. This was around the time Dr. Wright would stop in. She was a young doctor and full of spunk. I was convinced that she had a frappuccino every morning on her way to work, because she was energetic when the sun was still down. She would always ask, "How are you feeling?" in a way that a friend would ask. She had a hearty laugh and would speak to me in colloquial terms, not medical jargon. Then around 8:30, Jack, my mom, and/or my dad would normally arrive.

This particular morning, Dr. Wright did not come by. I figured she had a day off. Around 8 a.m., Dr. Wright popped her head in. I got a huge smile and exclaimed, "Dr. Wright, I did not think I was going to get to see you today! I thought maybe it was your day off."

She replied, "Oh no, girl, I do not have a day off for a week. You are stuck with me. I just had an emergency that needed my attention. That is why I am later than usual."

I responded, "Well, I am sorry for your sake that you don't have the day off, but I am selfishly glad that I get to see you. I wanted to tell you that I have had several manly farts." We both laughed. I loved that Dr. Wright could make bodily functions funny and silly.

She checked my charts and examined my incision. "You look good, friend. You just need to have a manly BM and then you will be ready to go home."

I cheekily responded, "I will do my best to make you proud, Dr. Wright." As far as medical doctors went, she was the most vivacious and my favorite. I would later find out that she was moving to Philadelphia. I certainly was thankful for her presence during my hospital stay.

Goin' Home (Take 2): Update from Jack sent 1/19/13

Today was the second day in a row that Becky didn't need any additional pain medication. She also didn't need any nausea medicine. This is indeed reason to celebrate. She continues to eat and tolerate food – and best of all, she enjoys the food she eats. We took several walks throughout the day, and Becky continues to get stronger and gain energy. All of this leads us to some very good news – Becky gets to come home tomorrow!

Now I know we've been here before, when we thought Becky would come home on Friday, and we were certainly disappointed when she didn't. But things have definitely progressed to a point where continued hospitalization would no longer benefit Becky's recovery. Her bags are already packed, and, as she told me, she is ready to blow this Popsicle stand.

We are certainly amazed and very thankful for God's healing work in Becky's body. We are also thankful for the incredible people and facilities at MUSC. Everyone has been wonderful, and so many people have gone above and beyond to ensure that Becky's stay here has been comfortable and recuperative. But most of all, we want to thank all of you reading this, who have sustained us with your prayers, well wishes, and loving support. God has worked a multitude of miracles already, and we look forward to even more revelations of God's power as Becky continues to recover at home... beginning tomorrow.

Home Sweet Home: Update from Jack sent 1/20/13

Becky is home. I am so thankful to have her back. I think it goes without saying that she is also thrilled to be back home. It has been a long day, with lots of "hurry up and wait" moments, and Becky didn't leave MUSC until 2:15 p.m. It was a long drive with lots of jostling along the way. Becky arrived home happy but tired, and although she had hoped to make it through Downton Abbey, *she just went to bed. We pray she'll sleep well and wake up refreshed and comfortable.*

Thanks again for all your prayers and support. Please continue to hold Becky in your prayers as she relearns her daily routines and new ways of eating. We know there will be bumps along the way, but we are confident that before too long, checking blood sugar and counting carbs will be as routine as putting on socks or brushing our teeth. Blessings, peace, and grace to you all.

I also felt like a huge victory was accomplished by leaving the hospital. I was free from IVs, hospital gowns, daily blood work at 5 a.m., nurses and doctors, having my urine measured, and sleeping in a single bed. Of course, after an hour-and-a-half car ride, the thrill of being out of the hospital had worn off.

I squeezed a pillow against my abdomen the entire ride home. Every bounce made my incision hurt and added to my nausea. When the car finally stopped in the driveway, I would have danced if I had been able. Like after a long plane trip, I could not wait for my feet to be on the ground.

As I got closer to the house, I noticed a sign on the door. It was a "welcome home" sign with water lilies made from tissue paper. My friend Sara from my birthday lunch had remembered that water lilies are my favorite flowers. On the poster board were messages from my church family. When Jack opened the door, I could not believe there were more posters – posters everywhere with Scriptures and pictures. There were little bouquets of flowers sprinkled around the house like surprises, including one on my bedside table. Denise and her daughters had asked Jack for permission to come over and decorate. Even though I was weary, the thought and kindness that covered the walls and windows provided a boost of energy. I was also really looking forward to sleeping under the same roof as Jack.

FIRST MONTH

When I was discharged, the hospital staff stressed that I needed a caregiver. I had thought my mom's primary purpose in that role would be to make sure I did not fall down, and to help with meals and cleaning. Our church family provided meals three times a week for two months. However, I needed my mom for so much more.

The two hardest adjustments were checking my blood sugar and eating. I had to check my blood sugar four times a day. I had trouble getting enough blood onto the meter strip and remembering the order of the buttons. I had to space out my meals far enough apart so that when I checked my blood sugar, I had not eaten anything within two hours. I also had to remember when to take my different medicines. With a fatigued body and a mushy brain, it was hard to figure it all out.

My mom helped me write out my schedule. Having everything written down was a tremendous gift. I kept the schedule at my place at the table and referred to it often. I knew with time I would be able to accomplish all of this on autopilot, but like most things new, it took a lot of concentration in the beginning.

Not only did I have to time when I ate just right, but I had to make sure I did not consume too many carbohydrates. To me it seemed like everything I liked was a carbohydrate. I was used to grazing and not worrying about counting carbs. Now, I felt like I was on a weight-loss diet for the first time in my life, and it was not easy.

The other challenge was nausea and pain. Once I got my blood sugar checked and figured out what I could eat, then I had to try and eat. For example, one day I decided that a half of a grilled cheese sandwich sounded appealing. I knew one slice of bread counted for two of my four servings of carbs for the meal. I was going to have an apple for my third carb and some raw carrots for my fourth serving. However, I took one bite of the grilled cheese sandwich and felt full and nauseous, and I had intense abdominal pain. My mom tried to encourage me to have one more bite, but the nausea and pain won. I had been told that pain and nausea after eating was normal as my digestive track healed. Thus, I was not concerned or shocked by the pain. But I became discouraged by what seemed to be wasted time and energy, when energy was so precious. I had planned and calculated for nothing.

Getting in and out of bed was also a challenge. The acts of lying down and of getting up hurt. I would roll over to one side and use my arm to push myself up. I had pillows all around me and they helped me feel comfortable in my bed. Unfortunately, they always needed a little adjusting. My mom was patient and would adjust each pillow as many times as I would ask. My body required a long nap in the morning and the afternoon. In addition, I would sleep for ten to twelve hours at night. It did not take much to wear me out.

Thankfully, during my first few days at home, my healing seemed to have a linear progression. Every day I felt a little stronger, had a little more energy, and got a little more confident with my diabetes equipment and regimen. In addition, I was able to eat a little more, and the pain and nausea after eating began to decrease.

The highlight of each day was going for a walk outside. South Carolina's moderate weather was a gift in the winter. The fresh air always lifted my spirits. Every day my mom and I walked a little further.

I also enjoyed sitting out on the screened-in porch with my mom. My mom got both of us a new Bible study workbook by Priscilla Shirer entitled *Discerning the Voice of God; How to Recognize When God Speaks*. We silently worked on our own at the same time. We often broke the silence with comments like,

"Did you read this part? I never thought of it that way before!" Everything seemed to be moving forward – until I hit another setback. On Wednesday, January 30, almost two weeks after being discharged from the hospital, I woke up at 4:45 a.m. feeling like I was choking. I had a sore throat and it hurt to swallow. I had a phlegmy cough and did my best to cough up some mucus, suck on a cough drop, and adjust my pillows. By 7, I was soaked with sweat, had the chills, and thought I was going to vomit and pass out. I had stomach cramps, back pain, and diarrhea. I checked my blood sugar and it was normal. I took my temperature and it was normal.

That was when I realized I was experiencing pain medication withdrawal. Three days earlier I had dropped back from two pain pills a day to just one. I had experienced these same unpleasant withdrawal symptoms in the spring. I told myself, *Becky, the good news is you don't have a stomach bug, you know you aren't dying, and eventually the symptoms will go away.* The hard part was coughing with a sizable abdominal incision. I would try and suppress the coughs just to avoid the pain. I felt discouraged to have made such progress and then to feel so awful.

I started to feel sorry for myself, thinking, *Why must I suffer? Why must anyone have to suffer? I am so ready for a sabbatical from pain! How much longer? How much more must I endure? Shouldn't I be a pain expert by now? Why can't I handle this pain? Am I being punished?*

I went into the guest room, where my mom was sleeping on an air mattress, and broke into tears. I felt so fatigued and was not up for a new round of battle. I confided to my mom, "I don't feel strong enough for more pain. I know I am not going to die, but it feels like it."

After that, my mom did her best to break up the long days and keep me distracted with silly old movies. When I started to question if I could outlast the pain, my mom would get out her figurative pom-poms and be my personal cheerleader. We would repeat together our latest mantra: "I am going to make it. The pain will not last forever. The best is yet to come."

The same day my intense withdrawal symptoms began, I

came across a Scripture in my Bible Study from Isaiah 50:4: "The Sovereign LORD had given me his words of wisdom, so that I know how to comfort the weary. Morning by morning he wakens me and opens my understanding to his will" (NLT). I felt comforted by so many, but I was terribly weary. I sensed God was telling me via the Scripture that through this experience, I would be able to comfort others who are weary. Once again, having a nugget of purpose lifted my spirits.

In fact, the day before reading this devotional I had received an e-mail from someone I had never met, stating that one particular blog entry really touched her and encouraged her. My response was, "Well, I am not the one with wisdom, but God is. I guess in a way it is a miracle, how God can use my experience, brokenness, and request for prayers to encourage others."

The long days of pain medication withdrawal lasted two weeks, and the symptoms intensified to the point where I could not sleep without the aid of prescription medication, had constant pain and nausea, could not get comfortable, felt like I was going to pass out and vomit simultaneously, and continued with sweats and chills. I did a lot of crying and walking. I joked with my mom, "We'd better pull down the shades, so our neighbors don't think we are taking some sort of illicit drugs as we march around the house listening to praise music." I would try and tire myself out so I could sleep. Sleep was my only escape from pain.

"Discouraged" does not begin to capture how I felt. "Defeated and confused" gets a little closer. I just could not think straight, let alone comprehend that my healing was moving forward. I was pleading and begging God to eliminate the withdrawal pain, as well as the incision pain. The pain had exceeded my threshold, and exhaustion was making me extra miserable. Not having a timetable for when the pain would let up was daunting and overwhelming.

On Friday, February 11th, I had my first follow-up appointment with the surgeon. I was embarrassed to share on my blog that I had subconsciously put my hope and trust in the surgeon to erase my pain. I asked the surgeon why I was experiencing so much pain and what to do to prevent it. Dr. Adams replied, "Pain is normal after surgery. You should anticipate pain for six months after this surgery." I felt crushed. His answer was not what I wanted to hear.

I met with a dietician, and she made some recommendations to help with sour belches and to get good bacteria back in my system. I also met with a pharmaceutical doctor to go over when and how I should be taking different medications. She suggested taking nausea medicine every time I took pain medicine, because pain medicine can cause additional nausea.

Three days later, I had a follow-up appointment with my primary care physician. He explained that the source of my pain, in my case the pancreas, was gone. However, there were a lot of nerve endings attached to the pancreas that were still active. Dr. Kessel informed me, "The nerve endings will heal, and you are progressing in the right direction." His instructions were, "Keep smiling and don't get discouraged. It is going to get easier." This physician also suggested a different nausea medicine.

Making the minor adjustments that the surgeon, nutritionist, pharmaceutical doctor, and PCP suggested led to significant relief. I concluded my blog update by letting friends and family know that for the first time in two weeks, I was not gripped by pain or nausea.

I am hopeful that I have turned a corner. Regardless, this little respite from pain has reminded me of how wonderful and enjoyable life can be. God heard my weary cries and the pleading by many on my behalf. I feel encouraged to press forward. My prayer is that you too may feel encouraged, trusting and knowing that God hears your prayers and pleas. As we approach Lent, a season of preparation for Easter, I hope you will listen and hear God's persistent voice through prayer, Scripture, and mentors.

CHAPTER 32

POCKETS

One of the traditions I had carried with me since childhood was celebrating the small stuff. As a numbers person, I loved celebrating benchmarks. On February 20, 2013, I celebrated one month home from the hospital. The next day, I celebrated meeting the six-week post-surgery mark. I was not quite sure what made six weeks so special, but many of my discharge restrictions were lifted after six weeks. I was most looking forward to being able to take a bath.

As had become my custom, I updated friends and family on passing these benchmarks and encouraged them to celebrate victories in their own lives. At this particular benchmark, I had a lot to report, I declared that "pockets" was my new favorite word for the day and it summed up my recent victories and challenges.

My mom had recently purchased for me a pair of dark blue sweatpants with pockets. They quickly became my favorite pair of pants and I wore them almost every day. With a sore and bloated abdomen, I only wore pants that had elastic or drawstring waistbands. My mom noticed that none of my wearable pants had pockets. As a result, when we went for our daily walks outside, I would have to carry my cell phone, keys, and tissues in my hands. But once I had pockets, my hands were free. I loved to talk with my hands, and so the addition of pockets made me smile. Furthermore, when I was in the house, I did not have to worry about remembering to pick up my cell phone and carry it around with me. It stayed with me in my pocket. Once again, I was celebrating the small stuff.

I also liked figurative pockets and thought about time in

terms of pockets. I felt like I was in the midst of a slow and lengthy season of healing, and that was overwhelming at times. My days continued to be long, so I liked thinking of each day as containing several pockets. In the past few weeks I had some marvelous pockets: I walked on the beach, got my hair cut, and was serenaded by a barbershop quartet that came to my home on Valentine's Day. I had pockets of time to read, to watch *The Carol Burnett Show* episodes, and to pray.

Most of my days consisted of pockets of laughter and pockets of tears. Pockets of epiphanies and encouragement, and pockets of confusion. Through the guidance of Scripture and of Priscilla Shirer in *Discerning the Voice of God*, I was reminded that God's voice was not one of guilt or condemnation (Isaiah 54:4, Romans 8:1, John 8:11). Instead, God's voice was one of love, truth, and peace (James 3:17).

A major revelation for me that came out of this study was that the Holy Spirit, which was the only one to know the thoughts of God (1 Corinthians 2:10-12), could lead two different people on two different paths, and both paths could be holy for those specific individuals (Romans 14). For example, what job to take, what food to eat, what movies to watch, what books to read, etc. For years I had felt confused about why some people felt called to avoid certain things and others did not. Romans 14 explained these differences and how we are to live in peace. I was so thankful for this explanation and to serve a God of peace and not division. In the back of my mind, I was beginning to wonder where God might call me to work and serve after I fully recovered from surgery.

I had been asking God for help in taking my eyes off of my circumstances and fixing them on the Lord. I hated pain, like most people, and felt it was my Achilles' heel. I believed I could handle just about anything – except for pain.

Now several weeks post-surgery, I was gaining confidence. I had the blood sugar testing down. I was able to get a drop of blood with my first stick and no longer required much concentration to check it. In addition, I was walking farther and faster, sleeping less, eating more, and overall progressing in the linear way I preferred. My pain had decreased to a point where I was able to go two days without any pain medicine. I thought I was ready to go to church and keep moving forward. Unfortunately, on February 16, a Saturday night, I was hit with horrible pain and could not fall asleep until 6 a.m. I rationalized that I had just let the pain get too bad before taking any medicine and therefore was unable to sleep. I was relieved Sunday night when I could sleep. Regrettably, Monday night felt like a replay of Saturday night; however this time the insomnia was accompanied by horrible stomach cramping. I quickly realized I had a stomach bug. I tried really hard to look on the bright side – that my mom was home with me, and I did not get the bug on a day we had doctors' appointments in Charleston. I thought, *Yes, I am looking above my circumstances.* My mom even encouraged me that this stomach bug was possibly accelerating getting toxins out of my body. *Yes, I will think positively.*

My pride started to swell. By Wednesday night I had survived forty-eight hours of running to the bathroom and not sleeping at night, while not taking any prescription pain medicine and managing to keep my blood sugars under control through my first bug. I hadn't purchased a billboard ad to say, "Look at amazing me," but I was feeling like I had licked this recovery. To be honest, I could not wait to gain some strength after the stomach bug, so that I could report on my progress via my blog to friends and family.

Then on Wednesday night, my pain quickly escalated to a 12 on a 1-to-10 pain scale. I cried as I took the breakthrough pain medicine, because not only was the pain unbearable, but my record was now broken. I also could not fall asleep until after 1 a.m. On Thursday night the pain came back, and again Friday afternoon. I humbly reported to friends and family that I was back to taking my pain medicine daily. My blood sugars also spiked because of the pain. I felt like I was back on my knees begging for mercy, and my eyes were primarily focused on my circumstances.

My beloved church family in Lancaster has a Lenten theme each year. In 2013 the theme was "Strength in Weakness." The devotionals helped to encourage and remind me that in my weakness, God's strength more clearly shines. I hate weakness in myself – about as much as I hate losing control. "Strong" and "in control" would be underlying descriptions of my ideal day, but I learned some sweet blessings from weakness and letting go. Before having chronic pain, I did not truly grasp Paul's words when he asked God to relieve him of a thorn that tormented him. God replied, "My grace is sufficient for you, for my power is made perfect in weakness." Paul's response was, "Therefore I will boast all the more gladly about my weaknesses, so that Christ's power may rest on me" (2 Corinthians 12:9-10, NIV). I certainly related to Paul begging Christ to relieve him of his pain. However, I would not have stopped asking for relief after only three requests.

I pondered, "God's grace is sufficient for me." I began to ask myself if I truly believed and accepted that God's grace is sufficient for me – When I am in pain? When I cannot sleep? When I am weary? This was a hard concept to swallow. I tried, when I got anxious, to breathe the prayer, "God's grace is sufficient for me," letting the truth sink in and rebuke lies.

In the midst of my pain and insomnia, I continued to do the Bible study with my mom. The words in Exodus 3:7 leapt off the page. God said to Moses, "I am aware of their [Israel's] suffering." I felt that God was reminding me once again that I was not forgotten.

I concluded my update to friends and family on February 22, 2013, with the following:

Thus, with hope and anticipation, I look forward to sharing how God's strength will continue to shine during this dry pocket.

I gratefully and humbly ask for your partnership in prayer. My prayer requests:

1) Wisdom and discernment to hear God's voice, particularly with knowing how to take care of this body. I am still waiting for the manual. :0)

2) Endurance for my husband, Jack. Needless to say, his sleep has been impacted this week by my insomnia. This weekend and next weekend he is leading retreats, and he is preaching this Sunday and next Sunday.

3) Peace for my parents. My parents have made a tremendous sacrifice to be apart so that my mom could care for me. I am grateful for so many who have encouraged and supported both of them. Friday, March 8th, my mom is flying home after being in SC for two months. My prayer is that my mom would feel at peace when she leaves, knowing I am okay, and that my parents would have peace right now as they miss one another.

I will conclude with a Scripture that has been extra special to me over the past ten years. In John 14:27, Jesus is quoted, saying, "Peace I leave with you; my peace I give to you. I do not give to you as the world gives. Do not let your hearts be troubled, and do not be afraid" (NIV).

Peace, love, and gratitude,
Becky

CHAPTER 33

SAYING GOODBYE

My mom invited me to come into her bedroom and wake her whenever I could not sleep. Prior to my hospital stays, I had been a sound sleeper, so I was not well-prepared for insomnia. Then when I was prescribed a strong sleeping pill, it helped me to fall asleep but made me disoriented in the middle of the night. I would enter my mom's bedroom crying uncontrollably and would bang my head against her bed in distress.

Regardless of the hour or of how much sleep my mom had gotten before I woke her up, many times out of a deep sleep, she would calmly pray over me, read devotionals, and get me hot tea to drink. I needed her soothing, tranquil voice to combat the frantic voice in my head. I would start to fall asleep in my mom's bed, and then I would wake up again. The scenario replayed countless times. However, my mom never made any amendments to her invitation for me to wake her.

My mom and doctor both felt I needed to stop taking the sleeping medicine, because it was actually making things worse. Stopping the sleeping medicine made me feel less crazy in the middle of the night, but I still could not sleep two consecutive nights in a row. In addition to the insomnia, I was battling diarrhea. Both of these were symptoms of pain medication withdrawal. I was irritable and cantankerous during the day from sleep deprivation and feeling literally depleted, but my mom continued to cheerfully take care of me despite her own limited energy. This was our pattern for about three weeks. I decided that my mom was a cross between Superwoman and a saint.

My mom and I continued to work on our Bible study each day, which gave me tremendous encouragement. My mom would remind me of each step of progress I had made so far in this recovery. It was so easy for me to get discouraged. My mom understood – on a level deeper than most of my friends and family – the physical anguish of narcotic withdrawal, as well as feeling like one's body would never be strong again. My mom's recovery from emergency surgery, only two years prior, gave me confidence when she told me, "Becky, the withdrawal symptoms will end. You are healing, and you are going to keep getting stronger."

Sometimes I would ask my mom multiple times in a twenty-four hour window, "Am I really going to get better? Are the withdrawal symptoms really going to end?" What I couldn't fathom, but my mom would remind me, was that God loved me even more than my mom did, and God had divine timing.

I knew before I even had surgery that the plan was for my mom to stay with me for two months. It was extremely generous of both my parents to sacrifice time together. My mom also forfeited time with her friends and her routine. But as the date for her flight home grew near, I became anxious. Many questions not only bounced around in my head, but I also asked my mom, "Who will go on walks with me? Who will help me count my carbs? Who will calm me down when I cannot sleep?"

My mom kept reassuring me that I would do just fine after she left. My mom also had great suggestions, like calling friends on my cell phone when I went for walks.

While it was bittersweet to say goodbye to my mom at the airport, God lavished my mom and me with hope in the days leading up to her departure and even the very day she flew out. On that day, Friday, March 8, my mom, Jack and I drove to Charleston for my two-month follow-up appointment with the surgeon. Dr. Adams exclaimed, "You are a star patient! You have put on a few pounds and maintained them. This is not typical at all during the first three months of recovery."

I could not take credit for this accomplishment. My mom's

encouragement to eat another bite, and the wonderful meals that our church family provided, were key to my weight gain triumph. I also believed all of the prayers and notes of encouragement had kept my spirits up and helped to propel me forward.

I shared with Dr. Adams my struggle with insomnia. God gave the surgeon wisdom to suggest medicine to help relax me before bed. Also, the surgeon increased my enzyme dosage to help me properly absorb my food. Thus, when we dropped my mom off at the airport that afternoon, she had extra reassurance that I would be okay.

It took me six days after my mom left to write a blog update. Typically, my procrastination on updates was fueled by difficult news. But this time I had lots of answers to prayer to share. I struggled to sit down at my laptop and write an update because, while I was doing so well, the memories of the long stretches of intense pain and thinking I would never survive were still fresh and tender. Every time I started typing, I would get a lump in my throat and my eyes would get watery. Finally, on Thursday, March 14, 2013, I took a big gulp, brushed my tears aside, took a deep breath, and courageously began to write:

> *I proclaim today with great joy and thanksgiving that I have gone ten days without pain or breakthrough pain medicine. A miracle indeed!*
>
> *I can hardly believe it myself.*
>
> *The absence of pain was initially overshadowed by insomnia and diarrhea. After over three weeks of wrestling with insomnia and having to take Imodium like it was candy, I am delighted to share that since Friday (March 8), I have had only one sleepless night and have not had to take any more Imodium.*
>
> *I believe in God's divine wisdom and love. He allowed the really hard stuff to happen while my mom was with me.*
>
> *I ended my last update with three prayer requests. All three have been answered far beyond how I could*

have imagined. Praise be to God!

1) Jack found an app that helps me keep track of my carbohydrate intake so I stay within my limits. It is easy, fast, and specific; it knows that a small Fuji apple from Trader Joe's is 22 grams of carbs. With time and technology and lots of prayers, I am slowly learning how to take care of this refurbished body.

2) Both of Jack's retreats went well, with stronger relationships formed, and there were no major disasters. God also gave Jack the words and energy to deliver two sermons, two Sundays in a row. The best part was having my dad, my sister, and my brother-in-law join me and my mom for a long weekend in February for my first Sunday back to church AND getting to hear Jack preach.

3) My parents are reunited in Pennsylvania after my mom spent two months showing me sacrificial love. It was bittersweet to say goodbye to my mom, but it helped that I got a star report from my surgeon the day my mom flew home.

Those are the answers to the three prayer requests from my last post. I have more answers to prayer to share. However, some have required patience.

My biggest headache was trying to get enough strips to check my blood sugar. My prescription was for four strips a day. Unfortunately, some of the strips were defective. Also, when my blood sugar was low, I was instructed to check it every fifteen minutes until it normalized. As a result, I could easily go through six or eight strips per day. Not surprisingly, in my first month I ran out of strips before my insurance allowed a refill. My pharmacy ended up giving me an emergency supply. I realized that this would be an issue each month going forward. I tried explaining the dilemma to my insurance company. They said I had to have my doctor write a letter. Therefore, I had my endocrinologist write a letter. This still was not sufficient. My request *had to go before a board. It was all very exhausting and aggravating. I was only trying to get enough supplies to follow my doctor's instructions and take care of my body. Of course, what it boiled down to was money. The strips were very expensive, and while I was paying over five hundred dollars a month for prescriptions, my insurance was paying even more. I kept feeling like everything that I thought I had insurance for was a façade. I have disability insurance, but every month I have to battle with them to prove I cannot work. I have health insurance, but now have to battle to get adequate prescription coverage. Now after many phone calls to my insurance company and the help of my doctors, my prescriptions are all approved for the quantity I need each month. This is a major victory and relief.*

My mom helped me and Jack complete our federal, state, and local taxes. With moving and having limited energy, gathering all of the information and entering it was a huge undertaking and accomplishment. I ended up having one hundred thirty-two medical receipts in 2012 that tallied up to over $11,000 in out-of-pocket expenses and close to three thousand miles driven for tests, doctor's appointments, hospital stays, and medication. It took me a total of three days to collect and sum my receipts.

I finished the Bible study I had worked on with my mom entitled Discerning the Voice of God *by* Priscilla Shirer. *Jack mentioned a new study to try called* The Grand Sweep. *Not only that, but we are doing it together! This is like a triple answer to prayer – 1) I was looking for a new study; 2) I wanted to do something with Jack that did not involve doctor's appointments; and 3) I was praying for something to spiritually nourish Jack as he works long hours leading and guiding others.*

Naturally after my mom left, there was a void. Jack is at work, and I am slowly recovering from my weeks of insomnia. We both needed something to look forward to and focus on. God knew just the thing. Friends from Lancaster are visiting Beaufort this month. It came as an unexpected surprise that has given us something to anticipate with joy.

With spring and Easter around the corner, there is a sense of new life and new beginnings. I am SO ready for a new beginning! I asked the surgeon this past Friday if my recovery time would be shorter, since I am doing so well. He said, "No, you still have four more months of recovery." While I would like to hit fast-forward and be done with this whole ordeal, I am thankful to have two hard months behind me.

I am getting anxious thinking about when or where I may work and how I might serve others. As I read over my last blog update and could see how faithful God has been to my prayer requests, I feel at peace boldly asking for prayers for those things that are weighing on my heart.

1) Prayers for discernment and direction for future employment. May I be patient and not be anxious about researching and prematurely applying for jobs.

2) To let my body continue to rest and heal even on days when I feel really good.

3) Prayers that I may offer this really raw and hard time to God with thanksgiving and ask for God's will to be done, that God will use this time to bless others.

I would be delighted to pray with you or for you regarding anything weighing on your heart. May joy and hope abound in your spring.

Blessings and gratitude,
Becky

After this update, I continued another eleven days without pain, totaling a twenty-one day stretch of pain-free living. I felt like I was experiencing euphoria like never before. It was hard to capture in words, but after such a long period of time with daily pain and the fear of daily pain, the absence of pain made me feel like I was flying. Maybe this was what Isaiah was referring to when he said, "Those who hope in the LORD will renew their strength. They will soar on wings like eagles; they will run and not grow weary, they will walk and not faint" (Isaiah 40:31, NIV). I could think and do things without being physically, mentally, and emotionally consumed with pain.

Praise be to God, I was also sleeping, eating without nausea, continuing to go for daily walks outside, and not feeling the grogginess of daily pain medicine. My blood sugars were behaving. I had followed through on my mom's idea to talk with friends on my phone while I walked. I was enjoying getting caught up with friends. In addition, some snags with my insurance paying hospital bills got reconciled, and I was even getting a reimbursement check. I also met someone who was visiting our church who had a connection with my alma mater. This small connection helped make me feel closer to friends far away. None of these things escaped my notice.

Palm Sunday I was singing Hosanna and waving my palm branch with more joy and thanksgiving than in previous years. As far as I was concerned, I was on top of the mountain and there was not a cloud in the sky.

On Sunday night, March 24th, as my new palm branch rested next to my bed, I had a horrible attack of pain. I was experiencing something called phantom pain; the source of the pain was gone (in my case, the inflamed pancreas), but the pain paths were still active and the pain was very real. It felt exactly like a pancreatitis attack. Very quickly my pain level went from bearable to excruciating. Thankfully Jack was with me and got me my breakthrough pain medicine, and within an hour it was under control.

It may sound strange, but I felt out of shape for dealing with pain. It felt more painful to me, because I had gone three weeks without pain. However, the worst part was that I no longer felt invincible. Like aftershocks from an earthquake, I had tremors of pain throughout the next week. Did I mention this was Holy

Week? Not a great time for a minister's wife to feel weak. I heard one minister refer to Holy Week as "holy-moly" week.

Praise be to God, I not only received the strength I needed to get through the week, but I was given a burst of energy for Easter weekend so that I could enjoy and celebrate it. Emotionally, my discouragement was instantly transformed into encouragement when friends from Lancaster arrived for a visit. This family had been a source of encouragement and inspiration long before I became ill. They had five beautiful children, and they had grown their family in part through adoption. One of their daughters was from Ethiopia. When I dreamed of our future family, I often thought of theirs.

Easter weekend was full of celebration and provision. The weather was beautiful, flowers were bursting with color everywhere, and a missed turn led to an amazing discovery. After we missed a turn while driving to the beach, our friends spotted a nature center and asked if we could stop there. There were fascinating hands-on activities and live animals inside the center. The family visiting us had asked about fishing, and the nature center provided free fishing poles to borrow.

In addition, we got to meet a vibrant turtle that only gets fed twice a week. Her feedings take place at noon, and it just so happened that we arrived at 11:45 a.m. on a day the turtle got fed. Any earlier or later and we would have missed this experience. Many times God does take care of the details, yet I fool myself into thinking that I am responsible for making things happen.

The holy week services were also saturated in provision and God's handiwork. Jack preached on Maundy Thursday and at the evening service on Easter Sunday, and God clearly provided the messages. The services wove together themes carried by the music, the Scripture, the litany, the prayers, and the sermon, which were all done by different people. I love the reinforcement of themes, and I view it as affirmation of God's hand at work.

I crashed physically and emotionally the next day, Easter Monday, which happened to be April 1. My friends were on their way back to Lancaster, Jack was back at work, and my energy was non-existent. I quickly took inventory and decided a day of rest was due. I reflected on my recent, joy-filled interactions with children, and I remembered Jesus' words to have faith like a child. *Goodness,* I thought, *I have some work to do!* On this same day, I found out that my dad's mother (my Nana) had fallen and broken her hip. This was no April Fool's joke. Instead of being the one in the hospital, this time I experienced what it was like to be far away from a loved one who was undergoing surgery. I felt helpless. I was thankful that prayer was not limited by spatial or geographic boundaries.

I am notorious for underestimating the time needed for a project or for recovery. My one day of rest stretched into a week of twice-daily naps. During this week of post-Easter recovery, I began reading a book entitled *One in a Million: Journey to Your Promised Land* by Priscilla Shirer. Priscilla talked about the strong parallels between the Israelites and Christians today. God freed the Israelites from Egypt, and God freed us from sin. The Israelites journeyed through the wilderness, and still Christians walk in our own wilderness of circumstances and choices. Of course, I was most focused on and excited about how to arrive at the land God has promised us.

As I read, I saw my Egypt as the bondage of pain, and I perceived the healing from pain as the parting of the Red Sea. However, like the Israelites, I had quickly forgotten the miracles and provision and started to grumble and complain, thinking, *Why am I so fatigued? Will I ever have the energy to be gainfully employed or to raise children?* I had gotten away from my attitude of gratitude and was sinking fast.

Thank goodness for reality checks. I reminded myself, *I am only three months out from major surgery. Healing takes energy, so fatigue is normal.* I felt like a newsflash went through my brain in big neon letters: *You are free from daily pain, and you are complaining about being tired?*

Time and time again, God has shown me that following His nudges leads to blessings. However, for some reason I get wimpy and become concerned with looking foolish. I took a step of faith (my faith sometimes feels like the size of a mustard seed) and asked someone I did not know very well if she would mind getting together and praying with me each week. I was glad I did. I needed to be re-centered for the week ahead. As I neared the one-year anniversary of my traumatizing ERCP at Johns Hopkins, my mind was flooded with flashbacks. The more I tried not to think about it, the more the memories and details haunted me. I kept telling myself, *I am safe. I am pain-free and tube-free now.* So why the fear? I prayed and prayed for peace and forward movement, but I felt not only stuck, but also in a downward spiral.

On April 8, 2013, I had a cleansing cry and let out all of the emotions and feelings I was trying so hard to suppress. I realized that if I wanted to have freedom, I had to forgive. I had to forgive the physicians at Johns Hopkins who made mistakes and compromised my health. I praised God for His help in giving me the strength to forgive, because it was hard and not natural. Reading the parable of the unforgiving debtor (Matthew 18:21-35) helped me to put things in perspective. To paraphrase the parable, a king forgave a huge debt, approximately $20 million, for Servant A – who immediately turned around and grabbed Servant B by the throat and demanded he repay his debt of $20. I grappled with how God, who knows everything I have done and everything I will do, still loves and forgives me. I concluded, *Surely, after so much forgiveness has been shown to me, I can forgive others.*

The next day, Tuesday, April 9, I felt at peace.

CHAPTER 34

THREE MONTHS

On Wednesday, April 10, I celebrated three months without a pancreas. I continued to celebrate my pain-free state. However, I noticed all week that my blood sugar levels had been lower and my energy was dwindling. I beefed up my carbs, but by Wednesday afternoon, I barely had the strength to get out of my chair and realized I really was not feeling well. A thought entered my head that said, "Check your temperature." I did, and I had a fever. I rarely ever have fevers. I checked my blood sugar. It was not going up like it should have after all I had eaten. It was actually dropping.

I started feeling shaky like I was going to pass out. Jack was in meetings and I did not want to call him, even though I was scared to my core. I texted a friend who was going to the church and asked, "When you see Jack, could you ask him to call me?" Next I unlocked the front door and called my amazing neighbor, Denise. She answered the phone, but she was at the school picking up her children. She told me not to move and that she was going to call another neighbor. Within a few minutes, a retired woman with dirt all down the front of her clothes came storming through my front door. Barbara had received the call from Denise while gardening and had immediately run over to my house.

It took her a minute to catch her breath, but I was so thankful to have someone with me. My biggest fear was passing out by myself. She sat next to me on the couch while I continued to drink apple juice and check my blood sugar. Barbara sat with me until Jack came home.

Jack was supposed to lead a class that evening, but the

senior pastor said, "Go, we can cover this." I was well aware that not all bosses would be so understanding. I continued to feel affirmed that we were at the right place.

I went to bed that night feeling defeated; fear started to creep in. I began to ponder, *Can I ever be in the house by myself? What if this happens again?* I could not sleep; this was my fourth night in a row of not being able to fall asleep until 2 a.m. or later. I was not in the mindset to be thankful, so I believe that the Holy Spirit nudged me to thank God. I started saying, "Thank you, Jesus," over and over. The more I said it, the more at peace I felt.

The following evening, I slept the entire night and was not even affected by a thunderstorm that woke Jack up at 3 a.m. I was especially thankful for the rest, because Friday, April 12, I had a marathon of doctors' visits in Charleston.

The first doctor I saw was a psychiatrist, which was a requirement for all transplant patients. I had only met this individual once before, and it had been for my psychological evaluation prior to surgery. During the previous visit I was concerned about the surgery, and I had just had sixteen vials of blood drawn. I was not really in the mood to talk. Now that the surgery was behind me, I felt much calmer and ready to talk. The psychiatrist was helpful, validated my feelings, and gave me great encouragement. She said I was in really good shape physically and emotionally for being three months post-surgery. I had little perspective on what was normal, but hearing from others who had seen patients undergo the same surgery gave me some understanding.

Next, I saw the surgeon who had said I was a poster child for the surgery. He was not concerned about my fatigue, because according to him, "after chronic pain and major surgery, you aren't going to just bounce back. Your body is healing, and that takes time." He also stated, "Many of my patients who are six months post-surgery are not doing nearly as well as you are doing now." This was definitely a perspective-bender. I had thought my recovery was creeping along.

The nutritionist said that eating more frequent small meals would help with my energy, but echoed the surgeon in saying that fatigue was normal three months after major surgery. She also gave me some new vitamins to try.

I shared with the endocrinologist, the diabetes doctor, about my low blood sugar episode. He explained, "When your immune system is fighting a virus, your blood sugars are going to be lower. You reacted perfectly when you started to feel shaky. The best thing to do when you are sick is to rest and stay hydrated." The endocrinologist then asked if I would be willing to talk to another doctor. At first I was confused, thinking my beloved endocrinologist no longer wanted me to be his patient. My endocrinologist quickly clarified that his coworker had seen my chart and heard talk of me and just wanted to meet me. Now I understood his question.

I replied, "Sure."

An elderly woman with a walker entered the room. She exclaimed, "I wanted to meet you and see that you really exist. I could not believe how well a person without a pancreas could be doing. Your blood sugar levels amaze me." I could not believe a doctor was excited to see and meet me.

All of my doctors said they did not need to see me for three months. Since I had always seen them monthly, this felt like a huge vote of confidence.

I returned home from Charleston feeling pretty humbled. I had been grumbling about my slow progress, and it turned out I was way ahead of schedule. I still felt weak and was fighting this virus, but I was emotionally back to soaring.

I had read in the study by Priscilla Shirer that the Israelites were in the wilderness for *three months* before they heard from God at Mt. Sinai. Since I was now three months post-surgery, I took this as encouragement and hope that I would also hear and discern God's voice – in my case, about future employment.

VACATION

Three and half months after my surgery, I was more than ready for a celebration vacation. My parents generously paid for my sister and her husband, as well as Jack and me, to all sail together with them on a nine-day Caribbean cruise. This vacation was to celebrate my mother's sixtieth birthday. The original date for the voyage had been set for January 2012. However, it had been postponed because of my illness and frequent hospitalizations. Now fifteen months later, the full celebration was about to begin.

Once again it felt like divine timing. I was ready for a vacation from isolation. Jack was ready for a vacation from the stress of beginning a new job. My parents were ready for a vacation from being apart and from caregiving. This was our first family vacation with my new brother-in-law, Michael. We were all eager to get to spend some non-wedding-related time together.

I had been on four previous cruises, so my anticipation grew with each day. However, this was going to be Jack's first cruise, and he was a little apprehensive.

As I began packing for our trip, it occurred to me that I had never previously flown as a diabetic. Questions began swirling through my head: *Do I need a special note from my doctor to carry syringes and insulin? Do I need to get clearances ahead of time, like those who fly with guns?* Thankfully, a close and dear friend of mine had been a diabetic since childhood. I picked up the phone and called her. My first question was, "How do you fly?" After a few minutes of clarifying my abrupt and out-of-context question, I was reassured that the TSA workers would not confiscate my needle caps, insulin, or syringes. I packed plenty of all my medications. Not only would I be out at sea, but the ports were not in the United States. I wanted to be sure I was prepared and could really relax on vacation.

I breathed a sigh of relief when I went through airport security and did not even have my carry-on searched. When our flight landed in San Juan, Puerto Rico, my parents, sister, and brother-in law were there to greet us at the baggage claim. Their flight had arrived several hours earlier, so they had already had lunch. My parents asked if Jack or I wanted anything to eat. I answered, "No, I just want to get on the cruise ship."

We all piled into a taxi van and headed to the cruise ship.

As soon as I stepped onto the long gangway that connected the cement dock to the *ginormous* boat, I felt officially on vacation. No more thinking or planning needed to be done.

Jack and I explored the boat. Our first stop was our cabin room. I warned Jack that the cabins were small, but not to fret because we would not be spending much time awake in them. All of my previous cabins had just enough space for the bed, and no natural light. I was shocked when I opened the door and saw a sitting area and carpet. This room had floor space and a porthole window. We quickly dropped off our carry-on luggage and set off to find some food. Jack inquired, "Honey, do you think they have food out now?"

"Oh yes!" I answered, "There is always food out on a cruise."

Jack seemed surprised when we walked into a room that had a huge buffet with all sorts of salads, fresh fruit, side dishes, main dishes, and desserts. It may have been 4 p.m., but we were not alone in eating. Many other guests had also found the buffet.

We then stumbled upon the theater, library, pool, and spa, and we walked through an art gallery and casino and did some window-shopping. After flying, it felt wonderful to be walking. We had to scurry back to our room to get changed to arrive at the dining room on time. I put my glucose meter and prescription medication in my small purse. I could not wait for Jack to experience the attentive care of the wait staff and enjoy the delicious multi-course meal.

After we ordered, I checked my blood sugar level. I was horrified when I realized that I needed insulin. By getting off my regular eating schedule, my blood sugar was higher than normal. I had not given myself any insulin in over two months, so I had left it in our cabin. I embarrassedly excused myself from dinner and quickly walked back to the cabin. It was a good half-mile or so back to our room, so I was out of breath when I opened the cabin door. I pulled up my skirt and looked away as I injected my thigh. I quickly hurried back to the dining room. I had joked with my endocrinologist that he could not look at my blood sugar levels from the dates of the cruise. The one thing I had not considered was that while individuals can take breaks from work, diabetics cannot take a vacation from monitoring their blood sugar. I was a little upset that I had not even misbehaved and already had to take insulin.

The rest of the cruise, I enjoyed fresh fruit and desserts, but in moderation and spaced out. Thankfully, I did not need any additional insulin during the trip. At some point it dawned on me that at this time a year ago, I had a PICC line and could not eat anything. Now I was on a cruise and was sinking my teeth into lots of tasty treats. This quickly turned my discouragement to praise.

Before the cruise was over, Jack was ready to book our next one. We really enjoyed a stress-free time of reading by the pool, walking around different ports, and enjoying a variety of delicious meals.

Returning home had both easy and hard adjustments. Returning to our spacious house was not difficult. I had prepared myself for missing my family. But I was shocked at how easily I became exhausted. While I had felt fine on the cruise, I had not been doing laundry, preparing meals, washing dishes, or doing any other housework. I quickly became discouraged by what felt like steps backwards in my journey to recovery.

Even with fatigue, I searched and read job descriptions for several hours a day. In some ways it was like an addiction. I had trouble stopping. I did not put any filters on my job searches with the exception of distance. Subsequently, I looked at everything from travel agent to vet assistant.

I came across two amazing-sounding jobs and did some research to inquire further. The first one was a math tutor. The company was a tutoring franchise that specialized just in math. Unfortunately, the commute was an hour, the pay was close to minimum wage, and there were no benefits. I also discovered that they tutored in small groups, and I preferred tutoring one-on-one.

The second job I came across was a teacher for the homebound. The employee would go to the homes of students who could not come to school due to health issues, and she or he would teach them one-on-one. It was a part-time position and it sounded perfect. I could use my experience as a medical patient to have true empathy for the students. Prior to my illness, I would have been freaked out by PICC lines and IVs.

The job was posted through the county school district and required a South Carolina teaching certification. I called to find out if I could apply with my expired teaching certification from another state and was told no. I looked into what was required to earn a South Carolina teaching certification. In my case, I would need to get a master's in education first. I felt discouraged. I had teaching experience and nine years of professional math tutoring experience, not to mention an undergraduate degree in mathematics. I regretted not finishing my master's in education right after college. However, I could not justify now spending time or money on a master's to qualify for a part-time job.

I had a strong desire to glorify God through my employment, and I felt like I needed some spiritual duct tape to put myself together after the door shut on both of these "dream" jobs.

My mom and Jack gently reminded me that I still had two more months before I could work, and maybe pouring so much energy into job searching was premature. However, I really wanted to get my ducks in a row. I wanted to be productive in my waiting. Plus, the idea of working gave me hope that I would have a routine and meet some new people. I now lived in a small community, and job opportunities were very limited. I did not want to miss an opportunity.

After four months without a pancreas, I asked for continued prayers for peace, healing, and discernment. I wanted to be realistic about the type of work I pursued.

Unfortunately, over the next few weeks I became more and more obsessed with online job searches. I stressed myself out over trying to find something that made financial sense, I was qualified for, I was passionate about, and I could handle energy-wise. Instead of staying grounded in my trust of God and the peace the Lord provides, I floundered in distress. My mind became so future-focused that I had little energy or concentration for anything else.

It took the unexpected death of a beloved church member on May 23 for me to remember that life is short. Jim Wescott had fought cancer bravely for many years. Jack and I had visited him at MUSC and shared details about our cruise. He was an avid boater and shared dreams of places he would like to visit.

By God's grace, the funeral was twelve hours before we had to leave for the airport to fly to Chicago for my dear friend Annie's wedding. I was blessed to be present at the celebration of one man's life and then able to be present with my husband at the celebration of a new life through marriage.

The week after the wedding felt like a crash from a very high building. I had anticipated being tired after a week of high energy and emotions. However, I did not anticipate the pain and its various forms. I started having pain and passed out at our kitchen table early Tuesday morning, only three days after Annie's wedding. I attributed it to my sleep schedule being off and my body tired from travel.

Then on Wednesday evening when Jack came home from work, I was not feeling well. He knew that sometimes I would not feel well just because I had been at home all day by myself. Thus, Jack encouraged me to go with him to a potluck dinner at a church member's home.

I checked my blood sugar at home before we left, as I continued to be self-conscious about checking my blood sugar in public. My blood sugar was normal, so I took my dinner medicine with a few gulps of water and then was ready to go. I didn't want to mess with a purse for the medication – and the church member only lived a few miles from our home.

The large home was packed with church members. I knew that one woman worked on a military base as a civilian. I decided to strike up a conversation with her about what it was like working on a military base, and to ask if she knew about any job openings that I might qualify for.

After a little while of standing and chatting, I excused myself. I was starting to feel nauseous and lightheaded, but I did not want to make a scene. I found a chair and sat down, thinking my blood pressure must be low. I tried looking around to find Jack, but did not see him. I asked someone if they had recently seen Jack. Since Jack was a pastor, everyone knew who he was – even if I didn't know who I was speaking to. The woman asked if I was feeling okay. At this point, I was in a lot of pain and was soaked with sweat. I replied honestly, "No, I think I need to go home. Would you mind getting him?"

The next thing I knew, I was horizontal on a couch with people crowding around. I felt a cold washcloth on my forehead. I did not recognize all of the faces, but thankfully one of them was Jack's. Jack had apparently caught me just as I was slipping off the bar-stool-height chair. He had carried me over to the couch. I thought, *So much for not making a scene.*

The civilian employee that I had talked to, Jodie, was a nurse. Jodie knew how to take action. She shouted to the hostess, "I need some orange juice and some cheese." She looked at me and said, "Becky, I think your blood sugar dropped. Where is your meter?"

I felt like the worst diabetic and confessed, "At home. I checked my blood sugar before we came over, and it was in the low one hundreds. I usually only check it before meals and bed."

Jack offered to go home and get it, but I did not want him to leave me. I was so scared and embarrassed. I drank the orange juice and ate the cheese. I was informed that my color was coming back. As soon as I felt strong enough to stand up, I asked Jack to take me home.

When we got home, I checked my blood sugar and it was normal. I did not know what to think. My pain level was still high, so I took some breakthrough pain medicine.

The next day, I once again was shaken to my core and felt vulnerable being home alone. However, the pain medicine made me groggy, so I slept most of the day.

The following day, Friday, I had an annual appointment with my new South Carolina gynecologist. I mentioned my recent passing out. She asked if I had any changes to diet, medicine, etc. I was not sure why I had not made the connection earlier, but over the previous few weeks I had been slowly decreasing a nerve blocking pain medicine in hopes of increasing my energy. Her hypothesis was that my pain had previously been masked and now my body was responding to the pain by shutting down. She wondered if the cause for the pain may be scar tissue or an adhesion that was affecting my digestion. She shared, "The good news is because you are not vomiting, you do not have a blockage."

This really did not feel like good news. My first thought was, *No, I am healing. I don't want complications, nor do I have time for them. I am flying to Pennsylvania in five days for another friend's wedding.*

I called MUSC and explained the situation. Fortunately, they got me an appointment the day before I flew north. I concluded my five month update to friends and family with three prayer requests: First, to pray that I could hold on to hope and not be discouraged by this pothole in the road to recovery. Second, to pray for conclusive answers on Tuesday, and a simple solution to the pain and ultimately to the issue. Third and lastly, to pray for another safe and joyful opportunity to celebrate and see loved ones.

CHAPTER 36

FUTURE PLANS

As I packed for my third trip in less than three months, employment continued to be in the forefront of my mind. I made a mental note: *I prefer a job with minimal to no travel.* While I loved traveling to see friends and family, my strength and endurance were decreased after each trip. Traveling for work would not be a good fit.

I smiled to myself as I packed my diabetic supplies this time without anxiety or fear. I reflected on the fact that almost every job search in our area resulted in medically connected job opportunities. I wondered if maybe I was to use my experience as a patient to be a compassionate nurse or physician's assistant.

Tuesday, June 11, Jack drove me to Charleston. We had a brief appointment with Dr. Adams. He believed my pain was nerve related, but in order to rule out any complications from surgery he ordered a CT scan, blood work, and an endoscopy. I appreciated that I could be seen by Dr. Adams on such short notice and that he could put our minds at ease. He prescribed an increase in my nerve blocking pain medicine.

As I checked out and paid my copay, I went ahead and scheduled the tests Dr. Adams had ordered. I was surprised when I was informed that I could have a CT scan performed that day, as well as my blood work. I thought, *Great, let's get them out of the way while I am here.*

The hospital employee informed me that I should go ahead and have my blood work done and she would call to receive authorization from my insurance for a CT scan. I was instructed not to eat before the CT scan.

An hour after I had the blood work completed, Jack and I checked back with the scheduler, because we had not received further instructions. She told us, "The typical time it takes insurance companies to approve a CT scan is between fifteen minutes and one hour."

After multiple phone calls and the intervention of several supervisors, my CT scan was finally approved. This process ended up taking five hours. Unfortunately, after nine hours of not having anything substantial to eat, my blood sugars were off and I felt weak. I began dry heaving and could not get down the radioactive, chalky drink that was required for the CT scan. I went up to the receptionist in the waiting room and asked if a clear drink option was available. The receptionist knew nothing of this option, but she said she would have a nurse come out and meet with me in the waiting room.

A few minutes later, a very kind and compassionate nurse came over to where I was sitting. The trash can at my feet gave away my dilemma. I explained to the nurse, "I had a CT scan done many years ago in the ER and they gave me a clear liquid to drink. I am trying my best, but I am not having any luck keeping the chalky drink down. I have really bad gag reflexes. I am so sorry."

The nurse sympathetically said, "No need to apologize. I will go check and see if the clear liquid is an option for your test." She returned with two cups filled with clear liquid. The nurse graciously stated, "Do the best you can. If you can get one cup down, that will be sufficient."

Once again I thought, *MUSC staff needs to provide tutorials for other hospitals.* I remembered being yelled at by nurses and technicians on more than one occasion for not being able to keep down a radioactive drink. Someone once gruffly told me that by not keeping down the concoction, I was wasting everyone's time. What a stark contrast. By God's grace and the friendly support of the nurse, I swallowed one cup of radioactive juice and had the CT scan completed. I tried to watch as the nurse inserted the IV for the test, but I felt queasy and ended up looking away. As much as I wanted to be brave,

I realized I was not wired to work in a medical field.

Wednesday morning we had a brief and direct flight from Charleston to Baltimore. We loaded our suitcases into a rental car and headed north. I shuddered as we passed the exit for Johns Hopkins. I sent up silent praises for MUSC. As we turned off the highway and traveled familiar roads to my parents' house, I had a weird feeling of returning home. This was both Jack's and my first trip back to Lancaster since moving to South Carolina. Because I had been blessed to see my family and friends, it had not dawned on me that we had been gone for nine months. For a moment, I felt like I never wanted to leave. On our two previous trips, I had not felt the warm-and-fuzzy "it is good to be home" feeling as we drove back to Beaufort. I wondered if Beaufort would ever feel like home.

Fortunately, I did not have much time to process my thoughts because of our full schedule. We had both sets of family, friends, former co-workers, and former church members to visit. In addition, Jack officiated my childhood friend's wedding. The wedding was fun and fascinating with Mexican decorations and traditions woven into the Pennsylvanian event. My dear friend Ashley, the bride, married a handsome gentleman from Mexico. As I thought about my adjustment to South Carolina, it seemed like an anthill of an adjustment compared to what Ashley faced when she moved to Mexico. She not only was immersed in a different culture, but had learned a new language.

I returned to Beaufort terribly homesick and, unsurprisingly, tired from another trip. I wondered if I would ever be able to return to Lancaster without my heart being ripped out. It didn't help that my pain's frequency and intensity continued to increase. The pain kept me from sleep, which caused fatigue and frustration. However, as I looked back at my three prayer requests from my previous update, I realized they had all been answered.

My third prayer request was for a safe and joyful opportunity to celebrate and see loved ones. Jack and I had the joy of seeing many friends and family in a relatively short period of time. Although I was always thankful for the phone and e-mail to stay in touch over a distance, my favorite form of communication was in person. God blessed me with opportunities to catch up with individuals who had known me for years and with whom my guard fell down naturally and instantly. I was more aware than ever of the gift of established friendships. I joked with my close friends and said, "Thanks for always accepting me just as I am, missing organs and all!" As I reflected, I realized that every day on my recent trip to Pennsylvania had been truly joy-filled. As a bonus, I met people I had never previously met, but who had been praying for me. This was a tremendous honor. God not only provided me with many wonderful memories, but I also was kept safe and had no health hiccups.

My second prayer request had been for conclusive answers Tuesday at MUSC and a simple solution to the pain. The CT scan and blood work came back normal. I had an endoscopy scheduled for the end of July. I followed up with my PCP, Dr. Kessel, after my trip, and he agreed with Dr. Adams' assessment that my pain was nerve related.

My first request had been to hold onto hope and not be discouraged by this pothole in the recovery process. This continued to be a daily plea for me. My mind was so ready and excited to work, but my physical body was terribly unpredictable.

I decided on the fourth of July to send an update to friends.

Happy 4th of July! Many thanks to all who have contributed to the freedoms Americans get to enjoy every day. I was reflecting on all of the freedoms I am blessed with. Many of the freedoms I have been offered are not mandated by the government, but instead have come in the form of invitation from friends: the freedom and space to vent, to cry, and to ask unanswerable questions. Thank you!

In six days I will reach the six-month mark of being

pancreas-free (on July 10th). I have longed for this day with great anticipation. I envisioned being able to work and being "normal." As my sister reminded me, normal is only a setting on the dryer. As a result, I am slowly accepting my "new normal."

I continued on to provide an update on my appointment at MUSC and note how my prayer requests had been answered. Next I humbly shared some of my vulnerable moments.

This past weekend I felt like my little world was shattered. I rode with Jack as we ran some errands. After a few stops, I was exhausted and felt ill. I had to come home and lie down. My stamina and strength were better three months ago. What was happening?! I e-mailed Lisa, the MUSC patient who had her pancreas removed in 2009. She encouraged me that it was normal to become tired easily, and four years after her surgery she continues to have to rest frequently. I had been so excited to begin working and was looking at online graduate school programs. Now I can't even go to the grocery store without a nap before and after. I came across the words from Isaiah 30:15 (NLT): This is what the Sovereign Lord, the Holy One of Israel, says: "Only in returning to me and resting in me will you be saved. In quietness and confidence is your strength."

I am attempting to rest and trust that my strength comes from the Lord.

This past Sunday morning (June 30th), after feeling like I was going to vomit and pass out, I lay down and cried out to God. I had not slept the past two nights, and the pain was becoming unbearable. I lamented that this was not the life I envisioned for myself. What child or student dreams of being disabled and weak at age thirty?! I desperately wanted hope and reassurance. I tried for a second time to get ready for church. As I was brushing my hair, I looked at a Scripture I had tacked up on my mirror. A very familiar verse from Jeremiah (29:11 NLT): "For I know the plans I have for you," declares the Lord, "plans to prosper you and not to harm you, plans to give you hope and a future."

I had read this verse so many times, but today the final words struck me. I am promised a hope and a future. That is what I want and need. I felt as if this verse had been written today to answer my cry. By God's grace, I made it to church and got to hear my husband preach an exceptionally powerful sermon. Guess what verse was in the bulletin? Jeremiah 29:11. I almost started to cry. God wanted to be sure I knew that I have hope and a future via the Lord.

Jack preached on Elijah and Elisha. To keep them straight, J comes before S in the alphabet. EliJah was a prophet who taught EliSha. EliSha's request was to have a spirit like his prophet teacher, EliJah. Jack spoke about how we can be EliJahs and be role models and leaders to EliShas in our life. Jack also encouraged the congregation to think about ourselves as EliShas and look for mentors, or EliJahs, in our life. I reflected on the EliJahs in my life, who have helped mold and shape me. My brain is like Jell-O, but I can think of ten off the top of my head.

I had hoped to be a teacher post-recovery, but at this point it is not looking likely. I started to feel sad and then remembered that I have hope and a future. There was a volunteer opportunity to help local individuals in the community prepare for the GED. I began to think, "Maybe I will be a teacher in an untraditional way. Only God knows. Regardless, I have hope and a future!"

What came next, I would have never imagined.

A lady in our church who has shown great compassion to many, including myself, came up to me and said she had to tell me what a wonderful sermon

Jack preached. My favorite compliments in the world are ones about my beloved husband, so my day was made!

Then she continued on to say that she had to tell me that she was reflecting on the EliJahs in her life – and that I was one. What?! I am half her age and she has only known me for nine months. She survived cancer and the death of her first husband. What could she possibly learn from me?! This is not a plug for myself, but a two-fold blessing. God heard my distressed plea for hope. I have felt stuck, like an al dente noodle thrown against a wall. I have had a narrow picture of what abundant life looks like, and God is showing me that there are many things I am oblivious to and do not see, like making a positive impact on someone's life. Second, this just goes to show, you never know who is watching and being influenced by you!

Your prayers certainly have influenced my life. I am so thankful and humbled that I am remembered in others' prayers.

Yesterday I stumbled upon a blog written by someone who had chronic pancreatitis and had the same surgery as I did to remove her pancreas and have her islet cells transplanted into her liver. The blog is www.mylifeafterpancreatitis.blogspot.com. She posted on January 2, 2013, "I have survived six years post surgery, taking each day as they come. I have attempted to be transparent to all. I still have pain, and there are days that are spent in bed flat, but there are days that are full of joy."

I scrolled through her posts and came across one that she wrote seven months after surgery. She talked about how she feels like someone has kicked her all around her ribs. I have been telling Jack how I feel like someone has taken brass knuckles to my ribs. There is hope and joy in knowing someone else has had a similar experience, especially because I start to feel crazy. This is an unexpected gift and blessing as I try to navigate my new normal.

Please know that prayers do get answered. I received a card in the mail yesterday that declared, "No ocean can hold it back. No river can overtake it. No whirlwind can go faster. No army can defeat it. No law can stop it. No distance can slow it. No disease can cripple it. No force on earth is more powerful or effective than the power of PRAYER." Can I get an Amen?!!!

Thank you for your powerful prayers. I pray that you may be encouraged that God has plans for you that include hope and a future.

CHAPTER 37

WHAT DO YOU DO?

One of the customary questions everyone asks when meeting a new person is, "So what do you do?" It was an innocent question, and in the past the answer had been simple for me. I would answer, "I am a commercial credit analyst for a community bank and enjoy tutoring math on the side." I used this answer until we moved to South Carolina. My answer then changed to preparing for major surgery and recovering from major surgery. Now that I was past the six month mark post-surgery, I felt like recovering from surgery was an outdated answer.

One particular day, Jack was introducing me to a new couple at our church. They immediately asked the dreaded, "What do you do for a living?"

Jack chimed in, "She takes care of me and keeps me in line." The couple picked up that Jack was trying to be humorous. However, they pressed further.

"Do you have a full-time job?"

I am not sure if Jack had thought of this response earlier or if it came to his mind at that moment, but he replied, "Becky's full-time job is working on healing." Well, that halted the questioning.

Later that day, Jack made a paper sign for me and put it at my place at our kitchen table. It stated, "I am working on healing."

When I discovered the sign and asked about it, Jack kindly replied, "To remind you of your full-time job. I don't want you to forget that you have a full-time job, and it takes a lot of hard work and effort. I am so proud of you." Jack also had business cards made with my name and the blog address. He did everything he could to restore dignity and remind me that my value was not tied to a job title or paycheck.

I did my best to cling to my new job description and take seriously "working on healing." I continued to monitor my glucose levels. I filled my gratitude journal with blessings. I prayed and continued to read things that nourished my spirit. I also continued to send updates in hopes of connecting with others with pain or suffering, and to glorify God through recounting answers to prayers.

My biggest concern about my surgery, besides the initial post-surgery pain, had been being a diabetic. But now I could take my blood sugar after one prick and rarely needed to give myself insulin. I tried to remind myself, *Becky, you had worried about something that now is not a big deal. Right now you are worried about being strong enough to work, but in the future you will look back and realize this was not worth stressing over.*

However, I did have two immediate concerns that needed my attention as I worked on healing. The first was having to run to the bathroom immediately after eating any food. If it had not been so painful, it would have been comical. I joked with Jack that if my digestive system got paid based on productivity, mine would be making some serious overtime. The second concern was controlling my nerve pain.

On Sunday, July 28, the day before my eighth endoscopy, I e-mailed friends once again sharing my challenges and hopes.

Sharp, stabbing pain has returned to my ribcage. The pain has increased to the point that this past Wednesday night, I prayed for the rapture to come. I am ready for a new body and to be in a place without pain or tears. However, God reminded me of my future children, and I could not help but change my prayer request to strength and wholeness to be a good mother.

I could not sleep several nights this past week due to pain, so I prayed for everyone I could think of. Due to my foggy memory, I am sure I prayed for many individuals multiple times. I also felt compelled to pray for groups of people, especially those who are treading water and just trying to keep their heads above water. I feel empathy for those experiencing loss – loss of a loved one, a job/career, or a dream. My heart is still adjusting to the longer than anticipated recovery from surgery.

Part of my current struggle is that I am a "math person" who likes to plot points and make projections. Right now my pain and energy are not trending in the desired direction. I have become discouraged because I am feeling worse now than I was three months ago. However, I am comforted by remembering God's faithfulness in the past. I picture myself holding a lantern, because figuratively I can only see one arm's length in front of me. Therefore, I ask for discernment from God for just the next step, even though I impatiently want directions for the next ten miles.

Tomorrow at 9 a.m., I will have my eighth endoscopy. I feel like I should be a professional at IV's and hospitals and medical tests, but I am not. The smells and the gowns cause a lot of past memories to erupt. My prayer requests are for peace and a simple solution to my latest pain and digestive gymnastics.

The consecutive days of pain, sleepless nights, and frequent runs to the bathroom have worn me down. The image that comes to mind is of ocean waves. It takes a sizeable wave to knock a person down, but once down, little waves can prevent a person from collecting herself, regaining orientation and balance, and ultimately standing up. I trust and hold on to the hope of better days and blessings rooted in purpose. I know that a good attitude is essential for survival. My toolbox of attitude boosters includes: scripture, music, inspiring stories, and thoughts of my future children. The latter, as previously mentioned, are what help me to keep fighting when I feel like giving up.

I have been reading about different individuals who

*have been conduits for healing, who have first
experienced suffering. This is not to glorify suffering, but
to acknowledge that transformation can be a by-product.
I want to be a conduit for healing. I would prefer for my
updates to have neatly tied bows with no loose ends.
However, my life has been significantly improved by
others' transparent sharing. Thus, I humbly aspire and
hope that sharing my work-in-progress life will nourish
others who are struggling.*

*With gratitude and love,
Becky*

The following day, Jack and I woke up early and headed to
MUSC. Even though my brain was groggy from an early
morning alarm, my mind still swirled with questions. I
wondered what the doctor would find and if correcting the
issue would require an additional surgery.

As the nurse was getting me prepped for the endoscopy,
she said, "I have some questions for you." She began reading
down a list, "Do you have heart problems?"

"No," I stated.

"Any lung problems?"

"No."

"High blood pressure?"

"No."

"Cancer of any kind?"

"No."

With each answer, gratitude began to well up inside me. I
had been so focused on and used to sharing all of my health
issues and medications that I had overlooked all of my body's
organs and systems that were properly functioning. The
reminder of all of the health in my body provided me with
tremendous peace and joy.

When I woke up and saw Jack's face, I informed him that I
was next in line for the endoscopy. I was confused and dazed
when he told me it was all over. The procedure was over

literally before I knew it.

However, the best news was that my esophagus and stomach lining looked good. In addition, where I had surgery was healing properly and I had no adhesions. I felt so relieved.

The only issue seen was that food was still sitting in my stomach – after fifteen hours of fasting. A normal stomach empties forty-five minutes after eating. This may sound twisted, but this was an answer to prayer. I wanted the doctors to find something small, so that they could address the source of the pain.

After the endoscopy results, I could not wait to get home to type up an update. I always loved the image of being held in God's hand. At this moment, I imagined the prayers of others lifting me up as if I was crowd surfing. I felt the outpouring of prayers were a way God's hands were at work.

The day after my endoscopy, I began volunteering at a GED camp. It was held at a church, but not the church where my husband was a pastor. It was a four-week camp, and I helped to review the math concepts and problems one-on-one with a young adult for two hours a day. Most of the other volunteers were retired. I felt blessed to be able to help and knew this would not have been a possibility had I been gainfully employed. The tutoring also confirmed that I was not ready to work outside the home full-time. The two hours of tutoring consumed all of my day's energy and concentration.

I also began eating smaller meals, which helped my digestion, but unfortunately did not diminish my stabbing rib pain. Instead, my rib pain continued to increase in intensity. Jack suggested that I make an appointment with Dr. Kessel, my PCP. I reluctantly called to schedule an appointment and could be seen the same day. My PCP predicted I had a muscular-skeletal problem and ordered an X-ray, prescribed an anti-inflammatory medication, and referred me to a physical therapist (PT).

Although the X-ray came back normal, the anti-inflammatory medication provided some instant relief. My hands and knees had felt swollen, but I thought this was from

**Sell your books at
sellbackyourBook.com!**
Go to sellbackyourBook.com
and get an instant price
quote. We even pay the
shipping - see what your old
books are worth today!

Inspected By: martha_chavez

00043274272

0004327 **4272** S

the humidity. After just one dose of the medicine, all my joints felt better and I had less rib pain lying down.

Going to a physical therapist required me to find courage once again. I hated meeting new individuals in the medical field and having to retell my medical history. I felt judged. Of course I projected the judgment on myself, believing that others looked at me as someone who just could not get it together. I look healthy, so why could I not just be healthy?

The physical therapist's office reminded me of a mix between a doctor's office and a gym. A large room had all sorts of exercise equipment, and several little rooms each had a medical exam table.

The physical therapist that Dr. Kessel had recommended discovered that two of my ribs were stuck and not moving properly. In addition, three of my vertebrae were out of alignment. My posture has been compromised over the past two years from hunching over in pain. My treatment plan was physical therapy twice a week and daily stretches to strengthen my core and improve my posture. Almost instantly my sleep quality and energy improved. I felt better than I had in over a year. I still tired easily and required naps, but I was grateful to take fatigue over pain any day.

Between the PT and the tutoring appointments, I was getting out of the house and feeling really positive. However, with one phone call I temporarily let go of my joy and celebration.

I received a phone call from my private disability insurance company. They usually sent letters requesting additional paperwork, so the phone call caught me off-guard. In this phone call, the insurance employee asked harassing questions like, "Aren't you young to be on disability? Don't you want to work?"

I called Jack, totally distraught. He reminded me that I am working on healing. Jack also instructed me to, in the future, only take calls when he was present. I tried my best to unsubscribe from the guilt and the lie that I was not trying hard enough.

I shared with my neighbor and friend Denise my struggle with the disability insurance company. Denise was as appalled and irate as Jack was. She reassured me that they were just bullies and to ignore their twisted jabs. She understood, because she, too, was used to hearing, "You don't look sick. You look fine." While many times this was meant to be a compliment, it was hurtful. It implied that we somehow were exaggerating our health problems or that we just really did not have serious medical issues.

I always felt better talking to Denise. I asked her if she thought I would be strong enough to be a mother in the future and asked how she continued to be a mother to five energetic daughters. Denise shared that she prayed every morning for the strength for that day. The request reminded me that God had provided enough manna in the wilderness each day for the Israelites.

Denise also shared that she and her family were moving. Her husband had received a job offer for a position four hours away. I felt heartbroken to be losing the one person in my new community that I felt like I could really relate to. I tried once again not to focus on my circumstances and instead on Jesus. I tried to be grateful for our time that had overlapped in Beaufort. Denise's family moved in August of 2013.

In September, I half-joked that in the past two years I had worked on a master's degree in suffering. As a new school year began, I was optimistic that a new degree was underway. I ended my September 2nd update with:

> *I pray that I would be open to the lessons that each day holds. Ecclesiastes reminds us that there is a season for everything. May you encounter a season of purging what is not from God (fear, lies, etc.) and instead clothe yourself with God's armor.*

CHAPTER 38

HEALTH OVER JOB

With the absence of Denise and her family, I was ready to move to a different neighborhood. It was painful driving by their former home every time I pulled in or out of our driveway, and Jack and I were interested in purchasing a house. Jack and I worked with Greg, the same realtor who had helped us find our rental home. Several homes appeared to match our criteria and budget – but any that we were interested in seemed to go under contract immediately after we had a tour. The ironic thing was several of the houses had not had any offers in over six months. We joked with Greg that we should be hired to walk through sellers' homes, because we seemed to attract other buyers.

The first house that we made an offer on reminded me of my childhood home. It was a two-story brick home with four bedrooms. It was spacious. We wanted a home that would be comfortable for hosting holiday parties and having family and friends visit. This met all of the criteria and then some. Unfortunately, we got into a bidding war and lost.

Our offer on a second house ended up falling through after we received the home inspection report and found that some serious and costly repairs were required – and the owners were unwilling to make them. The house cosmetically looked fine and was less than twenty years old. However, it had mold issues and was not structurally sound.

The third house we made an offer on was a short sale. It was by far our favorite of the three. It had been a house I had admired from the street during a walk with my mother after my surgery. I appreciated the architecture so much that I had made Jack stroll past it with me on our next walk. Jack had been confused about why I wanted him to see the outside of a house that, at the time, was not for sale. But I saw this house, with its unusual architecture, as a sign of hope. Most of the homes in our area were "cookie cutter" homes that looked very similar to one another. Jack and I missed our old, character-filled home in Pennsylvania. I had thought that just seeing this house would encourage us, proving that there were some unique homes in our community. This particular house reminded me of a Vermont home with its A-frame structure. Now eight months after I first noticed this dwelling, it was for sale.

When we toured the home, we were blown away by all of the "extras." The house had built-in dressers and bookshelves. It had hardwood floors without a square inch of carpet. Jack and I both felt that carpet was hard to keep clean and anticipated hardwood floors being ideal with children. The living room was spacious, yet cozy, with a wood-burning stove and a two-story ceiling. The previous owners had taken an old Singer sewing machine stand and converted it into a sink stand. The kitchen had an island, which would be perfect for entertaining. There was a lot of exposed wood, and the house even had a loft. However, what made this home truly unique was the sunroom connected to a screened-in hallway out to a screened-in gazebo. We later found out that the house was originally built by an architect for himself and his wife. It truly was one of a kind. This was our dream house.

We made an offer. The buyers accepted our offer in October, but we then had to wait to see what the bank that held the mortgage would decide. Our realtor told us that short sales tended to be slow, so not to anticipate hearing anything for months. We continued to look at house listings, but nothing else really caught our eye.

The fall seemed to be a sea of paperwork. We completed paperwork for preapproval for a home mortgage. I continued to complete paperwork for my disability insurance company and made daily phone calls to appeal their decision to terminate my coverage, and then I wrote a complaint for unfair claim practices against my disability insurance company. Everything required documentation and certified mailing. It truly felt like a part-time job. Thankfully, after an investigation my disability insurance company ended up extending my coverage through the end of 2013. The one good thing about all of the paperwork was that it made me aware that my strength and stamina were improving.

My confidence also started to grow as I made it several months without insulin and passed the one-year benchmark of living in South Carolina. I was feeling like I knew more people at our church and in the community.

In December I went back to applying for jobs and writing cover letters. I contacted my references and updated my resume. I was ready to start the new year with a new job.

On my one-year anniversary of being pancreas-free, January 10, 2014, I had a job interview at the county treasurer's office. This interview lasted several hours, and I arrived home exhausted and with diarrhea.

I tried to select jobs that aligned with my passions or were low-stress. Living in a small town, the options were limited. The treasurer's office position was not something I felt overly passionate about, but I figured it would be low-stress like a bank job and would keep nine-to-five hours. As I found out more details during the interview process, however, red flags went up. I had assumed the position was low-stress because the compensation was lower than my first job out of college almost ten years ago. The reverse was true. The person filling the position was expected to manage ten employees at three different offices. A time card was used to punch in and punch out. I had not been required to do this at any of my jobs after college. If an employee was late, she or he got written up. I tried my best to be punctual, but my digestive system was not always reliable.

After I was offered the job, I asked about paid time off and was horrified to find out none was allowed for the first six months, and after that less than one day of vacation accrued per month. I inquired about being able to take time off without pay for going to the doctor's or seeing family during the first six months. After all, I had to be seen by my endocrinologist every three months. In addition, at Christmas I had found out I was going to be an aunt and was excited to be able to meet my new niece or nephew. The office told me that unpaid time off was not an option. Working a stressful management job with low compensation and only six vacation days my first year seemed ridiculous.

I shared my concerns with my doctors at MUSC as well as Dr. Kessel. I was concerned about having digestive issues at work and not being able to take a nap. I averaged ten bowel movements a day. Dr. Kessel explained that stress can increase the speed of digestion. Up to this point, I had not gone two consecutive days without a nap. In what my doctors said and did not say, I realized I needed to find a flexible and low-stress job.

I prayed and wrestled with what path to take. It seemed crazy to turn down a job when it was the only one I was offered. However, for the first time in my life I was truly valuing my health over income. I had worked so hard to gain strength and health that I was not willing to lose it over a mediocre job. I took a leap of faith and declined the job offer.

In addition to my job search, interview, and discerning process, January was packed with some other milestones and revelations.

I decided to contact my friend Janae to find out more information about adopting from Uganda. Janae was the persistent friend who had visited me in Lancaster and prayed boldly for a job for Jack to be provided that day. She had also started a foundation over a year ago in honor of her first daughter, to help orphans and women in Uganda. Last summer, while at a wedding, I found out that the bride's brother had been to Uganda on several occasions and had designed solar-powered computers and had taken them to Uganda. The youth director at our church raised funds for her daughter to be a missionary in Uganda. In January, a lady from our church gave me a book entitled *Kisses from Katie* about a recent high school graduate who traveled to Uganda to teach and ended up caring for hundreds of children.

Jack and I had learned that when God nudges us, we need to listen and pay attention. Janae provided the contact information for a woman named Faye who was American who took care of orphans in Uganda.

Around the same time, I was introduced to a health and wellness company through which I could work, but set my own hours. It was a business opportunity unlike anything I had ever heard of before. I would get to share amazing products with people while they were pampered with a free facial and foot soak. It also had an educational aspect. I would get to share information about skincare. For example, what is put on one's skin is absorbed into the body in twenty-six seconds or less. I felt it was important for individuals to be educated about what is going into their bloodstream. Many ingredients that are allowed in the United States are banned in Europe because they are not safe or beneficial to the body. When I first learned this I was shocked. I had always thought the United States had some of the safest products.

I had some major fears to overcome to start my own business, including picking up the phone and asking relatively new friends if I could practice on them, and speaking in front of others. I was also fearful of commissioned-based income, because no income was guaranteed. However, I loved pampering others and was willing to go outside of my comfort zone to earn income for the adoption fees. Once again, the desire for my future children spurred me on.

In February, Jack and the other associate pastor led a group from our church on a trip to Israel. My mom came down to stay with me while he was gone. My mom and I traveled to visit friends and family in the area. We even got to visit Denise and her family in their new community. While Jack was in Israel, I received news that the bank owning the home we were interested in buying had approved our request to purchase. We had thirty days to settle.

March truly felt like madness as I packed up our belongings and kept running my own business. We also got news in March that twins had been born in Uganda, and Faye had guardianship of them. Their mother had died a few hours after birth and the father did not feel that he was capable of raising them. Their names were Wassua (a boy) and Nakato (a girl). Oh my goodness, God was providing our dream house and now babies. I felt like the stars were aligning. I had their pictures on my phone and on my computer. I could not help but think about them all day and pray for them.

I was told by an adoptive mother in our area to keep myself busy, or I would drive myself crazy waiting. I had no trouble staying busy. We talked with Faye on the phone, and she started the paperwork on her end to legalize the adoption. I started contacting agencies to find out about getting our home study updated.

I realized that if I had taken the job at the treasurer's office, I would not have had the energy or time to be packing or working on adoption paperwork. I was thankful for the flexibility of owning my own home-based business. I continued to feel healthy, but my body did require quite a bit of rest, including naps, and I had physical therapy twice a week from January to May. I kept an eye out for job opportunities in our area, but I was not finding any that were the right fit with my health and my credentials. However, I did not fret or stress over not finding a salaried or hourly job because I anticipated being a stay-at-home mother. I realized, prior to my illness, I would have never considered this as an option.

CHAPTER 39

NEW PURPOSE

I was nervous and excited as I packed up boxes. I could not wait to be settled in our new home, where we could paint the walls, change the landscaping, and start making memories. The idea of this being the last move for a while was comforting. Jack and I joked that we wanted to retire in this home.

I spent several hours each day boxing up items. I was making a dent, but I was nervous about packing up everything in time for our move. One afternoon when I felt tired, I decided to pack up one more box. As I was coming down the stairs, I felt a burning and itching sensation in my leg. I got to the bottom of the steps and pulled up my sweat pants. To my horror, the vein on the side of my left shin was sticking out an inch. My first thought was that I had been bitten by a spider. I started to feel lightheaded, so I lay down on the floor and called Jack on my cell phone.

Jack answered, "Hey honey. How are you doing?"

With panic in my voice, I quickly said, "I think I was bitten by a spider or something. My leg feels funny and a vein is really distended."

"What did the spider look like?"

"I didn't see a spider, but there's a bulge and it seems to keep swelling. I don't know what else could cause this. It really hurts. Can you come home? I am afraid of passing out."

"Where are you now?"

"I'm lying down in the guest room."

"I'll wrap up what I am working on and be home in a few minutes. Don't move."

I focused on taking deep breaths and staying calm. I was

thankful that Jack only had a ten-minute commute. When Jack got home, he took one look at the vein and agreed it needed to be checked out by a medical professional. Jack tried calling Dr. Kessel's office, but they were already closed for the day. We decided to go to urgent care and avoid the emergency room.

Jack drove me to the urgent care office and I hobbled inside. Now it hurt to put any weight on my left leg. The doctor at urgent care scratched his head and declared, "I've never seen anything like that before. It's not a spider bite, but I'm not sure what it is. Have you ever had a blood clot before?"

I answered, "Yes, but it was in my arm while I had a PICC line."

"Hmm. Well, to be safe you should have an ultrasound done to make sure it isn't a blood clot."

We were instructed to go to the emergency room. I reluctantly went to the dreaded local hospital. After only a few minutes of waiting in the emergency room lobby, an ultrasound tech took me back. I was pleasantly surprised by the speedy service. The ultrasound confirmed that it was not a blood clot. The following day, I went to see Dr. Kessel and he said I had blown out a vein from lifting too much. I was instructed to keep my leg elevated with ice on it, and it should feel better in a few days.

I did my best to pack boxes with my leg elevated. Jack teased me at not being a good patient or knowing how to rest. However, I could not relax when boxes needed to be packed.

My mom once again flew down to graciously help with the move. This was a much easier move, because the two homes were located less than a mile apart. We moved all of our things over several days with the help of some church friends. I stayed away from any heavy lifting, but I rejoiced that I could help with this move.

Two days after moving, I boarded a plane headed west and my mom boarded a plane headed north. My mom was flying home, and I was going to a conference connected with my business. I didn't feel great the morning we left, but I assumed my body was fatigued from the move. I was traveling with a friend, her husband, and their nine-month-old son.

We had a layover in Houston, Texas. I felt a little lightheaded and nauseous, so I purchased a smoothie. I suddenly felt much worse. I checked my blood sugar, but it was normal. My pain escalated quickly, so I took a breakthrough pain pill. This did not stay down. I began vomiting violently. I handed my friend, Nicole, my glucagon kit and informed her that if I passed out, she should inject me. Nicole looked horrified and passed the kit to her husband. She went to the gate agent and asked for help. I called Jack on my cell phone, thinking he might know what to do. I told him, "I am vomiting and not feeling well. Oh, paramedics are here. I'll talk to you later. I love you." I hung up the phone.

As our flight was boarding, the paramedics gave me oxygen and placed me on a stretcher. The paramedics took me by ambulance to a local emergency room. Nicole and her family rode with me in the ambulance.

After I received some IV fluids and pain medicine, I felt okay to continue on the trip. The ER doctor wanted to keep me overnight, and both the doctor and my husband said there was no way I could go to the conference. But if I could not go to my conference, I just wanted to get home and be with Jack. I signed paperwork to discharge myself against the hospital's recommendation. My friends and I returned to the airport. I quickly realized how weak I was and asked for a wheelchair. Once Nicole got me to my gate to fly back to Charleston, we parted ways.

I was wheeled onto the plane and, by God's providence, I was seated next to a medical doctor. He saw my arms taped up from IVs and blood work, along with my hospital bands. He asked if I was okay. I explained my unexpected trip to the ER. I felt reassured that if I had any trouble on the plane, I would be well taken care of. My luggage did not make it back with me, but that was the last thing on my mind. I was just so grateful to be back with Jack. I could not believe I had spent five hours flying, just to end up back in the airport I had departed from earlier that day.

This event really shook me up. My independence seemed to be shattered. However, I tried to focus on the blessings. I figured my body was in desperate need of rest. I didn't see this episode as a long-term setback.

Fortunately, we had a time of respite scheduled that month at our favorite bed and breakfast on a lake in western Maryland. The wraparound porch was sprinkled with rocking chairs. The rooms were spacious and the sheets had high thread-counts. Homemade chocolate chip cookies were made throughout the day. The smell of the warm chewy morsels made the tranquil setting feel like heaven. We had five nights there. It was a truly great opportunity to rest.

Each evening there were hors d'oeuvres followed by a boat ride. There was something invigorating about going out on a lake in a speedboat after spending the day reading, eating, and dozing.

Each evening concluded with a toasty fire outside on the brick patio. Guests congregated around the fire pit, roasting homemade marshmallows and chatting. We enjoyed finding out where other guests had traveled from and what adventures their days had included.

One young couple was there on their honeymoon. They were from Baltimore, Maryland. Jack and I shared that we used to live in Lancaster, Pennsylvania, but had moved to South Carolina a year and a half ago.

The couple asked, "Have you been here before?"

Jack answered, "Yes, we were here one time before and became hooked. It is our favorite bed and breakfast."

The couple shared that friends of theirs had highly recommended the place.

I asked how long they would be staying and was surprised when they replied only two nights. The husband explained that he was completing his residency at Johns Hopkins and could not take much time off.

I do not know what compelled me to ask, but I did. "Do you by any chance know Dr. Cole?"

The husband replied, "Yes, I've worked with him. He's a

great guy."

Like lava spewing uncontrollably out of a volcano, I declared without stopping to take a breath, "I was a patient of his and he was awful. I had chronic pancreatitis and the first time I met him he said there was nothing wrong with my pancreas. I ended up staying in the hospital for almost two weeks after he did an ERCP. I think all people in the medical field should visit Medical University of South Carolina in Charleston. They provided excellent care. I had my entire pancreas removed and was home in ten days."

It was like diarrhea of the mouth. I could not stop. Initially, I had felt empowered to tell someone who knew Dr. Cole that his care stunk and that there was a hospital with less prestige that provided a million times better care. However, I quickly realized by my husband's mortified look that I had taken a casual conversation and made it awkward. Fortunately, the recent groom did not debate or question my views. However, shortly thereafter the newlyweds got up and went back to their room. When we got back to our room, Jack asked, "What came over you? That poor couple is on their honeymoon."

I honestly replied, "I don't know. I thought I had moved past my bitterness towards Dr. Cole. I didn't realize I still harbored such deep anger. I'm used to telling people in Beaufort about how great MUSC is. I wasn't prepared for someone to like Dr. Cole. Do you think I should apologize to the couple?"

"No. I just think you shouldn't bring it up again."

With the recent move fresh in my mind, a moving analogy popped in my head. I felt like I had been all unpacked in a new house – but then I opened a bedroom door and found a room full of boxes. I had thought I was all done with Dr. Cole but clearly hadn't finished "unpacking." I was so embarrassed. I hated that I had heart work to do on vacation. However, I took the experience as an invitation to pray and ask God to help me forgive, let go of the past, and replace anger with gratitude.

A wise friend in Beaufort suggested praying for blessings for Dr. Cole and his family. This felt like the last thing I wanted to do, but over time it truly helped me to heal and to replace bitterness with peace. I felt a new level of wonder and challenge to follow Jesus' instructions to "love your enemies and pray for those who persecute you" (Matthew 5:44, NIV). The rest of the trip was not eventful. We returned home refreshed. However, I had started planning different projects to tackle before we even pulled in the garage. The inside of the house was pretty well settled. I was ready to tackle the yard. I knew the soil was sandy where we lived, so I would need some guidance as to what to plant.

A family friend, Aaron, who had recently graduated with a master's in landscape architecture, was struggling to find a job in his field. I suggested that he come stay with us and take a break from living at home in Maryland. I knew that job searches were exhausting and frequently discouraging. I thought a change of scenery might be restorative. I also knew a few people from the church who I thought might be good references. Selfishly, I also thought he could help me select plants that would thrive in our new yard.

Our yard had a lot of potential, with brick pathways and raised flowerbeds. A week after Aaron arrived, we had eighty folks from the church signed up to come over for a potluck dinner at our house. I loved having a deadline and motivation for a project.

Aaron and I went around to local nurseries, so that Aaron could get an idea of the different options we had. I asked which plants were deer resistant. We had a lot of deer in our area and I did not want flowerbeds full of stems. Once we had a game plan, Jack, Aaron, and I went to a wholesaler and got two carloads of plants. We arranged them in their pots around the yard. I could not wait for the following morning to get started planting.

On Saturday morning, June 7, 2014, we got up early to beat the heat and get started planting. It didn't take long before I was covered in dirt and sweat. I couldn't wait to see the finished product. I thought after the planting was complete, we could take pictures for our adoption home study.

The ringing of my phone brought me out of my daydream and back to reality. When I answered the phone, it was Faye from Uganda. I asked the familiar question, "How are you?" She replied, "I am not doing so well."

"What is wrong? Is everything okay?" I thought maybe the biological father had changed his mind and was not open to Americans adopting his babies. I was glad to be sitting when I received the news.

"The twin girl, Nakato, passed away today. She stopped breathing and was taken to the hospital." I gasped in horror. This could not be happening. This orphanage provided food, clothing, and good medical care. I asked how Wassua was. Faye said that he was taken to the hospital to be monitored, but he was doing okay. I got off the phone and cried. Jack was sitting right next to me and picked up on what had happened. We had a cleansing cry together. I did not really know how to process the news. I was thankful for physical work.

I wished I could dig a hole and put my head in it like an ostrich. However, we had Aaron staying with us, and I had set up dinners and appointments to meet with church members involved with landscape architecture.

In addition, the week before I started sponsoring a business consultant, Melissa, and was training her to own her own health and wellness business, like me. I had promised to link arms with Melissa and help her get started. I had started my business to help my future children. Now that Nakato was gone, I felt like quitting. However, I wanted to be a role model for Melissa and help her achieve her dreams. As a result, my business during this season kept me busy and helped to keep me from slipping into depression. Plus, I still had a little boy who was counting on me.

Exactly a month later, on July 7, my niece, Ralli Elizabeth, was born. She was my parents' first grandchild. I was able to make a trip up to Lancaster to meet her. I stayed at my sister and brother-in-law's home and helped however I could. I felt an instant and special bond with this baby girl. Since I had never had younger siblings, Ralli was the first baby I held on the day of her birth. I could not help but think I was gaining training for being a mama.

Less than a week after returning home from helping with baby Ralli, I received an e-mail from Faye. She had wanted to call but was out of calling cards. Wassua had passed away. She explained it was the same type of scenario as Nakato: "Infection too far advanced before symptoms appeared." A thought entered my mind that I believe was from God, because my brain does not naturally think like this: the twins were now with their biological mother in heaven. They were in a place with no tears or pain, better than anything I could have provided them on earth. However, it still hurt.

Once again, I felt my purpose was swept out from underneath me. I was getting stronger and had the home for my future children. But I still did not have them. Why was this happening? My whole reason for not wanting to do domestic adoption was the chance the child might be taken from me. Now my biggest fear had happened.

I didn't question where God was, because I remembered all the times God was present through my dark season. Instead, I felt God gave me a peace that I clung onto. I trusted that God was not finished with me. I recalled a quote I had heard, "As long as you have breath, you have a purpose." Psalm 37:4 was also a knot on the rope I was holding onto: "Delight yourself in the LORD, and he will give you the desires of your heart" (ESV). God had clearly placed the desire to adopt on both Jack and my heart.

While I trusted God, I had no idea what my next step was. I continued to share my health and wellness business. However, this was also a painful reminder, because I had started it to earn income for the Uganda adoption fees. My passion was gone. As I put one foot in front of the other, I was blessed by meeting new individuals in my community. Several folks that I pampered with a free facial and foot soak really encouraged me to write my story. This had been a nudge I had felt by the Holy Spirit ever since my surgery was complete, but I had made excuses. At first the healing process was too fresh and painful. Then I was busy with preparing for the Ugandan twins. Now, I had no excuses. I secretly wondered if once I wrote my memoir, my child(ren) would be ready for adoption. In 2014, God provided me with opportunities to grow inner strength. I managed three ER trips when Jack was not with me. They were certainly not pleasant, and I was scared, but God showed me that I could survive, and I was stronger than I gave myself credit for. Not having Jack present was like not having my training wheels.

Naturally, my writing time was affected by ER trips and regular appointments to see doctors. My health hiccups at this point were related to vomiting and nausea, leading to dehydration and low blood sugars. Thankfully, in the midst of the unpleasant and hard work of healing, God gave me some additional blessings and income.

I took care of a three-year-old for three afternoons a week. I would pick Ross up from preschool, feed him lunch, read him a few stories, and then tuck him in for a nap. While Ross slept, I also took a nap. We would enjoy playing with a train set and other toys after his nap. Once again, I felt like I was getting some mama training. I also wondered if adopting a toddler might be a good fit.

In February 2015, Ross's family moved away. The same month, God brought a nursing student into my life who needed help with her college math course. While I could not provide any assistance on how to draw blood, I was able to break down the concepts and steps to solve for a single variable. I had never considered or thought about helping nursing students with math. However, God did – and heard my pleas and prayers to give back to the medical field. I was always grateful for advances in medicine and for the individuals who cared for me medically.

One day while I was at the hospital sitting in a waiting room, a small child arrived with his mother. I would guess the child was four or so. He had a PICC line in his arm. I thought, *Poor little guy. I can relate. I know what it is like to have a PICC line.*

I returned home that afternoon and said to Jack, "I think I

would be open to adopting a child with medical needs. I certainly know my way around hospitals. Plus, I've learned that distractions and giggles are the best remedy for waiting in hospitals."

Jack's jaw dropped. Three years prior, when we were at Temple Hospital after my first experience with a torturous test, Jack had suggested that a purpose and blessing for my health issues and pain might be to help our future children with their health needs. At the time, I thought this was a cruel theory. I had also thought my health issue was going to be cured within a month. Clearly, time had altered my perspective.

Jack and I decided to pursue foster-to-adopt (adopting foster children) and children with medical needs. I realized I was slowly gaining ground on the "comparison trap." I am not the *best* tutor or wife, nor will I be the *best* mother, but I will be the best I can be, and I am content with that. Clearly, we are all on a unique path; trying to fit into a mold is not only frustrating, but futile.

I was no longer embarrassed by checking my blood sugar or taking medicine. Similarly, I saw naps as part of my daily medicine. They are just what my body needs. Just like two individuals' eyeglasses prescriptions may not be the same, a lighter glasses prescription doesn't make one a better person. I am slowly learning to embrace my prescriptions along with my strengths and weaknesses. I certainly don't know what the future holds, but now I trust that with God's strength and presence, I will survive and thrive.

EPILOGUE

As 2015 drew to an end, I realized that yet again I had subconsciously set a deadline on my healing. Not only do I have a habit of setting time frames for when scars should be healed, but I also tend to underestimate the time it will take. I thought for sure I would be completely healed three years after major surgery.

Memories of these past few years still haunt me. I still feel sick to my stomach with flashbacks of IVs, hospital rooms, and uncontrollable pain. I have grieved the loss of a nine-to-five job. My heart continues to ache for the precious twins in Uganda.

But while I have certainly not lacked physical or emotional pain, I have also not lacked hope or joy. One of these great joys is knowing that I have been refined by the "fire" of these difficulties. Many times throughout my healing, I have been able to find parallels and metaphors in the beauty of the created world; these have encouraged me along the way. For example, I learned from a park ranger many years ago that some trees release seeds only in response to a fire's high temperatures, and that the fire helps to enrich the soil. Therefore, a fire births new life; it's not just destructive. I like to imagine that new seeds have been planted and tended in my spirit during my trials. I am aware of some of these, but other seeds may not germinate for years. I praise God for the encouragement of new growth.

In 2016, Jack and I started paperwork to become foster parents. By September 2016, we had fostered three babies. My heart got attached to each one, and I was devastated when their placement changed. The third baby left a few days before we evacuated for Hurricane Matthew. Jack and I stayed at my aunt's home. Once again God's timing was divine, allowing space and time to heal. I decided that I would rather surrender my dream to be a mother than to continue to have my heart ripped apart over and over. Jack and I returned home on October 10, 2016, and packed up all of the baby items. I sold some and gave some away.

On November 16, 2016, I received a phone call informing me of a one-year-old girl who was a pre-adoption placement; a committee had chosen us to be her permanent placement. Our daughter arrived two days later. Our church family once again rallied alongside us, quickly equipped our home with everything we needed in time for our daughter's arrival. There were some bumps in the road to adoption, but a year later on November 28, 2017, our daughter's adoption was finalized. We chose the name Amarissa for her, which means "Promised of God."

During Christmas 2017, everything seemed to be perfect. Then, the next month, my mom was diagnosed with Stage IV ovarian cancer. Both prayers of gratitude and petitions for healing continue to be present in our household.

One mind-blowing lesson I learned from the Bible was that many of God's blessings occurred over generations. For example, Ruth's courage led to the birth of her great grandson King David and ultimately to the birth of Jesus. Hence, I trust and believe the best is yet to come. I may not see all of the rippling blessings and benefits in my lifetime, and that is okay. I get glimpses of where God is at work, and they sustain me. I like to think of God weaving our lives together to create a beautiful tapestry. In our lifetime, all we can see is the tapestry's back side with knots. I cannot wait to see the front side, the full picture, from heaven.

Another nugget of wisdom that I have held onto came from an alum who came back to speak at my high school's chapel. He said, "Never think that God isn't going to use something. I thought I would never use geometry, and now I am a missionary and use geometry almost every day." I love that God does not waste anything that we have learned.

When I was a child, my family affectionately referred to me as the story teller. I was a gabber. My mom would always joke that I would never die from indigestion: I would talk so much at the kitchen table, I was always the last one to finish eating. Typically, my mom would have all of the dishes washed and the kitchen cleaned up before I was done eating, just because I had been talking so much. But although I have always enjoyed telling stories, I always viewed them as entertainment at best, not as something useful.

Through this illness and time of reflection, I have realized that stories can be more than entertainment; they can be avenues to share and see God's hand at work. They don't even all have to be serious and intense stories.

Another powerful element I've learned about stories is that illustrations stick. I know this because with my brain fried from pain medicine and anesthesia, it's a miracle I remember anything! Even after a phenomenal sermon, what I usually remember is the children's homily. Why? Because there's a prop or an illustration. This sticks. If by chance I can recall something from the sermon, it usually is a personal story. Again, personal stories stick. The Bible is full of personal stories.

My hope is that some of my story will stick with you. However, more importantly, my prayer is that my story will encourage you to reflect on your own story and to see where God's hand has been at work and where it is pointing. If you share your story, you will not only recall God's presence, but your eyes will also refocus to see God at work in your present circumstances. This has been my experience. And if your story then sticks with others, then they hopefully will reflect on their own stories, share their stories, and have keener eyes to see God at work. It's a domino effect.

I imagine everyone starting out holding an unlit candle, like in many Christmas Eve services. But when we each light just our neighbor's candle, a dark room quickly becomes illuminated. Can you picture the entire globe, and candles being lit all over the world? I believe the Holy Spirit works in many unique and mysterious ways. However, one *un*-mysterious way the Holy Spirit works is through relationships. How do you get to know someone? By sharing stories.

I recommend collecting stories that inspire you and bring you joy. For example, print out emails, comics that make you smile, and pictures that make you laugh out loud. I would tell you to put them in a box, but I tend to forget to open boxes. Therefore, I recommend you put them on the wall, your desk, or your mirror, or carry them in your wallet.

When Jack and I returned from our honeymoon, we discovered a wonderful gift from some friends: fun post-it notes all over our house. They put jokes and words of encouragement on food in our cupboard, in the freezer, in the shower, behind pillows, in drawers and shoes, etc. I believe God has sprinkled each life with these love notes and reminders. Be on the lookout, and plant your own reminders of them in places where you often look.

I also find that focusing on blessings redirects me away from judging – judging others and judging myself. It frees me to dance in body, mind, and spirit. Dance for me is the ultimate form of celebrating and expressing joy. I realize this may look different for each person.

During 2013 and 2014, the word I clung to was "hope." A beloved friend of my Nana's, Hazel Burhman, shared with me after my major surgery that butterflies are a symbol of hope. Regularly Hazel would pop little gifts in the mail that incorporated a butterfly. Hazel passed away in early 2015, but every time I see a butterfly in a piece of art or outside in nature, I think of Hazel and the hope God has brought me.

In 2015 and 2016, my word was "trust." I trusted that in God's divine timing, I would become a mama, that I would have opportunities to serve and be used, and that our needs would be met. I have a tendency to overanalyze and worry. While I was not able to fully extinguish these old habits, I set out to battle them with trust. I have gotten back to keeping a gratitude journal. I have been amazed at how many blessings abound if I merely look for them.

In 2017 and 2018, "peace" was my word. Peace through the waiting and wondering if the adoption would go through. Peace while my mom endured chemo treatments. Peace in the midst of moving from SC back to PA and changing churches, home, doctors, etc. One resource I was introduced to that has helped me hold onto peace is yoga. Yoga helps to quiet my brain, and the gentle flow strengthens my muscles. My favorite yoga incorporates Scripture into the practice.

Now in 2019, serenity is the word I cling to. Serenity is a sister to peace and encompasses reconciliation and calmness. My prayer is to stay serene as I prepare to publish this book and have no idea how God will use it. I also pray for composure and poise as I continue to learn about the depths of God's serenity. I seek internal reconciliation as my islet cells have become weaker and my blood sugar levels have become more erratic. I pray for calm despite many unknowns on the horizons in my life, my family's life, and the lives of folks around the world.

I continue to have dreams and hopes for my life ahead. I like to think I now hold them in open hands with the understanding they may happen, or they may be taken away and replaced with something else. I learned from Priscilla Shirer to end my prayers with "or better." Thus, whatever I request, I ask God to provide that or better – realizing that the "better" may not fit society's or my limited earthly view of "better."

I would like to share one final Scripture passage with you. In John 16:20-22 (NRSV), Jesus is talking to the disciples and is foreshadowing his death on the cross and then his resurrection. The illustration seems to fit many painful scenarios.

"Very truly, I tell you, you will weep and mourn, but the world will rejoice; you will have pain, but your pain will turn into joy. When a woman is in labor, she has pain, because her hour has come. But when her child is born, she no longer remembers the anguish because of the joy of having brought a human being into the world. So you have pain now; but I will see you again, and your hearts will rejoice, and no one will take your joy from you."

I continue to trust that the best is yet to come, and to believe that pain can birth joy and blessings. Now, it is time for you to reflect on your journey and to share your story.

AUTHOR'S NOTE

Many times throughout my illness, I heard people express, "Becky, you are so courageous." Or "I admire how brave you are." Truthfully, I was not brave. I had no choice. I was in pure survival mode. If I could have flipped a switch or opened a door and escaped the pain, I would have. I never would have chosen to endure such intense pain for so long.

On the other hand, writing this book has taken tremendous courage. It has not been pleasant remembering the pain and agony of waiting. I had always thought that once someone survived a traumatic experience, it would be easy to retell the story, because they would know how it ends – that they are safe or cured. The opposite has been true for me. I love sharing God's miracles, but the miracle cannot fully be appreciated without describing the painful circumstances. Even though I no longer have a pancreas, I still feel pain, nausea, and fatigue recounting the details. I mention this to support and encourage others to share their stories of God's provision and presence. It is not easy, but it can bring healing to the storyteller as well as to the listener.

It also takes courage to let go of control, including control of one's own story. Through this season of suffering, I realized that in order to receive God's blessings, I had to figuratively open my hands; this meant relinquishing my own white-knuckled grip on the reins. So I am choosing to let go of trying to be in control. My purpose is to bring glory to God. I have no idea how God will use my story, and I am okay with that. His plan is far better than my plan.

Honestly, I believe everyone has encountered trials in some

form and has a story to share. No one is immune to scars. What becomes hard is when we compare our brokenness and struggles with airbrushed images of friends and celebrities. Most people want others to see all that they have going right in their lives. It is important to be grateful and positive – but painting an incomplete picture benefits no one. When people project the image that they have it all together, they isolate themselves with hidden shame. Lies can easily creep in: "If people knew the whole you, they would not like you or be friends with you." Yet the opposite is true, as a perfect façade is not relatable. It creates a barrier to even close friends and family confiding their struggles.

A healthy approach allows us to have gratitude, and to thank God in the midst of a messy life. Grumpiness and negativity are as offensive as body odor. But our focus is what differentiates someone who is wallowing from someone who is genuine. My focus, while shaky at times, has been on glorifying God and seeking to learn and grow. There are many forms and ways you can share your story. For example, a phone call, a letter, an email, a blog, or a post on social media.

May blessings of hope, joy, peace, and love abound as you share your story!

QUESTIONS FOR
REFLECTION AND DISCUSSION

Chapter 1: Admit

➢ What is your biggest fear right now?
➢ What areas of your life are overshadowed by fear?
➢ What would confronting your biggest fear look like?
➢ What do you try to control, but feel nudged by God to let go of?

Chapter 2: The First Step

➢ I mention how Audrey Hepburn inspires me. Does anyone famous inspire you? If so, why?
➢ Is asking for help hard for you? Why or why not?
➢ Do you have a prayer partner? If not, who could you ask?

Chapter 3: Business or Pleasure?

➢ What are your top priorities that guide your decisions?
➢ Have you ever accidently stumbled upon a gem of a location? If so, where?
➢ What situation/experience made you feel like you were experiencing a slice of heaven on earth?

Chapter 4: Trick-or-Treat

> What are some fun traditions you enjoy?
> On a scale of 1 to 10, how much do you care what others think of you? If this number is high, why do others' opinions matter so much to you?

Chapter 5: Divine Timing

> If you could go on a vacation with anyone and anywhere, where would you go, and with whom?
> When has a delay to your planned timing led to a divine appointment?

Chapter 6: Thanksgiving

> Have you ever won something?
> What do you give thanks for this year?

Chapter 7: Twelve Days of Christmas

> Have you ever had a "pay it forward" experience?
> What is something you are looking forward to?

Chapter 8: December 27

> Who do you look up to, and what specific qualities do you admire in her/him?
> What tools do you utilize when you are in a figurative waiting room?

Chapter 9: Gratitude Scavenger Hunt

> Do you keep a prayer list or gratitude list?
> Recall a time when humor helped a situation.

Chapter 10: Purpose in the Pain

➢ Why might it be important to share your story?
➢ How could you share a piece of your story today? (Letter, email, phone call, social media, etc.)
➢ What is your favorite room in your home? Why?

Chapter 11: Cabin Fever

➢ What labels do you use to describe yourself? How would you feel if those labels were taken away?
➢ What experiences (suffering or otherwise) could you use to relate to someone struggling?
➢ Have you ever felt punished when something bad happened to you?
➢ Make a list of all the things you can do.

Chapter 12: Roller Coaster Drop

➢ Who do you instinctively reach out to when you receive disappointing news?
➢ Describe a time you felt like a figurative finish line was moved further away. (For example, when finishing a project or anticipating a promotion.)

Chapter 13: Battle

➢ How do you process frustrations?
➢ Have you ever experienced a time when you felt someone who was supposed to help you didn't?

Chapter 14: Empty

➢ Can you recall a time when you were totally dependent on God?
➢ Have you ever felt hopeless?
➢ Where do you find hope? About what are you hopeful?
➢ To which Bible character do you relate to best today? Why?

Chapter 15: Easter

- ➤ How do you define your worth?
- ➤ Did you ever believe or trust in something that you later found out was untrue or untrustworthy? How did you respond?

Chapter 16: Confused

- ➤ When has God's will pushed you out of your comfort zone? Did you protest?
- ➤ Do you have dreams for the future? If so, what is one of them?

Chapter 17: May Day

- ➤ What is something fun you can do today?
- ➤ What food or smell sparks a fond memory for you?

Chapter 18: Acupuncture

- ➤ Have you ever intentionally tried something that frightened you? If so, what was it?
- ➤ Is there a "luxury" that you would make a priority even on a tight budget?

Chapter 19: Janae

- ➤ What was a big prayer request in your life that you have seen directly answered?
- ➤ Can you recall a time when God answered a prayer in a way that you had not considered?
- ➤ Do you pray with boldness and gratitude, expecting that God will answer your prayer requests?

Chapter 20: Turned a Corner

- ➤ What is something you took for granted until it was taken away or lost?

Chapter 21: Squeezed

> ➢ Where do you feel squeezed in your life?
> ➢ Is there a phrase or passage of Scripture you cling to during difficult times?

Chapter 22: Called

> ➢ Have you ever been so engrossed in something that you temporarily forgot about your circumstances?
> ➢ Have you ever prayed for someone you never met? Are you aware of individuals praying for you that you haven't met?
> ➢ What was a tough decision you had to make in the past? What helped you with the discernment process?

Chapter 23: Wrong Turns

> ➢ Have you ever felt like you took a wrong turn while trying to follow God?
> ➢ Do you ever worry what complete strangers think of you and feel compelled to explain your situation?

Chapter 24: Struggles with Boxes and Tears

> ➢ Have you ever celebrated something prematurely and then regretted it?
> ➢ Have you ever met someone who you thought was an angel?

Chapter 25: Surprises

> ➤ What type of news do you procrastinate sharing with friends and/or family?
> ➤ How do you respond to your own wounds and scars? Do you...
>   • stay stuck in the past and shackled to fear?
>   • pretend everything is perfect and project an airbrushed image?
>   • view your scars and trials as gifts and opportunities to relate to others and place your trust in God?
> ➤ How, specifically, do you stay grounded and accountable?

Chapter 26: Waiting

> ➤ What helps you avoid throwing pity parties for yourself?
> ➤ What have you anticipated (whether positive or negative)? What did you do during the interim?

Chapter 27: Final Month

> ➤ What Scripture has spoken to you recently?
> ➤ If you could have any friend come over to your house and celebrate, who would it be?

Chapter 28: Surgery Eve

> ➤ What is your dream job?
> ➤ Have you ever focused on a "Promised Land"? What was it?

Chapter 29: The Big Day

> ➤ What is the scariest obstacle that you have ever faced?
> ➤ Who is an advocate for you? For whom do you advocate?

QUESTIONS FOR REFLECTION AND DISCUSSION

Chapter 30: Recovering at the Hospital

➤ Who has been a figurative cheerleader in your life?
➤ What has been your most unusual prayer request?

Chapter 31: First Month

➤ Recall a time when you had to rely on someone else. Who can you always count on to be there if you need help?
➤ How do you hear God's voice?
➤ Are you surprised when trials occur in your life?

Chapter 32: Pockets

➤ What is your Achilles' heel?
➤ What small victory can you celebrate today?
➤ Is God's grace sufficient for you?

Chapter 33: Saying Goodbye

➤ Who is the hardest person for you to say goodbye to?
➤ Like the Israelites, are you in "bondage" to work, an unhealthy relationship, addiction, etc.? Have you sought the freedom God offers?
➤ Do you experience flashbacks to a traumatic experience? If so, how do you work through the flashbacks?

Chapter 34: Three Months

➤ Are you able to thank Jesus when you are not feeling well or are upset?
➤ Recall a time when reality did not match up with your expectations.

Chapter 35: Vacation

> What obligations or responsibilities do you have, even on vacation?
> What do you fall asleep thinking about?

Chapter 36: Future Plans

> What Bible passage do you turn to for encouragement and support?
> What has helped make difficult transitions easier for you?
> Who is an Elijah (a mentor) in your life?
> Who do you mentor, or who could you mentor?

Chapter 37: What Do You Do?

> What do you sense your purpose is in this season?
> Do you find communicating with individuals who have similar struggles to be helpful?

Chapter 38: Health Over Job

> Have your top priorities that guide major decisions changed over the years?
> Have you ever had an experience when it felt like "the stars aligned"?

Chapter 39: New Purpose

> Recall a time when your façade has been cracked. (Maybe you had felt invincible.)
> How, specifically, do you combat bitterness?
> Have you ever had a dream that you were taking steps towards – but it abruptly changed or ended?
> What does your story equip you to do for others?

GRATITUDE:
ACKNOWLEDGMENTS

It took a village to help me survive this ordeal and to write this memoir.

First and foremost, I must thank God – for without God, I would not be here. I am extra grateful for God's divine timing and attention to detail, reminding me of the Holy Spirit's constant presence during my darkest season. It was the Holy Spirit's persistent nudge that led to feeling called to write this memoir.

I am grateful for my husband, Jack Miller, for showering me with love even as we went through the trenches.

My parents, Ed and Sue Young, for not only giving me life, but for repeatedly demonstrating unconditional love and sacrifice.

I was humbled by friends, family and even strangers who were willing to hold me close in prayer.

I am thankful for all the medical personnel who aided in my care, especially Dr. Adams, Dr. Granger, Dr. Kessel, Stephanie Owczarski, and Betsy Shuford.

I am thankful for Stacey Studley Collins encouraging me to start my memoir and connecting me with Melinda Copp. Melinda helped to guide me through the writing process by asking detailed questions to develop scenes and reveal transformation.

The memoir writing process was blanketed in prayer by some heavy-lifting prayer warriors in my life: Alisa Bair, Annie Michaels Liao, Ashely Sanders, Denise Bono, Janae Hostetter, Jessie Linn Chapman, Nancy Pratt, Rhonda Brinkley, Rila Hackett, and Sarah Sgro.

My brave and talented friends who were willing to provide feedback on my very first draft: Allison Hutt, Annie Michaels Liao, Elizabeth Stevenson, Eric Doss, Kris Lehman, Stacey Studley Collins, and Stephen Stanley.

Alisa Bair was not only instrumental in the initiation of my blog, but she also connected me to a phenomenal editor, Stephanie Hanna. Stephanie took a fine-toothed comb through my writing and made it the best version possible.

Thanks to Amy Royal for introducing me to yoga, and Carrie Bauer Carper for teaching Holy Yoga. Yoga has been a daily gift during the writing process.

Music has always played a significant role in my life. Throughout my memoir writing process, I have been impacted by Lauren Daigle's music, specifically her lyrics. Knowing that she overcame a health crisis as well makes her words even more powerful and touching to me.

My gratitude to Beth Kernaghan for the cover painting and for answering my 101 diabetic questions.

Aaron Miller is responsible for the graphic design and layout of this book.

Credit and gratitude to Clay Wegrzynowicz for taking the family photo featured on the back cover.

If we have crossed paths, I am grateful for you.

Made in the USA
Columbia, SC
09 February 2020